HOW TO
GET OUT OF
A RUT

Dr. WILLIAM J. KNAUS

A SPECTRUM BOOK

PRENTICE-HALL, INC.   Englewood Cliffs, New Jersey 07632

Library of Congress Cataloging in Publication Data

Knaus, William J.
    How to get out of a rut.

    A Spectrum Book.
    Bibliography: p.
    Includes index.
    1. Success. I. Title.
BF637.S8K55   158'.1   81.17735

ISBN 0-13-409318-6

ISBN 0-13-409300-3 {PBK}

10   9   8   7   6   5   4   3   2   1

Printed in the United States of America

Editorial/production supervision by Cyndy Lyle Rymer
Manufacturing buyer: Cathie Lenard
Cover design by Jeanette Jacobs

PRENTICE-HALL INTERNATIONAL, INC., *London*
PRENTICE-HALL OF AUSTRALIA PTY. LIMITED, *Sydney*
PRENTICE-HALL OF CANADA, LTD., *Toronto*
PRENTICE-HALL OF INDIA PRIVATE LIMITED, *New Delhi*
PRENTICE-HALL OF JAPAN, INC., *Tokyo*
PRENTICE-HALL OF SOUTHEAST ASIA PTE. LTD., *Singapore*
WHITEHALL BOOKS LIMITED, *Wellington, New Zealand*

FOREWORD

Psychological self-help books flow from the presses like bottles of wine from a winery. Few, however, do more than offer problem descriptions or inspiration to the reader who is seriously looking for an approach to deal with his or her problem.

Dr. William Knaus has written an exceptionally fine self-help book that describes how people get into ruts, how they maintain rut patterns, and, most importantly, what they can do to break free. In this work, the author describes virtually hundreds of strategies to aid people in coping with problem rut patterns. Furthermore, he has incorporated into his work numerous fresh and creative approaches that the reader interested in self-application of powerful cognitive-behavioral counseling strategies can learn to apply. Dr. Knaus has accomplished this in a clear, comprehensible style.

The reader will quickly comprehend that *How To Get Out of a Rut* is a serious book created to help the reader design a framework for building self-confidence and developing self-tolerance through the process of getting out of a rut. It is not intended as light fireside reading or as a complete and quick cure to a complicated problem. Instead it is a rather complete resource that the reader can review many times, and gain more from each reading.

L. René Gaiennie, Ph.D.
University of South Florida
Strategic and Planning Associates
Tampa, Florida

CONTENTS

IV UP FROM DEPRESSIVE RUTS

V GUILT, ANGER, AND RUTS

VI RUTS AND PROCRASTINATION

PREFACE

Dr. William J. Knaus, the founder and director of the Fort Lee (New Jersey) Consultation Center, is a psychologist and business consultant in private practice in Longmeadow, MA. In addition to his membership in numerous professional organizations, Dr. Knaus has published, lectured, and worked extensively in areas concerning therapy, mental health, and human resource development. He is the author of several books, including *DO IT NOW: How To Stop Procrastinating* (Spectrum Books, 1979).

I assumed in writing this book that the person reading it would be interested in improving the quality of his or her life, but, like most people, would tend to be a bit on the reluctant side when it came to taking the actual steps to change. But if the reader happened to be especially precocious in using sound psychological principles, he or she could probably move more rapidly through the program outlined in this book and modify the strategies to fit his or her abilities. Too many books, however, give too little space to the person who wants to change, but who resists breaking an unwanted pattern. So, I have carefully planned the book to include multiple strategies to assist the reader to break free.

The format of this book may be called an *awareness-action* format, and was written to assist the reader in planning and organizing counter-rut efforts. It is designed to help the reader: 1) demystify the therapeutic process; 2) determine for him- or herself if what is written accurately reflects the dynamics of his or her rut; 3) know this counter-rut system well so that he or she can be free to challenge it, change it, or embrace it.

In the awareness-action format, basic concepts are spelled out to heighten the reader's consciousness of the psychological issue pertaining to a rut. Action strategies that can be used to counter these concepts follow. If the steps outlined in these counter-rut strategies are carefully followed, what might appear at first glance to be difficult becomes familiar as it is practiced—and may prove easy.

The book is also designed to show how one can identify and counter rut-creating thinking and feeling. It describes how to accentuate positive desires, interests, and capabilities. Its principle intent, however, is to describe the awareness-action approach one can use to increase self-confidence, tackle tension, and advance possibilities for personal success.

vii

Do not try to tackle all your problem areas simultaneously. If you do, chances are you will end up frustrated, disappointed, and discouraged.

If you spend as much time in the next six months, working to improve the quality of your psychological and physical existence, as you would on a difficult college course, at the end of that period you are likely to notice that:

1. Your thinking is clearer.
2. You more rapidly recognize and disqualify erroneous or irrational thought.
3. You talk more constructively to yourself.
4. You better recognize that it does not make sense to bite into a negative self-statement and exclude alternative ways of thinking that are positive. In other words, you will be less inclined to jump to conclusions.
5. You will be less apprehensive about your future and more constructively active in your present.
6. Your study of yourself will be progressing and you will feel increasing confidence in yourself.
7. You will tend to be more objective in your assessments and humane in your actions.
8. You will be more open to your experiences and willing to look at life as it is, not through the mist of illusion.
9. You will be more tolerant of discomfort.

All nine of these advances are *possible*, but *not guaranteed*.

Acknowledgements

Thanks go to the following for aid in manuscript development: Michael Cann, Bud Gaiennie, Arthur Greenspan, Nancy Haberstroh, Wendy Johnson, Gregory Raiport, Jim Thompson and Doreen Pierce.

Special thanks goes to John Gallup, President of Strathmore Paper Company, and Charles Mulcahy, Strathmores' Director of Employee Relations. I would also like to acknowledge Lynne Lumsden, Editor-in-Chief of Spectrum Books, for her encouragement and support, and Cyndy Lyle Rymer, my production editor.

I
THE NATURE OF RUTS

According to Greek mythology, Sisyphus was the legendary king of Corinth who defied Pluto, the god of the underworld. For his disobedience, Sisyphus was condemned to roll a heavy rock up a hill, only to have it roll down again each time he neared the top.

Practically all people from time to time feel as though they are working against themselves, like Sisyphus with the rock. Unlike Sisyphus, however, who had no choice but to yield to the power of the god, people in ruts can break free. This first section starts the ball rolling in the direction of positive change. It spells out what is a rut, when a rut is a habit, resistance to changing ruts, strategies for change, and rut patterns in peoples' lives.

This section is designed to help the reader counter the negatives in his her life and develop strengths and positives. Thus, it follows the framework shown in Figure 1.

Part I contains three chapters. The first describes the anatomy and dynamics of ruts. Chapter 2 details the process of changing from a rut to a fulfilling pattern. Chapter 3 describes the sorts of patterns in peoples' lives that typify rut patterns. It also describes how rut patterns have hidden assets.

Figure 1

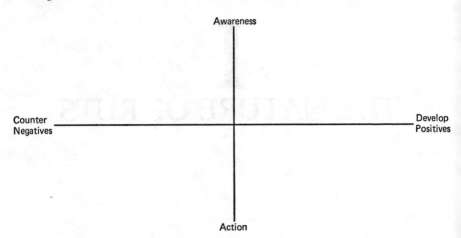

chapter one

ANATOMY OF A RUT

Joel Chandler Harris tells a story of Brer Rabbit, who, on his way to the cabbage patch, paused to greet a warm tar baby sagging on a cornfield fence. When the tar baby did not return his greeting, Brer Rabbit boxed this gooey warm ball of tar until the tar baby and Brer Rabbit were one and the same.

Now if Brer Rabbit, bent on revenge, continued to attack tar babies, he would literally be in a rut. He would be getting nowhere, caught up in a tar baby, spinning his wheels.

Unlike Brer Rabbit's arousing but frustrating encounter with the tar baby, ruts are generally monotonous, boring routines. They are like weeds that sap space and energy from the more desirable plants in the garden. In many ways, they are similar to television reruns; eventually the scene becomes so dull and predictable that the viewer watches inattentively.

Although there are no precise statistics on how many people are currently in a rut, casual observation illustrates that ruts are universal. Everyone gets in one from time to time; some stay longer than others.

The person in a rut typically experiences him- or herself as "stuck," "bored," "really trapped," and "unable to do anything." This sense of entrapment or resignation is seen in the agoraphobic housewife fearful of venturing beyond the kitchen door; the locksmith who hates fixing locks; or the woman who continues to date the same man of whom she has long since tired. This pattern is also seen in the person unhappily traveling from bar to bar searching for adventure; the "burned-out" teacher passively awaiting retirement; the college student who concentrates solely on studies and has no time for recreation and fun; the person afraid to express deeply felt feelings; the man who eternally ponders what to do with the remainder of his life; the problem drinker; the compulsive gambler; the able retired person sitting in silent solitude; and last but not least, the multitudes entrapped in unwanted patterns generating from false responsibilities, exaggerated security needs, invented duties, and groundless loyalties.

Ruts are unpleasant, monotonous, and unfulfilling patterns that pervade your life or are specific to only one or a few sectors of your life. They differ from a helpful pleasant routine in that they are boring, energy-sapping patterns that build on their own momentum and lead to ill effects.

Debilitating as ruts can be, the habit can be broken. If you choose to change and are willing to work to change, your chances are better than a person who gets caught in his or her own personal tar baby and hopes for a miracle to free him- or herself.

Admittedly, there is no guarantee that you will break free, even if you read the words that follow and put the principles into action. However, your chances will be enormously better compared to the person who sits life out on the sidelines as do, for instance, the characters in Samuel Beckett's play, *Waiting for Godot*.

Like the characters in Beckett's play, some people do not even recognize it when they are in a rut. For example, the man who goes to work, goes home, reads the newspaper, watches television, and simply falls asleep may be in a rut even though he may not realize it.

Rut or Value Choice?

Sometimes people appear to be in a rut when they really are not. Let's take Kurk's case as an example. Kurk worked as a foreman for a large fabrics manufacturer. His position was secure and it paid him a comfortable wage. Although he was unenthuasiastic about his work, he held the job because he realistically knew it would be difficult to find a better paying position. Besides, creating junk art, his real passion, would not afford him a living wage.

Many years earlier, Kurk had quit this same job and tried to succeed as an artist. Alas, he financially failed. Now with three teenage children rapidly approaching college age, mortgage payments, and his wife, Tony, suffering from early arthritis, he viewed himself as hardly in a position to go back to the full-time business of producing and selling junk art. Instead, he creates his junk art in his spare time, and resigns himself to a career at the fabrics company.

Kurk's choice is a value choice. He could try to make it as an artist, however, experience has taught him that such action would jeopardize family welfare and finances. And so he places the financial welfare of his family over his interest in a career in art.

Kurk is unenthuasiastic about his foreman job. He repeats a work pattern that is at variance with his true interest. He is not, however, in a rut. He could choose to leave the job. His actions reflect a free value choice.

Ruts and value choices are different. The person in a rut thinks she is helpless to change the pattern. In comparison, the person acting out of a value choice knows she has the freedom to act differently, but makes her choice on the basis of her value preference.

How To Tell a Rut
from a Routine

Patterns or routines need not be unpleasant, frustrating, or destructive. Indeed, some routines reflect a healthy preference. Some individuals simply enjoy a stable, predictable schedule. Indeed, stability and constancy make up a happy state for these persons. For example, John Smith, who has enjoyed working as a gardener for ten years and who enjoys a weekly routine of bowling and contributing his thoughts to his reading group, hardly feels in a rut.

So, what are the major components of a rut that distinguish it from a pleasant self-satisfying routine? Ruts reflect nine related features, which pleasant routines generally do not.

The nine features are:.

1. Repeating unsatisfying routine(s).
2. A sense of going nowhere.
3. A sense of boredom and monotony.
4. Serious self-doubts.
5. Strong desire to dodge discomfort.
6. Compensatory strivings, such as perfectionism.
7. Fear of change.
8. Depression over inaction.
9. A sense of resignation.

Although a rut need not contain all nine features (and may contain features not on this list), most characteristics will be present.

When a Rut is a Habit

A habit is an automatic way of behaving. For example, a man might routinely tie his left shoe before tying his right. Unless asked, he might never think to question which he tied first.

Like putting on a shoe, a rut is an automatic pattern, a pattern that has self-fulfilling mental features most people do not think to watch out for. For example, if you believe that you cannot change your life, your actions are likely to follow according to your expectation. In other words, you live your life through the expectation that you cannot change it.

Mental rut habits are sequential: one idea triggers an association of related ideas. A person in a rut may have a depressing stream of ideas, such as "I'm stuck," "I can't do anything to break free," "woe is me," and so forth. And this "no change" expectation becomes a mental habit that locks the person on a set course.

Gordon Allport (1937) believed that although a proportion of our motivations are obscured from conscious awareness, our *conscious* thoughts, the *conscious* meanings we ascribe to events, and our *conscious* intentions assert considerable influence on our feelings and actions. In this view habitual, rut-creating, "cognitive processes" (including expectations) can be identified and changed through re-education.

Resistance to Changing Ruts

Breaking from a rut means changing an unwanted living pattern to one that is better because it is more satisfying. But change can be tough. Most of us are creatures of habit and find it difficult to step out of character and consistently act in our self-interests. This resistance to constructive change can be quite perplexing: why would one not act to improve the quality of his or her existence?

One of the great mysteries of humankind concerns why a person resists changing a self-defeating habit pattern. Eric Hoffer, for example, made it clear that resistance to change is in the nature of the human condition. It is also in the nature of the human condition to be inquisitive, curious, and constructively creative. But choosing to follow one's positive and healthy inclinations sometimes seems like walking the wrong way through a wind tunnel, while continuing a self-defeating path seems like going with the breeze.

Sometimes resistance to positive change goes to ridiculous extremes. The emphysema patient who refuses to give up smoking, the coronary-prone person who refuses to exercise properly and reduce from his or her obese condition both resist *life-saving* changes. Although most of us are not obese, coronary-prone, or emphysemic, our resistance to positive change is often less extreme, but still serious. Who does not, for example, have a habit or routine that is self-defeating and should be changed?

Psychoanalysts explain this resistance to change by saying that the person is unaware of his or her motives and mobilizes him- or herself against gaining awareness by transforming personal observations through unconscious ego defense mechanisms. The person does this primarily to avoid painful recollections and sexual and aggressive impulses. The behaviorist avoids using the phrase "resistance to change," and instead talks of rewarding and punishing conditions that shape a person's destiny. The person caught in a rut would, in behavioral terms, follow a pattern of conditioned responses where change-promoting responses are penalized and avoidance responses rewarded. A child, for example, who is penalized for curiosity may act with conformity to avoid punishment. The child might be reinforced for conformity behavior, and may live his or her life in an overly restrained manner as a consequence of this early conditioning. The child does this because he or she has learned to be overly socialized and that to act differently risks punishment.

Routines are partially self-created and partially shaped by religious upbringing, formal education, observing parental models, peer influence, and other forms of educational circumstance. Undeniably, each person's cultural experiences have exerted powerful influences. However, as A. Thomas, Stella Chess, and Herbert Birch (1968) have shown, the individual also teaches these cultural forces how to treat him or her, and the individual influences the behavior of others.

Influenced by others and influencing others, the person also influences him- or herself. One of the means of self-influence grows out of a human tendency to prefer the familiar.

Ruts can and often are painful. But they reflect a *familiar* chronic discomfort. Paradoxically, there is security in the familiarity of the rut condition. The known evil appears safer than the unknown; in the unknown, one could be clumsy, inept, exposed, and vulnerable. So, resistance to change can also represent a means of self-protection against uncertainties of the unfamiliar.

We are not talking about protection against life-threatening circumstances when we talk about the unfamiliar. Self-protection against uncertainties of the unfamiliar is a psychological reaction to *anticipated psychological discomfort*. Even when the results of actions to promote change are likely to be highly beneficial, people often resist because change is uncomfortable, the change circumstances ambiguous, and the actions leading up to change unfamiliar.

People prefer to avoid uncomfortable ambiguous circumstances, or at least hesitate when they are not sure where they are going. They also do not like to feel trapped. Thus, a person in a rut often feels "caught between a rock and a hard place." What "is" is unpleasant, what "could be" is uncertain, and action seems uncomfortable. And the person freezes until action for change is the lesser of two evils or the pathway to change is *more clearly illuminated*.

Resistance to change occurs partially because a person fears facing discomfort. Discomfort dodging can also reflect a *reluctance* to act. Whereas the resistant person thinks he or she has no choice but to avoid discomfort, the *reluctant* person thinks he or she chooses to delay. In *contrast* to resistance, which is oppositional and steadfast, reluctance is a reflection of indifference and of giving in to the feeling or urge to avoid what seems uncomfortable.

Discomfort dodging, whatever its origin, is the greatest obstacle to surmount to get on the pathway of self-realization and joyful living. As I said in *Do It Now: How to Stop Procrastinating* (Knaus, 1979), "if a person is not afraid of discomfort, outside of real danger, what else is there to fear?"

Change is resisted for yet another reason. Erroneous thinking and false beliefs result in action that distracts a person from seeing what the reality of his or her situation really is. Because of these misconceptions the person is side-tracked. The grooves of misconception form the borders of his or her rut.

So, there you have it—change is resisted because of

1. our discomfort-avoiding tendencies;
2. our natural tendencies to continue with familiar routines;
3. our false beliefs that give us an unclear picture of reality.

This book is designed to aid the reader in dealing with each of these areas of resistance and it emphasizes coping with discomfort-avoiding tendencies and debunking false beliefs.

Levels of Concern

This "rut" book clearly points out *connections* between a person's attitudes, feelings, actions, and life-style. It provides well-structured approaches to countering life-style ruts and to approach life positively. The focus is, therefore, on current problems and their solutions. This is not to say, however, that the antecedents of the problem are unimportant.

Sometimes it is important to understand primordial critical instances that negatively influence a person's present. For example, a client, Larry, was in conflict with his wife because he did not want her to become pregnant and bear the children she wanted. Through his therapy, Larry learned that he did not like the kids who teased and tormented him when he was growing up. He had been a bright, sensitive child who was an easy mark for the bullies in his neighborhood. He was unable to defend himself against them because he feared them. Now, later in life he subconsciously feared that if his wife had children, they would grow to bully him. Furthermore, they would be a constant reminder of his own painful childhood.

Larry needed to identify this specific source of his aversion to children and work through his fears. Formal therapy was required because he had no clear conscious awareness of the source of his aversion to children. But by talking the problem out in therapy, he developed a fresh perspective, saved his marriage, and now has a family he loves dearly.

Larry's problems existed at the level of *historical connections*. At this level, a person's progress is likely to be aided if the historical connection between critical events in the past and current behavior is laid bare. In the majority of cases, historical connections are interesting and informative, but not particularly helpful.

Three contemporary levels are highlighted in this book. The reader can make substantially better use of the knowledge of the three levels compared to the level of historical connection. These levels are: (1) superficial barriers, (2) problem-promoting attitudes and beliefs, and (3) life style issues. Each is open to self-correction.

Superficial barriers are weak mental barriers or circumstantial obstructions. For example, one might be in a rut because she thinks she does not have the resources to finance her education so that she can work in the field she wants. The solution may be quite simple and practical.

1. Make social and personal adjustments to accommodate an educational program.

2. Apply to a bank for a loan to cover expenses.
3. Work part time and go to school part time.

Generally, superficial barriers are dealt with at a practical level. If the person is unable to deal at a practical level, when practical solutions are available, his or her rut can be related to self-view, a view toward his or her ability to tolerate inconvenience, or other self-restricting beliefs and attitudes.

At this level of *problem-promoting attitudes*, the concern is with *what a person tells him- or herself* to arrest his or her own progress. A person who regularly doubts himself and beats himself down needs to learn *how* he does this and *how* he can work to change the pattern.

The level of *lifestyle issue* centers on major lifestyle problem. A person in a rut, for example, has a lifestyle problem. He or she could be in a rut in a career, a family relationship, or in the ways he or she satisfies avocational and recreational endeavors. At the level of lifestyle issues the person needs to recognize and deal with pseudo-values, self-defeating attitudes and behaviors, as well as act to promote lifestyle changes.

What Does it Take
to Get Out of a Rut?

If you are going to work your way out of your rut, the amount of time it takes to change may not be as important as the quality of change and the emotional muscle you develop. Emotional muscle is inner psychological strength built from positive self-challenge and discovery. In building emotional muscle, there is no time for pandering self-illusion or fooling yourself with this pandering.

Building physical muscle takes time and work. With effort you can build up even though there will be no guarantee that you will become strong. But chances are you *will* become stronger.

Like building physical muscles, well-directed efforts to build emotional muscles pays off in greater self-confidence and tolerance. But as physical muscles require continuous exercise, so does the development of emotional muscles. It requires every bit as much effort, time, concern, and consideration as building a biceps or building wind power.

Building emotional muscle by countering negative thinking and discomfort fears is your admission ticket. The implication for those who read this book and hope to profit from it is clear.

1. to benefit requires learning and practicing how to do better many many times, perhaps throughout your life.
2. to benefit requires patience. A child does not grow to adulthood overnight; neither should an adult expect to emerge from his or her rut overnight.

You may possess exceptional underlying *potential* to modify your actions and cut free from your rut. However, potential must be used. To use your potential, you must be willing to make three prime commitments.

1. Directly and honestly face your problem;
2. Commit yourself to accept whatever discomfort is required to initiate action to disrupt the rut;
3. Accept that you will have to develop functional new ways of thinking and behaving.

In short, you need to commit yourself to the task of disorganizing your rut and developing a productive lifestyle pattern if you want to feel successful and experience a more zestful, productive, and happy life.

By reading *How to Get Out of a Rut*, you are signaling yourself that you do not want to be counted among those effete, restless hordes who have laid down their spirit and are plodding through life's paces.

chapter two
PREPARING FOR CHANGE

Human evolution is mirrored in the development and advancement of thought. We advance according to the conceptualizations that reflect a combination of reality, imagination, and human capabilities.

Informally, the evolution of a person parallels scientific advancement. As Thomas Kuhn (1970) points out in *The Structure of Scientific Revolutions*, science builds upon the experiences and abilities developed in the past and adopts new models only if they reflect past abilities and serve to resolve problems that otherwise could not be resolved. Likewise, each person, like a scientist, generates his or her advances by building upon the past.

Part of the past is a reflection of personal dispositional tendencies. How you develop yourself will partially depend on your dispositional tendencies. For example, if you have a low-key disposition during your childhood, it is unlikely that you will develop an excitable-hysterical manner as you grow up. Instead, you are likely to advance according to your capabilities and build upon what you already know that suits you.

Science does not move straight ahead without peaks and valleys, no more than a person does. All areas of science periodically bog down, suspended in static thought, because of unscientific myths and misconceptions. So, our scientific advancement is not without hitches. Sometimes false ideas hang up progress.

Throughout history, people have adopted false and restrictive explanations to account for seemingly incomprehensible phenomena. For example, when the crops of the ancient Greeks seemed about to fail, they would make sacrifices to the god of the harvest so that their crops would be spared. Europeans once thought that the world was flat and that anyone venturing on the sea beyond sight of land would fall from the surface of the earth and be consumed by lurking monsters. During the Middle Ages, the mentally ill were thought to be possessed by demons. To be saved, these suffering persons required exorcism, trephining (boring holes in the skull to release the devils), or racking torture to punish the demon.

Personal advances, like scientific advances, can be limited by false assumptions that create self-fulfilling philosophies, which in turn serve as *mental barriers* to change. These mental barriers are often like high stone walls or holograms: they seem unbreachable, and we don't think to try to breach them. Once the hologram is recognized as a corporal fiction, we are free to move through it easily.

Roger Bannister, who broke the four-minute mile record in 1954, shattered the myth that a human could not run a mile in less than four minutes. And many runners have passed through the four-minute-mile barrier since Bannister's feat.

Until done, many acts seem impossible. Imagine the reaction of people in the fifteenth century to the idea that a human would fly to the moon on a ship that shot fire from its tail. Imagine the same fifteenth-century people learning that their portraits could move through the air to be seen again on a television screen. Such revolutionary ideas would surely have been denounced as witchcraft, impossible, or madness.

Reality, when it contradicts a theory in which a person has a strong investment, is likely to be greeted with ridicule and censure. The theories of the Polish scientist Copernicus (1473–1543) that the earth rotated around the sun was condemned by priests, who based part of their religious beliefs on what they thought was fact, that is, the earth is at the center of the universe. Because the theory of Copernicus advanced the science of astronomy, the truth of the system gained leverage over the myths of the priests.

As you retreat from false myths, you advance in your counter-rut campaign. Each new step will build on previous steps. However, just as human history reflects evolution through the medium of often opposing forces, you may find your personal evolution also reflecting this process. Like Copernicus, whose observations and insights changed the state of astronomy, you too can come to new self-observations and insights and act against the forces that oppose your advancement. Ruts can be changed in the same manner as scientific discoveries are made. Sometimes a vital awareness occurs for accidental reasons and results in a breakthrough. Sometimes you can set your mind to look for new opportunity and when opportunity comes, you are prepared to recognize it. Sometimes change and discovery come about through carefully planned change. In short, there are many means of breaking a rut pattern.

To start our examination of strategies for change, we will consider these three vehicles for change: accidental, incubational, and planned.

Accidental Opportunities

You have precious little control over accidental opportunities. The skill is in recognizing an advantage when you see it, then using what you see.

These positive accidents depend on luck. They are completely haphazard and unpredictable. Unfortunately, when they are recognized by someone, they are often scoffed at by others, just as new ideas and discoveries have been scoffed at through the ages. Copernicus was ridiculed when he proclaimed the world was round; Thomas Edison was ridiculed when he proposed to light up New York with electricity.

Perhaps the greatest scoffers at our accidental discoveries are ourselves. For example, a normally unassertive person might on one occasion speak up for his rights. But he thinks his actions are peculiar and avoids considering the possibility that inherent in that experience is something that could be repeated. The thought of repeating assertive actions seems just too risky, and the person acts as though he were saying, "Assertiveness worked one time, but what about the next? Better to be assertive in fantasy; it's less risky."

Accidental discoveries typically do not result in a complete lifestyle metamorphosis. They can, however, make an impact and a difference in one aspect of life.

A Time for Incubation

Some people are in a hurry when it comes to reversing their ruts. But acting as though getting out of a rut is a matter of urgency, and then demanding an immediate satisfying lifestyle, usually will get you nowhere. Demanding immediate change is often futile because urgency in getting out of a rut typically leads to mental anguish rather than positive change.

Constructive incubation, compared to urgent demandingness, often speeds change. Constructive incubation is like planting a seed in one's mind about what one would like to do and then setting one's mind to look for opportunities. For example, a person may seek new vocational opportunities, but not know exactly what she is looking for. So, through resting on the idea and trial and error experiments, new possibilities are visualized.

Leon's case illustrates constructive incubation. His main problem was that he saw himself in a rut in his work as a junior executive for a large hospital products company. The company had a well-planned developmental program for its young executives. It focused on giving each junior exec specialized training, such as how to market a specific product line.

Leon felt restrained. At heart, he suspected he was a generalist, a person who has the interest and ability to become involved in various types of management problems. His company, on the other hand, was training him to become a specialist in obtaining good distribution for a specific product line. Although he found the work interesting, Leon did not feel sufficiently challenged. So he thought about changing employment. While he let the idea sink in, he read and thought and talked with friends about new job possibilities. Later, when an opportunity developed to join a consulting firm, Leon jumped at the opportunity. Although he

had not specifically considered consulting as a career, it hau
he wanted: the firm was oriented toward providing trainees with a
wide range of experiences under the guidance of "expert" senior
management. When Leon saw the opportunity, he knew that was
what he wanted.

Constructive incubation is not the same as procrastinating. It is
an active, constructive *search* process. Procrastination is a non-
productive avoidance process.

Planning for Change

Of the three major means of change—accident, incubation, and
constructive planning—planning can benefit by the other two. A
plan is simply a design for the future. To plan effectively, however,
requires developing self-management skills, such as knowing how
to analyze the rut problem, designing a counter-rut change program, organizing time and resources, implementing and controlling the change process, monitoring and evaluating results. If a
happy accident does not occur and if incubation proves ineffective,
a good action plan may still help put destiny in the hands of the
planner.

Planning, obviously enough, involves *anticipation*. Constructive anticipation is a prerequisite for the *problem-solving* strategies
that become part of a good plan.

There is much in life that one can enthusiastically *anticipate*. A
gardener, for example looks at the seed catalogs in the winter and
decides what he wants to grow in the spring. He orders his seeds
and waits. Then he prepares the soil and plants the seed. During
the growing season, he maintains the garden and watches out for
the young growing plants. And after the growing season has
ended, he prepares the soil for the next beginning.

While the plants grow, the gardener does not sit idly by. Life
goes on. But the garden is something to look forward to, something that is renewed each year. It is filled with anticipatory revelation.

Anticipatory revelation is looking forward to discovery. For
example, if the gardener experimentally grows rhododendron, he

must wait with anticipation many years before he sees the color of the flowers his experimental plants produce. His revelation is in discovering the color of the flower, whose evolution he set in motion years before.

Joyful anticipations that bear an outcome occur in the world of action, not passivity. They occur as the by-product of *producing a product*! The person who is vitally absorbed in such production is hard to beat because he or she does not view life as a contest. Instead, it is a pathway for discovery. Building products is the way of expanding the pathway.

Products take many forms. A product can be conceptual, such as developing a new way of overcoming fear; artistic, such as creating a sculpture; physical, such as learning tennis; mechanical, such as maintaining a well-tuned automobile; or botanical, such as renewing a garden every season.

The product can be a relationship in which two people can work together. It can be the result of a team effort to discover a new immunization process or a team effort to have a successful business organization. A product is any *process* that you are developing and willingly committed to continue developing.

Problem Solving

Illusion can be shattered through problem solving. To devise a good plan and to achieve it requires solving problems.

A problem arose for the citizens living near Mount Saint Helens in the state of Washington after the volcano erupted in May 1980. The problem was how to get rid of all the soot that was deposited from the eruption. The reason for the problem centered on the fact that the soot when wet, became like cement. It hindered the growth of crops, and was a general nuisance.

Problems such as how to dispose of volcanic soot, how to grow a larger tomato, or how to break an unwanted rut pattern have a common definition: A problem is a set of circumstances that *deviates* from desired conditions; a problem is an impediment to a goal or objective.

In attempting to solve a problem, it is important to define it in clear, objective terms. Once accurately defined, solutions become more obvious. For example, suppose you have the problem of how to get out of a rut. If you spell your problem out in clear and honest detail, you have a better chance to break free, as opposed to going on a directionless campaign. By asking *specific* questions, you can often pin down causes and solutions.

Since our concern here is solving the problem of how to get out of a rut, the logical first step is to isolate the problem. The second step is to analyze your rut according to its anatomy. And the last step is to plan for action, act, and evaluate your progress.

Isolating the Problem

Ruts can appear in many forms but the most common ruts seem to arise in career, interpersonal, and recreational areas of life.

1. *Career* refers to work or vocation. You would be in a career rut if you were dissatisfied with your work, and were not working to change the dissatisfying pattern.

2. *Interpersonal* refers to your relationships with people. You would be in an interpersonal rut if your people contacts were strained, stressed, or boring and you were not working to change the pattern; or you were continuing in a destructive or largely unsatisfying marriage.

3. *Recreational* refers to leisure-time activities. You would be in a recreational rut if you were dissatisfied with how you spend your free time and were not acting to change the pattern.

Analyzing Your Rut

Your initial effort to isolate your rut pattern begins when you determine which of the three general areas involves your rut. To begin, take one of the above three rut dimensions and analyze it, using the Rut Rating Form that follows.[1] This chart enables you to

[1]You can define your rut outside of the career, interpersonal, and recreational categories I have supplied. I have chosen to use these three rut categories because they are the most common areas in which a person can become rut bound. You could, for example, modify this listing. You could substitute your own categories if you thought them relevant. For example, you could characterize your rut as personal where personal refers to how you feel inside about yourself. Personal is attached to career, interpersonal, and recreational ruts, but it has its own special

apply the nine features that distinguish ruts from routine. The intent of this exercise is to examine the anatomy of your rut by generating some ideas about why you are in it.

Rut Rating Form

Criteria	Topic: Frequency		
	Rarely (1)	Occasionally (2)	Often (3)
1. I repeat unsatisfying routines (give examples).			
2. I feel a sense of going nowhere (give examples).			
3. I feel a sense of boredom and monotony (give examples).			
4. I wonder if I have the capabilities of ever breaking free from this rut [self-doubts] (give examples).			
5. I avoid making myself feel uncomfortable even if it means I may not achieve my goals [discomfort dodging] (give examples).			
6. I often believe that I need to be in control, act perfectly, or gain support and approval from others in order to break from my pattern [substitute activities] (give examples).			
7. I fear change (give examples).			
8. I feel depressed over my inaction (give examples).			
9. I experience a sense of resignation (give examples).			
Total			

characteristics. You would be in a personal rut if you routinely doubted yourself, were fearful of change, and were discontented with regularly experiencing unpleasant feelings like fear, depression, guilt, resentment, or frustration, and were not working to change those conditions.

In using the form, you label the topic you are analyzing. If it is your career, beside the word *topic* on the rut rating form, write the word *career*.

The second step is to cite examples under each of the nine criteria that distinguish a rut from a satisfying routine. Your examples will serve as documentation to either *support* or *refute* the statement. For example, on item 1, a respondent might support the statement: "For the past five years I have been working for Leaf Brand Foods stocking cans on grocery store shelves. It is a routine that rarely varies, which I find extremely tedious and unsatisfying." A second respondent might refute the statement: "For the past five years I have been working for Leaf Brand Foods stocking cans on grocery shelves. Although the routine rarely varies, I amuse myself by placing the label of each can one degree to the left of the one below it."

But under criteria 2, the second respondent might state: "I want to obtain a promotion to field manager. I have been passed over for that position two times in the past two years. I believe I am not going to advance. I often think about my failure to get recognition and a promotion to a supervisory position."

The next step is to quantify your results. Assign one, two, or three points to each criteria: 1 = rarely, 2 = occasionally, 3 = often.

Use documentation you have compiled to make a decision about how many points you want to assign to each of the criteria. Assign your ratings, and then total your score. The maximum number of points you can receive is 27, the minimum, 9. If your ratings fall between 9–13, you perceive your problem as mild; 14–18, moderate: 19–22, serious; and 23–27, very serious.

The ratings you assign yourself are not absolute ratings. That is, they are not intended as estimates of how your rut problem compares with the rut problems of others. The ratings serve as a guideline for you to assess the extent to which you think you are in a rut. More importantly, your initial ratings can be matched against ratings you can make when you complete different phases of your program in order to evaluate change.

As a result of your analysis, you may find that your problem is quite mild (9–13). You can, therefore, proceed through the remainder of the book to learn strategies to *prevent* rut-type problems, as well as for learning new approaches to advance your interests. If your score is 14 or above, you will most likely want to read with the intention of changing your problem pattern, preventing future negative patterns, and to advance your interests.

Once you have completed the Rut Rating Form, you can move on to the Accountability Matrix to determine to what extent your problem is self- or situationally induced.

Self-induced means that your situation is self created. In other words, you could make opportunities to break free from your unwanted pattern, but you are locked into a negative mental habit pattern.

Situationally induced refers to circumstances beyond your immediate control. You could be in prison, for example, and your pattern and routine are established by prison authority. You could have a serious physical or psychological handicap that places limitations on some of your activities. You may have a large debt and are working at a dead-end career that pays you much more money than you could earn elsewhere. You may strongly dislike your job, but since you do have debts to pay, your restriction may be situational until you pay off your debts. Situationally induced restrictions are normally not rut situations. They can, however, be used as excuses for getting into and staying in a rut.

The following is an accountability matrix that you can use to specify the major determinants for your problem.

Accountability Matrix

Dimension	Self	Situation	Both
Career _____			
Interpersonal _____			
Recreational _____			
Other[1] _____			

The purpose of the Accountability Matrix, like other problem-defining steps, is to provide a system for organizing your informa-

[1]*Other* refers to any area outside of career, interpersonal, and recreational where you think you are rut bound. For example, "personal" could fit into this *other* category.

tion. Although it may temporarily feel uncomfortable to bluntly face your problem, facing problems will get you ahead faster than not facing them. Furthermore, you will want to be clear and honest with yourself about the "causes" so that your efforts can be properly directed.

Developing a Plan

Once you have gone through the problem diagnosis phase, the last step in the problem-solving sequence is to develop a counterrut activity plan or program. You can use the following Activity Sequence Form 1 for this purpose.

In using the Activity Sequence Form 1, target your efforts on one specific aspect to your rut problem. Set your objective. Determine the *steps* to meet the objective. Decide how you will know if you are achieving each step (criteria for accomplishment). You can complete this form now, or, preferably, skim through the book before coming back to complete it.

Activity Sequence Form 1

Statement of goal or intent:

Procedure

Objectives Leading to Goal in Graduated Step Fashion	Action Plans	Results

To illustrate how the form can be completed, look at Activity Sequence Form 2, the work of a young man who was agoraphobic (a person fearful of open spaces and crowds, who, therefore, fears going outside of the home). In addition to illustrating how the form might be completed, the example serves another purpose. It graphically states that an agoraphobic person will have to learn to deal with that fear as a prerequisite for getting out of a rut.

Note in the outline of the following activity sequence plan, the steps are graduated from simple to more difficult. In this particular case, the man listed the first two steps to take, and once accomplished, listed further steps at daily intervals until the problem was resolved.

Activity Sequence Form 2

Statement of goal or intent: To be able to walk out of my house and go to the corner grocery store.

Procedure

Objectives Leading to Goal in Graduated Step Fashion	Action Plans	Results
1. First day, walk as far as I can before I feel overwhelmed with fear, then mark spot with chalk, and return home.	1. Carry notebook, write down thoughts that run through my mind as I progress. Try to determine what I am really afraid of. Is it the discomfort, is it that I think I won't succeed? Purpose: pin down the problem.	1. Walked farther than I imagined I would. Discovered through my writing that I am afraid people will think something is wrong with me. Fear I might faint or lose control. Resolved that I can't go on living my life being fearful of peoples' opinions or of fainting.

2. Second day walk to chalk spot and walk beyond until I feel overwhelmed with fear, mark spot then return home.	2. Carry walking staff for "moral support." Determine if carrying	2. Walking with the staff seemed to help. I almost reached the store. I felt happy because I did not worry about what people would think of me for carrying the staff. Will try to record my thoughts about the staff tomorrow as I proceed toward the store.
3 . . . . . . enter store.	3.	3. . . . entered store.

chapter three
PATTERNS IN PEOPLES' LIVES

We all have behavior patterns that characterize us and make us distinctive. Some patterns we are pleased with, such as patterns of promptness, compassion, or truthfulness. Other patterns we wish were not so, such as a rut pattern. However, even our rut patterns have distinctive features that contain hidden assets. If properly recognized and used, these features can light the pathway out from a rut and become the vehicles for preventing one of the worst outcomes of a rut—burnout.

In the first section of this chapter, we discuss some of the more common life-style rut patterns also describing their hidden assets. The next section covers the control-fear-depression play-off, and the last section describes the foundation for most rut patterns, using the concept of the "wheel of misery." Also covered in this section is the "wheel of satisfaction," which is the wheel people move to once out of a rut.

Rut Patterns

Turning Rut into Asset

There is a story of a school master, Oscar the owl, who organized a school for forest animals. Oscar wanted to be sure that each animal who attended his classes would be strong in all the main areas of the curriculum: tree climbing, flying, jumping, swimming, running, and burrowing. Naturally, he tested his class to discover what they could and couldn't do. The frog could jump, but was a bust at burrowing. The duck could fly, but failed at climbing, and so on. So, Oscar individualized each animal's schedule and drilled each in the art of what he or she could not do. Then he retested them.

Oscar found to his dismay that not only had the animals not progressed in their remedial program (which he knew from watching them), but each had become worse in their original excellent skills. The frog, for example, could no longer jump; the duck could not fly.

The message is clear—it is better to build on strength than on weakness. Let us now identify some common ruts and see how each form has hidden strengths that can be built on. As you examine each rut pattern, you may determine that your pattern overlaps with two or more of the forms. If so, don't despair. This is not unusual as there are no pure types. Indeed, each pattern will, in some respect, overlap with another pattern. So, it is important to keep in mind that the patterns are presented to provide you with ideas that can help you break your rut pattern.

The Fallback Rut

Any lifestyle characterized by working in spurts, slumping, working in another spurt, and then slumping again illustrates this fallback style. For example, the person who wants economic freedom, saves her money, goes on a spending spree, blows her money, feels guilty, swears she will repent, saves her money, then blows it again is in a fallback pattern. The person who wants to lose weight, goes on a diet, loses the weight, then regains the lost weight also is in the fallback rut.

The fallback rut is most prevalent among people who work for themselves and set their own structures and routines. Outside sales personnel, along with private practitioners such as attorneys and enterpreneurs, fall into this high-risk group.

Don's case illustrates the fallback pattern. Don grew up on the streets. Although technically reared by an aunt and uncle, he was hostilely rejected by them. As a consequence, he spent most of his young years out of the house. He frequently begged food and slept in abandoned automobiles. In this phase of his life, Don learned to survive, and he dreamed of the day when he might be rich and powerful.

In his late adolescence, Don apprenticed himself to people who promised to teach him marketing and advertising. He was ambitious and in the formative years of his career, he spent considerable time teaching himself as well as trying to learn whatever and whenever he could from his employers. When he developed confidence in his talents and had acquired considerable technical expertise, he went into business for himself.

In his new business, Don immediately translated his early acquired survival skills into obtaining accounts. Within five years, he had made himself a multimillionaire. He used his newly earned wealth to buy the best automobiles and to live on an elegant estate in a most exclusive area. He surrounded himself with beautiful women and even married a national beauty contest winner.

At the peak of his success, Don began to drink heavily and gain weight. He became withdrawn to the point where he stood by and watched his wife and employees mismanage his business until he went bankrupt. The bankruptcy was followed by divorce. Bankrupt, divorced, and despondent, Don began to pick himself up. He worked to control his drinking, lost weight, and forced himself to restart his business. Within seven years, he once again joined the multimillionaire club, lived in an exclusive community, and remarried. At the height of his second success, he started to drink, gained weight, blew his money, divorced his wife, and lost his business. This pattern of meteoric success followed by a complete burnout occurred once again before he entered therapy.

In therapy, Don learned that at least part of his fallback pattern reflected a subconscious belief that he did not deserve success. He subconsciously set himself up to fail. But when he got to the point of great despair, his basic drive for survival gained strength, and he once again felt stimulated and excited, and started to act productively.

People act out of mixed motives. For example, not only did Don think he did not deserve success, but he also feared that he would not become successful enough. He feared he would never become the most successful person of all times. In essence, he did not want to face the fact that there were limitations on his capabilities. He also feared that having limitations made him vulnerable to psychological annihilation, which he defined as living his life as a "rummy" on the streets.

Don's pattern of coming back from defeat to obtain victory was arrested once he accepted that:

1. He deserved his success because he had the ability to attain it.
2. He had limitations, but he need not get wiped out because of them.
3. It is hardly a disgrace if one does not become the most successful person the world has ever known.

With the acceptance of these basic ideas, Don's successful business ability was stabilized.

A very common fallback rut pattern is seen in the behavior of people who procrastinate. Such people often work in spurts, rest on their laurels, slide back into the old procrastination pattern, drive themselves to pull away from the pattern, then lapse back once again. They follow a pattern of procrastination-action-procrastination-action.

The fallback victim can also be a person who spins in a circle of self-doubts, acts against the doubts, finds that he or she is capable, then starts to self-doubt again.

One of the most depressing self-observations a person in a fallback pattern has is that he or she is "getting nowhere fast" and that whatever he or she does will be undone.

Breaking loose. If you are in a fallback pattern, you must have arrived somewhere to fallback from. To have reached that position, you had to act reasonably effectively.

Although it is certainly true that "fading in the stretch" has negative consequences, the fact that you are in this fallback pattern shows that you are able to "run the race." What you now need to learn is to be consistent.

One method is starting to reverse the fallback pattern is a comparison of opposites. The comparison of opposites list below contrasts positive qualities and their negative counterparts. Contrasting opposites shows that one has alternatives to negative thinking and acting when one reverses a restraining negative belief or action. Sometimes merely articulating a positive healthy outlook can help to fix one's efforts on the positives. After all, who wants to go down a pathway of negatives when a positive pathway is clearly illuminated?

In setting up your comparison of opposites, identify the negative attributes you believe short your progress. List them individually on the right side of a sheet of paper. For each individual negative, write its opposite on the left side of the sheet. The list below illustrates the format.

Positive Attributes	*Negative Counterparts*
1. Willingness to take a risk.	1. Avoidance of risks, "playing it safe."

2. Perseverance toward objective.	2. Pausing, side tracking, and diverting from objective.
3. Intelligence.	3. Unwillingness to think clearly.
4. Tough-mindedness.	4. Thoughts of being inadequate and weak.
5. Active orientation.	5. Passive orientation.

Using your comparison of opposites, assess what you have done to allow your negative qualities to dominate your positive qualities. You can use the following as a guide:

1. You forgot your positive qualities.
2. You believe that once you start "downhill," nothing can stop you.
3. You think that if you have an urge to slide back, you have to give in to that urge.
4. You have miscalculated and thought once you obtain a certain level of success, you will automatically maintain that level without further work.

Once you have analyzed the reasons for sliding back, determine what you can do to reverse the fallback pattern. For example:

1. What can you do to keep your positive qualities in the forefront of your thoughts and actions?
2. What would you have to do to maintain a forward momentum and thereby resist your fallback pattern?
3. What do you think you can do to substitute constructive action for an urge to give up?
4. What can you do to convince yourself that maintaining forward momentum is like exercising? If you want the benefits of exercising, you have to exercise. If you want forward momentum, you have to paddle forward, not backward.

In short, it is important to figure out what you will have to do to make your positive qualities dominate.

People in fallback ruts often let their moods govern their minds. Practically everyone has low cycles where their energy and desire is low. Unless understood and checked, these inevitable low points can be the start of a descending pathway, and expanding malaise.

Although it is easy to revert to a fallback pattern, you can talk yourself out of lapsing by: (1) recognizing that you have the stamina to progress, and (2) the only thing stopping you is believing that you must slump while in a slumpy mood.

If you do not immediately break your fallback pattern, take heart. There are many strategies described throughout this book that you can use to help yourself counter your *stop power* and turn it to *go power*.

The Spectator Rut

People like different activities. Some of us enjoy skiing; others look forward to the Friday night poker game with the gang. Some prefer to spend time alone involved in their own hobbies and interests. For some people, a little interpersonal contact goes a long way. Others are likely to be unhappy unless continually involved with people. Most of us live between these two poles.

Some people prefer greater solidarity than do others and enjoy life more when they can actively amuse themselves. They are great advocates of self-entertainment. These persons are members of action clubs that differ considerably from the spectator club.

Members of the spectator club avoid action involvements and instead substitute watching others do what they wished they could do. Television addicts are members in this nonselective group, along with idle dreamers. Indeed, almost anyone who escapes into a passive routine to avoid the trials of living fits this category.

The spectator is prone to self-entrapment as in the conflicted fantasy world described in T.S. Eliot's poem, "The Love Song of J. Alfred Prufrock." Prufrock's life is measured in "coffee spoons of time." He passively waits to obtain the clarity of vision and confidence that only bursts from active experiences. The spectator, like Prufrock, may temporarily block awareness of the desperate and imprisoning rut he or she is in. Inevitably, this uncomfortable awareness becomes conscious, exposing the spectator to feelings of boredom and a nagging lack of fulfillment.

Resign your membership. Perseverance and observational skills are qualities that spectators rightly claim. In addition, there are some spectators who are "dreamers," who think deeply about life's possibilities.

The observing person with a good fantasy life can sometimes come up with unusual insights. Perhaps you can discover an area where your observational skills and imagination can be used. For example, such an area may be art where you translate your imagination through an art form. Through art, your ability to observe and to imagine blend into an activity in which you are an active participant. If you are more practical minded, substituting woodworking, gardening, or tinkering for observer activities might be the ticket.

You can also help yourself out of the spectator rut by identifying your favorite spectating activity as a prelude for identifying its "activity" counterpart. Start by identifying your spectator interests. The following is an example that illustrates the process of converting passive spectating to active involvement.

Spectator Activities	*Action Alternatives*
Watching soap operas.	Joining a drama club.
Reading adventure stories.	Researching the history of adventure stories.
Viewing comedies.	Creating your own comedy script.
Listening to musicals.	Taking singing lessons or lessons in a musical instrument.
Watching sports activities.	Finding a sport that you can enjoy and develop skills, or researching that sports field and becoming an expert.
Listening to the news.	Studying the history of the major world events and their relation to the present world situation or joining a world events discussion group.

After you have looked over the above contrasts between spectator and action alternatives, make up a list of your own spectator activities and identify the action counterpart that best suits your temperament and capabilities. Keep in mind as you make up your list that some spectator activities are normal; often, watching a television show or reading a book is done to gather information or for entertainment purposes. A spectating pattern, in contrast, is definitely a self-restrictive activity.

The Dark Glasses Rut

When immersed in the rut of the dark glasses, life looks just terrible. People are seen as menacing forces not to be trusted; the inequities of the world are magnified; fearfulness dominates the consciousness.

Entrenched in the rut of the dark glasses, the person finds it difficult to trust. He or she is readily suspicious of the motives and the intents of others. In this sensitized state of hypervigilance, to assure that harm is not forthcoming, the person protects him- or herself by avoiding others. It is too risky to become known and to show vulnerability.

Ruth has ensnared herself in the dark glasses rut. As she looks out at the world, she is appalled by the inequities, filth, crudeness, rudeness, crime, and corruption she sees. She thinks that no one is to be trusted, even family members. Her philosphy is "everyone is out for him- or herself." The more she thinks about the disparity between the world as she would like it and the world as it is, the more outraged and hostile she feels. Because she feels so hostile, she is afraid of expressing herself because she is afraid she will lose control, sound confused, and be vulnerable to assault from the "hostile" people she thinks are causing all the trouble.

This hostility-fear combination of emotions is a powerful destructive force instrumental to Ruth's rut. She is snarled in this miserable hostility-fear play-off of: (1) seeing unfairness and injustice because she expects to see it, (2) feeling hostile when she sees unfairness, (3) fearing that she will overreact because she feels hostile, (4) holding back from acting, (5) hating herself for her inaction, (6) feeling vulnerable because she does not experience herself in control, and (7) becoming hypervigilant to "danger" and hypervigilant to see what she expects to see, which is unfairness and injustice.

The rut of the dark glasses, filled with anger, fear, suspicion, self-doubts, and discomfort, is one of the most crippling forms of rut.

Out of the darkness. The rut of the dark glasses is built on anguish and torment. However, lurking beneath this pattern are such real strengths as:

Social consciousness.
Critical awareness of social justice.
Strong sense of fair play.
Sensitivity
Alertness.
Insightfulness.
Ability to persist despite suffering.

Although these capabilities, personal qualities, and attitudes can be stumbling blocks, they can also be used constructively. Following are some thoughts on how to get out of the dark glasses rut.

1. Whereas the world cannot be completely transformed to meet one's expectations, still it is possible to make a positive social impact by choosing areas where your contribution is likely to have an effect and then by working to make that impact.

2. One can use his or her sensitivity and insightfulness to analyze several sides of each social issue. This analysis can be used to develop a broad perspective. Armed with knowledge of positive as well as negative sides to issues, one is less likely to fall victim to the type of rigid singlemindedness that the general semanticist terms "allness thinking".

3. Recognize that one cannot get the world to live consistently by rules of "fair play." However, if one believes in fair play, why not turn that quality back on oneself. Face it; it is hardly being fair when one keeps him- or herself in a state of upset over the inequities of the world. Instead of bemoaning the plight of the universe, try to figure out how one can be fair to oneself.

4. Sensitivity is a two-edged sword because, although one may be sensitive to inequities, one has the tendency to personalize what is seen or heard. To maintain the sensitivity without all the personalized garbage that goes with it, it helps to be prepared to look at what motivates people to act as they do. In this analysis, you may find that most people generally are trying to advance them-

selves and are not out to purposefully make other people's lives miserable.

5. Alertness is a real strength that can be applied to identify positive detail that others might miss.

The Perfectionist Rut

People slip into a perfectionistic rut when they view themselves as inadequate, then feel they must compensate by acting perfectly. Whatever the spotlighted deficiency, whether intelligence, attractiveness, or sophistication, the outcome is the same—the person believes that whatever he or she does is not enough and that he or she is, therefore, not good enough.

Perfectionism is an attitude of *having* to be more adequate than one is. Clearly, the person hooked into this attitude is too sensitive to failure. Thus, he or she often seems so hard at work avoiding failure that the person fails to achieve a sense of who he or she is.

Fear of failure is analogous to a person treading water in order not to drown, rather than learning to swim or get out of the water. It is also analogous to a person straining so hard to become the best swimmer that he has precious little understanding of his world because he has not taken the time to learn about anything but swimming.

A need for certainty is a subvariety of perfectionism. Because he or she thinks that certainty is necessary, the perfectionistic individual fears making decisions. She fears that she will make a mistake, and she handles this fear in opposite ways: by making impulsive decisions or by compulsively vacillating. Often these opposite actions are misapplied. The perfectionist, for example, is likely to make an impulsive decision on something important, such as how to invest his life savings, then several hours later be unable to decide on something trivial, which of two pairs of socks he will purchase.

A client, Rick, was caught by uncertainty. In this perfectionism trap, he became emotionally and financially destitute when he dodged finding a job because he told himself he could not go to work unless he was absolutely sure that he made the *very* best choice of job. He continually immobilized himself trying to figure out the "very best" direction possible. Indeed, in his efforts to cover all possibilities, he wrote more than 3,000 pages about his sad plight, hoping that in the very next phrase he wrote, he might find the answer.

Despite the number of pages he wrote, Rick's problems could be listed under two basic concepts: I must be sure of choosing the very best alternative, or my life will be an effort in futility; I would be a real worthless lout if I failed to use my potential properly. These ultraperfectionistic demands actually were in opposition to each other. Rick thought his choices had to be perfect before he acted. But without taking action, he had little basis for a choice. Naturally, his obsessive preoccupation with certainty sealed the coffin of self-fulfillment.

A need for certainty is often complementary to a need to *appear* perfect. Rose, a highly proficient executive secretary, thought she would lose her job if her employer did not view her as perfectly competent. Because she thought she would lose her job if her employer saw white-out on typed materials, she redid imperfect pages and hid them in her pocketbook.

Fortunately, when Rose integrated the idea that the nature of humans is to be fallible, that erasers were put on pencils to correct errors, that white-out was invented to correct "typos", and that even ice skating champions occasionally fall, she was on her way out from her perfectionist rut.

Another form of perfectionism is seen in the person who acts as critical toward others as toward him- or herself. Mike, a research scientist, was highly critical of his colleagues' work. He covertly criticized them for having holes in their theories and put them down for their imperfections. Because he thought his colleagues would be as critical to his theories as he was of theirs, Mike feared leaving out a single detail when he presented his work, lest he be the victim of criticism.

Mike's work was confusing because it was overly detailed; he embellished simple concepts until they became obscure. Because of this extraordinary effort to be complete, he looked like someone who could not see the forest for the trees.

Some perfectionists don't see themselves as such. Randy was quite surprised to discover she had strong perfectionistic leanings.

She thought a person who acted like a perfectionist was one who had all his or her work neatly ordered. "That can't be me," she said. "I'm really sloppy. I rarely get my work done on time." Despite her protests, Randy definitely had perfectionistic ideas. She was continually nagging herself and putting herself down because of her slovenliness. Thus, she had a standard she failed to meet and she maintained a self-condemning attitude for failing to meet it. That is perfectionism.

Substituting excellence and quality. There is nothing wrong with striving for quality and excellence. There are advantages to attending closely to detail and doing a good job. Society tends to reward its quality performers. And people who are excellent in their work generally tend to experience a solid sense of work confidence.

Perfectionism is different from *striving* for excellence. It is *driving* oneself to meet often very rigid standards and condemning oneself at the slightest failure. In essence, perfectionism is an *attitude* that says "I must do well or I'm a big nothing."

The person in a perfectionist rut has hidden assets that can help him or her obtain excellence and quality in performance. The perfectionist is likely to be brighter than the average person, attentive to detail, sensitive, goal-directed and task-oriented, and has critical thinking skills. He or she tries to solve problems in order to rid him- or herself of unwanted frustrations.

The elimination of self-blame and of blaming others for their shortcomings is the single most important step out of the perfectionist rut. Freed of the tension of condemnation, the person is able to use his or her abilities wisely because he or she can direct them realistically and constructively.

To begin this process of getting rid of perfectionistic blame: (1) look for benign motives and reasons for human actions and try to view yourself and others through understanding eyes, which is not, however, to say that you should sanction what you don't like, and (2) try to determine just what it is that is so devastating about making a mistake; then, like a good detective, snoop around and come up with clues that would lead you away from perfectionism and toward truth.

Perfectionism can be countered through the concept of the

psychological pie. Everybody has one. Sometimes this pie is divided into pieces, sometimes it is whole. Sometimes the pieces have false labels. Sometimes the most important pieces are given the smallest space. Sometimes a piece can be removed and happiness is attained. But sometimes a person thinks he or she cannot be fulfilled without *all* the pieces. Here is where the perfectionism crisis begins.

A perfectionist thinks that if a piece of the pie is missing, the pie will fall out of equilibrium and tip. The crisis continues when the person thinks of what the *ideal* pie would be like and substitutes that pie for the pie that contains his or her basic values. Then the "real" pie appears like a vacuum, like a black hole in the universe that can never be filled.

In truth, a person has many psychological pies (see Figure 2).

Figure 2

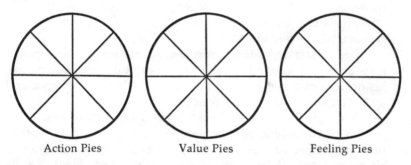

Action Pies   Value Pies   Feeling Pies

And when a person thinks badly of him- or herself because he or she does not approve of a particular piece of pie or dwells on a missing piece or looks at only one of his or her many pies, that person risks failing to appreciate the strengths that he or she has, as represented in those many pies.

If you think you are in a perfectionist rut, construct a few pies for yourself. Include action pies, value pies, and feeling pies. Then try to see yourself in light of the many pieces rather than restrict your view to only a few.

In chapter 4, on the *Perils of Inferiority*, this concept, that people are complicated and have many many positive qualities that they discount or are unaware of, is expanded.

The Personal Approval Rut

Vassalage technically went out of style during the Middle Ages. However, vassalage *is* alive today in a new and highly disguised form—the personal approval rut.

Because of an abnormal oversensitivity to rejection, a sizeable number of people are in psychological bondage by negating their personal rights out of fear of bothering or upsetting someone else. This overconsciousness is manifest in the person who eats an undercooked meal in a restaurant because he is afraid of troubling the waiter with his complaint. Approval needs are also observed in the person who fears to express her wishes to her mate out of fear that the mate would become angered and berate her (even if he had rarely done so). Approval needs are seen in the behavior of the supervisor who does the work of his people because he does not want to be cast in a role of a "slave driver." They are seen in the worker who doesn't work for the sake of work; rather she works to impress others, to get praise, to obtain approval, or just to do what is expected to avoid criticism.

The person dedicated to securing approval necessarily places him- or herself in bondage: the person can't offend, only please; his or her emotional survival depends on others' acceptance and approval; he or she can't be rejected.

A client, Bob, believed that he was inadequate and could achieve worth only if he could get people to love and approve of him. In this need-for-approval trap, he believed he had to watch his every word, always look terrific, be fully knowledgeable, be sensitive to others needs, be patient, tolerant, and self-sacrificing. He had to be all the above in order to gain acceptance. Of course, he failed to achieve his goal of universal acceptance. In fact, by maintaining the belief that he needed approval, there was no way he could win. For even if he acted according to what person A wanted and also according to what person B wanted (and they wanted different things from him), what would happen if he spent an evening with both A and B?

Make yourself number one. Clearly, there are advantages to wanting approval from others and working to get it. In our society, getting along with people is a sign of good mental health and is generally beneficial. Very few people in their right minds willingly and actively plot to disenfranchise themselves from all segments of society.

Wanting approval and working to get it differ from needing and requiring it. The person who wants approval does not make his total human worth contigent on getting it. The vassal does!

The person in vassalage puts him- or herself number two in order to become number one. This scheme is a scam. It simply doesn't work. To break from this vassalage trap requires caring about the rights of others, while making yourself important and worthwhile in your own eyes. This is what is meant by making yourself number one.

A person in a personal approval rut has at least two potentially positive qualities that can be used in the service of making him- or herself number one—social sensitivity and caring about the rights of others. Although social sensitivity is typically desirable, *over*sensitivity definitely is not. Indeed, oversensitivity deprives others of getting acquainted with you and can lead to excess cautiousness. Furthermore, if you are overcautious with others, they are likely to get the wrong impression and come to believe that since you seem to be so cautious, you may not care for yourself. Who wants to bother being friendly toward a potential self-hater? However, if you can be sensitive toward others and about their rights, you have the capability of caring about your own rights and of assuring your place and getting your share.

If you care about others' rights, the following five concepts are helpful to examine.

1. Do you find yourself caring more about what strangers think of you compared to friends and relatives? If so, rethink your priorities. Why, for example, should you care that much about a stranger's view about you and less so about the views of your intimates?

2. What is the worst that could happen if you spoke up for yourself and stepped on someone's toes in the process? Examine this possibility and consider how you would cope. Next, consider the *most* probable outcome of your speaking up for yourself.

3. Some people confuse acting in their self-interests with selfishness. Self-interests refer to self-improvement. Selfishness refers to a need to exploit others and get every thing for yourself. Be clear with yourself about what is meant by your vital self-interests and what selfishness really means.

4. If subservient actions reflect a subservient attitude, identify the assumptions you think that attitude is based upon and question them.

5. George Kelly (1955) described the benefits of temporarily adopting a new identity as a way of fostering constructive self-change. In Kelly's system, if you want to get better, you have to act better. To use this system, invent a character you would like to copy. Make this character self-expressive and self-interested. Act out this new self-script. When the time comes to stop pretending, take the positive knowledge you derived from this experiment and apply it to your daily life situation.

The Dilettante Rut

Some people get in ruts because most of their energy flows into continuous change. People in the dilettante pattern rarely experience a sense of accomplishment because they do not stick to a job or project long enough to put quality into it. That is because they allow their attention to be fleeting. When they stick "too long" to a project, they experience normal frustrations, then seek refuge from these frustrations in change and novelty.

The dilettante is continually on the run. He or she is always in the process of getting into or getting out of relationships. The dilettante makes frequent work and career changes and says he or she does this out of boredom. Because of making continual changes in their lives, dilettantes rarely fail or succeed because they are never in one place long enough to put their full talents to work and to discover what their capabilities really are. Instead, they back off on the verge of discovery almost as though they were saying that they fear learning the truth about themselves.

In quest of thoroughness. There is certainly advantage to exhibiting an interest in change and novelty. But the question is whether this interest is an excuse to avoid commitment, frustrations, and self-development. To test this hypothesis, one can start by planning to make oneself work to counter one's normal dilettante inclination by sticking with a project twice as long as normal. And see what results.

The Good Life Rut

A person who appears successful by conventional standards, but finds his or her experiences unrewarding and all too commonplace, is in a good life rut. Often this person's original definition for "the good life" was obtaining conventional goals, such as getting married, having a family, holding a steady job, buying a camping trailer, being a member at the local country club, and/or having an active social life. Once the conventional goals are obtained, the challenges cease to exist. Disillusioned, the good life ruttist might initiate family squabbling, become involved in extramarital affairs, gamble, overconsume alcohol—almost anything to disrupt the boredom.

The person in the good life rut tends to be obsessive-impulsive. This process is characterized by dwelling on lacks and dissatisfactions, which explode into such feelings as depression and anger, which in turn are expressed in impulsive action. That is why a person who normally appears calm and seems to have everything under control may unexpectedly burst out in an irrational, seemingly senseless tirade over something minor. But the tirade symbolizes the deeper issue of frustrations and disillusionment.

On to real life. The person in a good life rut is overflowing with positive attributes. He or she has demonstrated the capacity to: set goals and meet objectives, exhibit stability and perseverance, and maintain cordial social relations. These competencies can be adaptively reapplied to break out from the good life rut. Use the following for a start:

1. Consider if you like challenge. If so, you could be in a good life situation because you have set a goal, reached the goal, failed to

develop a new goal, and now feel a lack of challenge. If so, press the realistic limits of your imagination and try to see the next challenging step.

2. Steadiness and perseverance without novelty and variety can sometimes be a person's undoing. However, there is no reason why you might not be steady and persevering in enjoying routines in your life that you value and steadily act with perseverance in adapting some of the qualities of the dilettante by trying novel experiences.

The Control-Fear-Depression Play-Off

Of the nine distinctive features of a rut listed in Chapter 1, the sense of lack of control, fear of change, and depression over inaction are critical. They form a synergism, which means the interaction or combination of two or more factors that yield a total effect greater than if those factors operated independently. For example, two environmental pollutants that alone are not too harmful can be really harmful if they occur together. Sulfur dioxide from coal-burning furnaces in combination with asbestos particles burned off from auto brake linings can induce lung cancer; the sulfur dioxide interferes with the process by which foreign particles are expelled from the lungs.

Like environmental pollutants, mental pollutants operating in combination can have a deadly effect. A mental pollutant is a harmful, faulty assumption that is taken for fact. If more than one of these concepts operate in unison, the combined effect may be like a synergism. The thought that one cannot control his or her destiny may result in stress and fear; fear limits normal psychological coping strategies from being effective and can lead to a sense of depression and resignation. Depression draws attention from the normal psychological coping mechanisms that are effective against fear. Under this synergistic condition, a person's psychological coping system becomes overloaded, inefficient, and malfunctional.

The most debilitating emotional characteristics of the rut are tied to a sense of lack of control as reflected in the emotions of depression and fear. And when a person is both fearful and depressed, he or she is more inclined to feel resigned. For example, a person *deeply* into a rut *views* himself as helpless, hopeless, and incapable of breaking free from his entrapment in this unwanted pattern. Although he wants out of the pattern, the catch is that the *thought* of taking actions that could change circumstances evokes fear. When he avoids facing his fear, he feels resigned; nothing will change and nothing can be done to change the outcome.

Accompanying this symptom of resignation is a seesaw state of emotional numbness and agitation. You feel numbed because you don't see much hope; you feel agitated with yourself because you don't move to change your condition. Over time, this seesaw state becomes like a bad cough. You know it's there, you want to get rid of it, but it keeps recurring.

The depression–fear–resignation cycle is a manufactured mental state of anguish. When one is very deeply entrapped in this state, it is quite difficult to change because the restrictions flowing from this mental outlook *appear* overwhelming.

The fear-depression exchange is, of course, relative; some are more severely affected, and the process can be acute or chronic. The case of Barbara illustrates a more severe fear-depression play-off. It demonstrates the type of beliefs a person deeply entrapped in this play-off is likely to have. Although most readers will find their rut to be less pervasive and intense, the self-restraints evident in Barbara's thinking are easy to identify with.

Barbara says she hates her job and feels depressed about it, but fears change because she believes: (1) she may not succeed in finding a new job, (2) she might lose financial security, (3) if she finds a new job, people there won't like her, and (4) no type of job holds potential for her. Barbara is still living at home with an aging and complaining father. She is depressed over her living conditions, but is afraid to move because: (1) she thinks she would be acting irresponsibly toward her father if he had to fend for himself, (2) she thinks she won't adapt to living by herself, (3) she thinks she might not be able to afford to maintain herself financially (she has the equivalent of four year's gross income in her bank account), and (4) she thinks she might be attacked by some wild-eyed rapist. Barbara has never had a close intimate relationship with a man. She is depressed over her single state, but she is afraid that: (1)

men will take advantage of her, (2) men won't find her attractive enough to marry, (3) men will control and dominate her life, and (4) her life would be miserable because she would have to cater to a man's every wish. Barbara is depressed over difficulties in making decisions, but she is afraid to act decisively because: (1) she thinks she will make some disastrous goof, (2) she thinks that if she does not have an iron-clad guarantee of success, she will ruin her life, and (3) she thinks people will regard her as a fool if she errs in judgment.

Many of Barbara's feelings of depression and fear are closely tied to underlying self-doubts and to intolerance for frustration and anxiety. These self-doubts and discomfort fears are self-generated. And it is these mental pollutants that form the mentally limiting synergism that binds Barbara to an unwanted pattern of living.

The powerful fear-depression-resignation rut Barbara was in, is a prelude to the burnout rut. In the burnout rut, *resignation* dominates.

Burnout

People can get into ruts in their career and become "burnout" victims. *Burnout* is a term that refers to a state of mental fatigue where a person perceives him- or herself as unable to assert control over his or her job.

Burnout can occcur in any career, but the most outspoken burnout victims tend to be those involved in people-oriented professions, such as sales, medicine, dentistry, psychotherapy, teaching, and ministry. Burnout candidates also include persons with high stress occupations, such as air traffic controllers, airline pilots, police officers, business executives, and supervisors. Being a waiter or waitress also produces a high percentage of burnout victims.

The burnout victim overtaxes him- or herself, mismanages his or her capacities, and operates out of an environment that provides little personal support. Often the person goes into a career with unclear or unrealistic expectations. The realities of the career challenges are not spelled out clearly in his or her mind. Often, the person must deal with difficult individuals.

Regardless of the work setting, people in the sort of rut that leads to burnout behave in one or more of the following ways: they *rigidly* adhere to the rules of the organization for which they work; they psychologically drop out; they engage in self-defeating power struggles with their employers; they distract themselves by bitching, griping, or complaining.

People who feel burned out and do not physically leave their jobs, fulfill their work commitments in a minimal and joyless way. They behave as though they had no place else to go, but don't want to be where they are. They often exist in a state of agitated limbo, thoughtlessly repeating their routines and wearying themselves with the tedium. They are often disillusioned by the thought that what they do does not make any sense, is stressfully the same, and serves no real purpose.

This frozen, joyless, unfulfilling burnout state can have numerous physical side effects, such as chronic exhaustion, hypertension, insomnia, headaches, and a wide variety of other psychosomatic disorders, including high blood triglyceride levels associated with coronary heart disorder.

Burnout can occur in intimate relationships. If it does, the person feels numbed, detached, cooled off, and trapped. If she stays, she does so because of one or more of the following:

1. She is afraid of change.
2. She would feel guilty if she left.
3. She feels too burdened by mental depression to activate a change.
4. She believes that she needs financial security above emotional satisfaction.

Joy felt trapped in her marriage. She was frequently beaten by her husband during his many alcoholic binges. She stayed with him because she feared the children would hate her if she forced a separation. Thus, she lived in morbid fear of the next beating. But when she discussed her feelings with her youngsters, she discovered to her surprise that they very strongly supported a separation because they too were stretched and strained by their father's violence.

There are early warning systems prior to burnout—brownout and smolder.

In the *brownout state*, the person often does not recognize that he is heading for burnout. Instead, he feels confused. Circumstances do not seem to be getting better despite his efforts. He feels frustrated that his expectations are not being met. He begins to doubt his skills and capabilities and wonders if he will be able to get his act together. He expresses his frustrations to his friends. Nothing, however, seems to change.

In the *smolder stage*, matters have worsened considerably. A person's morale is low. If her problem is job related, she notices that her performance has slackened. She dreads getting up to go to work. She resists the very thought of work, but she can no longer dodge thinking about it. She feels empty when she complains because her gripes have no effect. She looks for excuses not to go to work and uses illness as a pretense. Her family relations become strained and she is too easily prone to irritability. She ceases to enjoy sex or uses it as a form of escape from routine. At the smolder state, a sense of stagnation has firmly set in, and burnout is but a step away.

Clearly, it is better to recognize the earliest warning signal. At this stage it is wise to discriminate between the inevitable normal stress and strains and the extraordinary tensions in any career or interpersonal situation. Then look for what can be controlled, opportunities to learn more effective skills, ways to discriminate between whether your circumstances reflect an interim or terminal problem, and data to decide objectively whether to exit or stay with the situation. Most importantly, recognize that one's career or interpersonal situation is but one aspect of life and can always be modified or changed.

The Concept of the Wheel

Each style of rut thus far described is a learning behavior pattern that can be replaced by new productive and flexible patterns. Sometimes all that is required to make this "replacement" is to reveal the strengths inherent in your rut pattern and use the strengths you possess to get out and stay out of this pattern.

Rut patterns reflect the mental mechanisms that fuel them. Perfectionism, for example, reflects *fear* of failure that can lead to a sense of defeat, failure, and depression. However, fear and depression are themselves symptoms of more basic attitudes, which produce these two forms of stress. O.H. Overstreet (1925) wrote that insecurity and frustration avoidance were basic to emotional stress. In my view, insecurity (self-doubts) and frustration avoidance (discomfort dodging) promote undesired emotional symptoms (fear, depression, hostility, guilt) and malfunctional attitudinal patterns that negatively influence a person's career, interpersonal, and recreational satisfactions.

It is possible to view the various forms of ruts just described according to the concept of a wheel. It depicts each type of rut as a spoke on a wheel linked to a central hub of misery at the center, and career, interpersonal, and recreational pursuits at the rim. Woven between the spokes, hub, and rim are stress emotion symptoms: fear, depression, hostility, and guilt. Figure 3 shows the "wheel of misery."

Figure 3

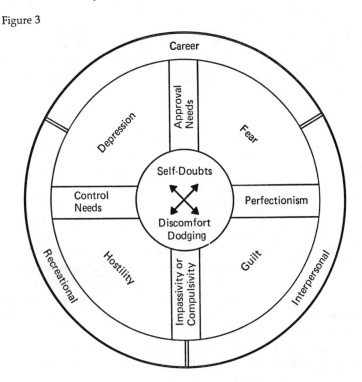

By using the concept of the wheel, the relationship between the various aspects of a rut can be visually displayed.

The wheel of misery has its positive counterpart—the "wheel of satisfaction," shown in Figure 4.

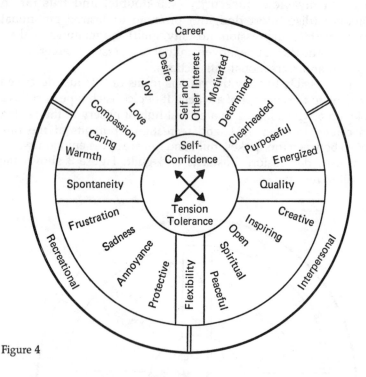

Figure 4

The wheel of satisfaction shows that a person who is self-confident and able to brave stress and tension is likely to show spontaneity, flexibility, quality in work, and interest in self and others. These qualities are the connecting spokes between self and activities. Woven between the spokes, rim, and hub of the wheel of satisfaction is a considerably broader range of positive as well as negative feelings and motives, a characteristic of many emotionally free and productive human beings.

People who ride the wheel of satisfaction know how to use their leisure time wisely. They recognize that leisure time-recreational activities are refurbishing activities which are important outlets for pent-up tension as well as prime sources of plea-sure. They also recognize that recreational activities are as much a matter of personal taste as a preference for pickles over ice-cream. Whether the activity is biking, acting, picnicking, gardening, sail-ing, photography, bridge, soccer, socializing, birdwatching, or spelunking, recreational activities are a vital part of a balanced lifestyle.

Obviously, to succeed in riding the wheel of satisfaction re-quires changing self-doubts and discomfort dodging tendencies and adopting a healthy, self-confident outlook and complementary ability to tackle uncomfortable problem situations without backing off. Thus, getting off the wheel of misery and onto the wheel of satisfaction involves *inner* (self) change as well as *outer* (career, interpersonal, and recreational) change.

In Part II, self-doubts and discomfort dodging are identified as the two basic dynamics that underlie the fear-depression play-off and the various styles of ruts, and that keep people riding the wheel of misery.

II

FOUNDATIONS FOR CHANGE

At the hub of the wheel of misery discussed in Chapter 3 are self-doubts and discomfort-dodging urges. Part II describes these basic human problems that often are the foundations of peoples' ruts.

Chapter 4 details the self-doubt process and how to deal with it. Self-doubts reflect the person's self-view. Self-doubts result in hesitation, second guessing, and lost opportunity. In a state of self-doubt, it is quite easy for a person to slip onto the treadmill of self-debasement. The *self-doubt-downing theory* introduced in this chapter shows how this process works. It also shows ways of getting off the treadmill.

Chapter 5 describes the dynamic ingredient that often goes unrecognized as a major mechanism in a rut pattern—discomfort fears, sometimes called *intolerance for tension*. A person who fears discomfort is often afraid of his or her own negative feelings. This chapter details methods of tolerating any type of emotional tension, including fear of feelings created by the self-suggestion that discomfort must be avoided. This chapter also makes clear that people will often act in self-defeating ways because they want to spare themselves from tension, not because they are inherently self-distructive.

chapter four
PERILS OF INFERIORITY

One day in the far distant past, one of our curious ancestors peered out of his Stone Age cave and came to believe that he was inadequate; not just because he couldn't run as fast as others or that she wasn't as skilled in starting a fire as others, but that he or she was decidedly *inferior*.

Unquestionably, inferiority concepts have been around for a long, long time and are as much a part of the human condition as hangnails and warts. Furthermore, the roots of inferiority can begin at any stage of life. And we can etch inferiority onto ourselves through self-creation as well as through being taught.

Inferiority: A Matter
of Self-Creation

A person can feel inadequate one hour and brimming with confidence the next. The self-view is not static. Rather, the self-view can change according to circumstance, mood, and what one happens to be *thinking* of at the time. Indeed, at times it seems quite easy to jump to negative conclusions about oneself and then to generalize such conclusions. This inferiority generalizing process can occur at any stage of life and can be self-created, as the following four cases illustrate.

Jill's feelings of inadequacy began in second grade when she moved to a new neighborhood and decided that the children in her new school were more capable than the youngsters in her old school. Jill had been accustomed to achieving at the top of her class. With the move to her new school, she began to feel inferior because she thought the work was easier for the other children. She believed she had to work twice as hard just to keep up. And work she did. Jill became a seven-year-old work-a-holic. Because of her dedication to her studies, she left little time for socializing. Jill's studies, however, paid off and her school performance was excellent. Not surprisingly, her peers began to view her as a brain because of her grades and as a snob because she failed to relate to them. Jill, in contrast, thought she was stupid because she "had to work harder than the others" and a "social moron" because she had no friends and was teased.

As Jill grew older, her self-concept took a second tumble when she concluded that she was not feminine. She noticed, for instance, that her mother could put makeup on more adequately than she could. She also noted that many of the girls in her class dressed better and seemed more attractive than she. These observations became two inferiority documents that led Jill to conclude that she was different from other people and *inadequate because she was different*.

Jill's inferiority views evolved from *critical conceptualizations*. She conceived of herself as inadequate because she believed she did not compare favorably to other people.

In her mid-twenties Jill went into therapy to break from her unwanted patterns. Once she could see how she was generating her own problems, she actively began to recognize her misconceptions, stopped blaming herself, stopped viewing herself as abnormal, and started acting in her best self-interests.

Sometimes, inferiority blooms in young adulthood. Ralph was an unusually attractive and bright child. He grew up feeling confident and secure. He found that people seemed to go out of their way to be helpful to him, and he was popular and successful.

After he graduated from college, Ralph worked for a major pharmaceutical company as a sales trainee. He worked hard, established himself, and won a promotion to sales manager. But he proved only marginally suited for management. Moderately well organized, he could not establish a viable leadership position.

Ralph began to feel inferior, demoralized, and defeated when he saw himself failing. He had not taught himself to deal with failure. Now he felt trapped in a management position at which he performed poorly, and he did not think he could step back to being a successful salesman. At this point in his life, Ralph had reached a crisis. He needed to face up to the fact that his talents were sales-oriented and that it was better to be a strong and successful salesman than an unhappy marginally successful sales manager.

The inferiority blues can emerge in midlife. Wanda was a beautiful actress whose beauty began to fade when she reached forty. In her mind her fortieth birthday marked her career's end. Furthermore, without beauty queen looks she no longer felt worthy, started to doubt herself, and began to think she was a failure.

Self-doubts and inferiority feelings also come to those in later years who are competent and who retire without a plan. Ted was a highly competent president of a successful corporation. On his retirement, he decided to sit back, relax, and enjoy life. Instead, he went into a mental dive. When he failed to immediately develop recreational interests, he began to think of himself as useless.

Jill, Ralph, Wanda, and Ted developed self-negating thinking habits. All four thought they were inferior for being who they were. This dip in self-confidence occurred with Jill early in life, with Ralph in young adulthood, with Wanda in her middle years, and with Ted in retirement. In each case the inferiority thinking process resulted from erroneous conclusions and misconceptions.

Instruction in Inferiority

Occasionally, a person's constitutional makeup is so good that even an incredibly negative environment has minimal poor effects, but such genetic strength is rare in children living in such negative environments. In a psychologically poor environment, the individual can be subjected to a wide range of negative experiences, which often influence self-concept. For instance, children developing negative self-concepts may be subjected to:

1. Constant parental squabbling and fighting where the child infers or is told that he or she is to blame.
2. An unstructured home environment with unclear or inconsistent limits.
3. Repeated beatings and assaults.
4. A reaction of disgust and avoidance by the parent toward the child.
5. Parental perfectionistic expectations.
6. A paucity of tactile and affectional contact.
7. Verbal viciousness:
   a. *invectives*: you're a rotten stupid person.
   b. *prohibitions with consequence*: don't you dare do that or you'll go to hell.
   c. *disregard for sensitivities*: we're going to drown that cursed pet hamster of yours.
   d. *double messages*: you know we love you; how could you have done that to us?
   e. *character assassinations*: your're disloyal, dishonest, and disreputable; you are rude, crude, and unattractive.
   f. *loaded questions:* Why do you suppose nobody likes you?

The same factors that negatively affect a child's concept of him- or herself can influence a person at any stage of life. A person working for employers who are time-urgent, demanding, inconsiderate, and pejorative will have a hard time avoiding the start of self-doubts that can lead to feelings of inferiority. A person harped at by his or her mate for minor infractions may, of course, retaliate or may begin to have self-doubts and come to view him- or herself as clumsy, neglectful, and inept, the labels supplied by his or her mate.

But people are generally not like rocks upon which indelible markings are carved. They are not mindless beings, so conditioned by the forces of their environment that they act like robots. So, even if a person has come to think badly of him- or herself, and acts self-defeatingly because of this view, there are ways out of the inferiority trap.

Inferiority: A Matter
of Selective Perception?

People who develop poor self-concepts blind themselves to their own better qualities. L. Frank Baum's famous tale, *The Wizard of Oz*, brilliantly depicts such blindness. In the story, there is a cowardly lion, a tinman without a heart, a scarecrow without a brain, and Dorothy, a little girl who wants to escape the clutches of the Wicked Witch of the West and return home to Kansas. These characters seek the Wizard of Oz to ask for what each lacks: the lion, courage; the tinman, feelings; the scarecrow intelligence; and Dorothy, the way home.

The lion, tinman, and scarecrow feel inadequate and want to be given the "gifts" of courage, feeling, and intelligence. Dorothy, on the other hand, appears as though she is a victim of circumstances who needs to find a way out.

What the Wizard asks of each of the four is to kill the Wicked Witch of the West, and so they set forth on their quest. At a point of confrontation, when it appears that the Witch will triumph, Dorothy accidently discovers that the Wicked Witch of the West will vaporize if splashed with water. The day is saved.

The Witch symbolizes the side of ourselves that is a distraction from self-discovery. By destroying this distraction, we destroy another illusion, that there is a Wizard who can cure all our ills. We discover instead that the solutions to our life circumstances reside within ourselves, waiting to be discovered.

The *Oz* story further dramatizes the point that blocks in self-awareness can, as with the lion, tinman, and scarecrow, lead to inferiority feelings. As the story unfolds, it becomes clear that each character already has the desired capabilities, but just can't see them.

In this quest, the lion learns that he has courage because he *acted* courageously; the tinman has compassion because he *acted* compassionately; and the scarecrow learns he can think because he *used* his thinking ability.

By concentration on gasps or lacks, the *Oz* characters blocked themselves from seeing their positive qualities and strengths, while highlighting "deficiencies.'" This process may be called *reifi-*

cation, taking mental myths or misconceptions (such as the scarecrow thinking he had no brain) and making oneself believe that the
myths are complete reality. This reification process produces
"smoggy awareness' because the absorbed person strongly de-
nounces his or her normal human faults and fails to see beyond
them to actual strengths. The expression "he can't see beyond his
nose" partially captures the spirit of this concept.

The person suffering from "inferiority reification" comes to
know more and more about personal weaknesses or lacks until he
or she knows everything about those weaknesses and practically
nothing about the strengths. For example, Pete, a highly capable
architect, takes on only simple problems because he believes he
will fail if he challenges himself. In this case, Pete's abilities exceed
his ambitions, so he fails to learn about his capabilities and resigns
himself to mediocrity.

Inferiority feelings come from inferiority thinking. At least part
of this process involves a person's failure to recognize personal
strengths, as the following two cases illustrate.

Paul, a participant in a psychotherapy marathon, had a serious
case of the "inferiorities." He believed that he had no redeeming
qualities. In his words, "I am a complete bust." Indeed, the depths
of his inferiority feelings would make the lion, tinman, and scarecrow characters of *The Wizard of Oz* seem to overflow with confidence.

As is true with many persons suffering inferiority reification,
Paul berated himself for what he lacked, while dismissing his accomplishments. Interestingly, many of Paul's accomplishments
were significant. He graduated from an Ivy League college with a
"B" average. In his career he had advanced to a middle management level. In his work he demonstrated intellectual astuteness,
leadership, and stick-to-it abilities. However, when his prior accomplishments were brought to his attention, he did not view
them as significant. Instead, he concentrated on what he thought
he lacked. Through the power of negative thinking, he skirted over
his positive abilities and magnified the negative.

The group tried to help Paul to get an honest perspective, but
we met with considerable resistance. He was just too heavily in-
vested in his symptoms for us to make a dent. Rather than engage

in a no-win power struggle, the group and I used a *positive blowup* approach, where the positive attributes necessary to make the accomplishment were highlighted. For example, the fact that Paul graduated from a fine college suggested he had perseverance, had mastered prerequisite skills, had above-average capabilities, and could comprehend and retain information.

Paul continued his "inferior human being" theory even after the positive blowup intervention. Then Judith, another marathon participant, admitted an identical problem.

Up to that point, Judith had maintained a low profile in the group. Like Paul, she was a victim of the power of negative thinking, and she viewed herself as an inferior being. Judith described her problem and took the offensive as she did. She argued that it was impossible for her to get out of her rut. Indeed, she claimed that attending the marathon was a futile action. Her reasoning: she was legitimately inadequate, whereas Paul was only a "pseudo-inadequate."

Judith did an outstanding job arguing her views. I pointed out that if she were so hopelessly inadequate, how could she be so articulate and talented in defending her inferiority? She snapped back that her abilities in defending her inferiority were hardly a virtue. (A point I heartily agreed with!) Then Judith and the group broke into laughter. Within this period of humor the group and I began to get Judith to accept that if she was that skillful in presenting her inferiority viewpoint she couldn't be inferior.

As Judith began to make progress in countering her inferiority thinking, Paul suddenly saw that his inferiority beliefs were similar.

Paul saw Judith as a person with superior qualities. Because he now saw how Judith's inferiority thinking served as a restraint that perpetuated her rut, he was better able to see how he had fooled himself, and how Judith, despite her high intelligence, had essentially done the same. So because of this marathon experience, Paul saw that he suffered from an *inferiority concept*: a pessimistic core of ideas he strongly adhered to.

Paul saw that he was not totally inadequate. Indeed, he was quite competent and worthy in many key respects. He also learned:

1. He previously discounted positive experiences.
2. In important circumstances his actions may reflect his negative self-view and thus result in the outcome he wants to avoid.
   a. The results of these self defeating actions are mentally recorded.
   b. They form a series of recallable negative documentations that support the core inferiority concept.

Negative documentations are past experiences that support a negative self-view. Often these documentations reflect valid self-observations that could be interpreted to mean that one is inferior. For example, many of Paul's negative self-observations were valid. Paul found it difficult to develop long-term relationships with women. He never had a friendship or love relationship that extended beyond six months. Thus he felt inadequate partially because of this documentable and valid observation. But the reason he had difficulty developing long-term relations was that he presented himself as a phoney by continuously trying to impress women to whom he was attracted. He figured that if he boasted and made himself sound like a great person, his *presentation* would gain him devotion. But his well-intended attempts to gain acceptance essentially put people off.

To change, Paul needed to take the medicine. He had to learn to *think* more objectively about himself. He needed to learn to *act* more responsibly to reduce the number of negative documentations. By learning the process of disequalization, Paul began his quest to think objectively.

Disequalization

Paul's conflict over how he could have positive capabilities when he considered himself inferior was resolved when the difference in strength between objective thinking and inferiority thinking were positively disequalized. David Berlyne (1960) describes disequalization as a way to allay conceptual conflicts by the *absorption* of new knowledge. In Paul's case, the new knowledge was acquired by learning to look at himself from a fresh perspective through giving adequate weight to his positive attributes and through recognizing their significance.

The Self-Doubt-Downing Syndrome

The inferiority reification process can be spelled out using the self-doubt-downing process and can, therefore, be confronted. The self-doubt-downing framework describes the basic steps to inferiority. Knowing the sequence will help us see how to reverse this malfunctional process.

Ken is a highly successful coach for a small college football team. He would like to coach a Big Ten squad, but he has blocked his own pathway because he feels inadequate. Part of his inadequacy feeling comes from his "inability" to speak in front of groups. Indeed, when he considers giving his team a pep talk, he hesitates because he thinks he may not get the words out correctly and may say something foolish. To compensate, he spends individual time with each of his players because he is more comfortable operating one on one. However, it is clear to Ken that if he is to advance, he must learn to speak before groups. Because he avoids learning public speaking skills, he defeats his goal; he downs himself and blames himself for failing to face his fear.

Ken is a victim of the self-doubt-downing process (shown in Figure 5).

Figure 5

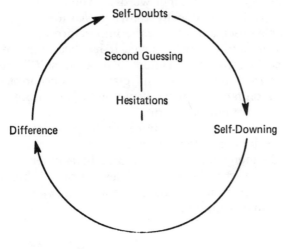

Ken follows a predictable mental pattern of doubting his abilities to portray his ideas effectively. This doubting is tied to second guessing himself (will I or won't I get my ideas across?), which results in hesitation.

This phase is self-defeating enough because time passes and opportunities are lost. However, Ken *interprets* his hesitations and lost opportunities as weaknesses and views himself as inferior because of them. He blames and downs himself for failing to act and for being weak. This part of the process is the self-downing, or garbage phase, because Ken "dumps on himself." He uses documentations of prior ineptitudes as ammunition for self-blame. At this point, the self-downing process becomes sheer misery. Ken views himself as different from other persons and thinks he is somewhat subhuman for having the problems he has. At the same time, he believes he is superior to most coaches and thinks that his tension keeps him from achieving a better coaching position. This leads to further doubts, second guessing, hesitation, self-downing, and the conviction that he is abnormal, weird, or different for so poorly containing his inner tensions.

Contending with the self-doubt-downing sequence. Alan Kazden (1974, 1978) has noted that the poorer the quality of a person's self-observation, the more difficult it will be for him or her to change constructively. In other words, if you do not see yourself clearly, you will have difficulty knowing *what* to change.

Kazden's observation about the importance of accurate self-observation is hardly new or novel. It has been repeated many times since Socrates first stated "Know thyself." However, whether new or novel or old and gray, the concept of accurate self-observation remains an excellent point of departure to uproot inferiority and get out from a rut.

The Scruffy cat story illustrates the importance of this self-awareness, self observation concept.

From the moment he was born, Scruffy let other cats manage his affairs. Even when he was an adolescent cat, his brothers and sisters brought him his food and his mother still washed him and played cat games with him.

One day Scruffy was adopted by an old man, Mr. Barker, who wanted Scruffy for a companion. Like Scruffy's brothers and sisters, Mr. Barker would bring him food and amuse him. However, washing was up to Scruffy, and since Scruffy had never learned to wash himself, he began to look more and more like his name. Indeed, he began to feel badly about himself because his white fur started to look dirtier by the day. The worse he looked, the worse he felt, and the more impossible the clean-up task seemed to be.

Mr. Barker was amused by his scruffy cat who seemed to avoid washing. Scruffy, however, was not amused. He lived with his affliction and his bad feelings about himself as one might live with the gout.

One day Scruffy happened to spy a number "ten" female feline. Overcoming his initial hesitation, he approached her. As they chatted, he fearfully made his interests known. Naturally, she was curious about what he had to offer her, but she trotted home when Scruffy had little to say.

Months passed and Scruffy was still amusing Mr. Barker with his scruffiness and still bemoaning his loss of the pretty feline. As it happened, a perky but scruffy female feline spotted him as he basked in the morning sunshine on the gray porch rail. She approached him. "Finally," she thought, "I have found someone who will understand me." Her conversation, however, was short-lived; Scruffy stuck his nose in the air and pranced back into the house to sip his milk. As he did so, he thought to himself, "Who wants to bother with that scruffy looking female!"

Time passed and Scruffy continued to dwell on how sad his life was, how unable he was to change it. But Mr. Barker one morning sat down with his scruffy friend. He pointed out that whether Scruffy liked it or not, if he wanted to be more appealing, he would have to work to develop a new habit of keeping his fur clean and attractive. Neglecting himself hardly created the sort of image that would impact positively on others. Furthermore, rather than being critical of the other individuals for exhibiting similar problems, Scruffy would be wise to recognize that his evaluation of the scruffy feline was a reflection of self-dissatisfaction.

Scruffy growled at the words, but he knew they were true. And if he wanted the advantages of change, he had to change.

Like Scruffy, to break free from a rut, it is important to commit yourself to work toward developing a satisfying and productive life-style. This will, of course, involve getting clear with yourself about what you are interested in doing, what skills you possess or can develop that will enables you to succeed at your interests and what blocks you from moving forward.

Expanding Self-Perspective

People are the best sources of information about themselves; yet most know precious little about themselves despite the fact that they have been living inside their own skin all of their lives. Self-knowledge can be limited by all sorts of misconceptions and poor mental habits, including self-doubts, exaggerated expectations, fears, and so forth. And discordant outlooks, as vented by our mistaken thinking, lead to the pattern we call a rut.

Most people would agree that getting rid of misconceptions through enlightened self-awareness is strongly prefered to self-oblivion. But people who seek change through enlightenment know it can be difficult to be bluntly honest and self-accepting at the same time. To be otherwise, however, lends to a pathway filled with thorns of disillusionment and unhappiness.

I once wrote a manual on how to help children develop psychological coping skills. I outlined how to develop self-enlightenment skills. A fundamental concept of the manual was the concept of positive self-knowledge, as this is a most powerful psychological coping tool.

A realistic perspective is the cornerstone of self-knowledge, so to begin to telescope your positive perspective, fill in the details on the Perspective Chart, using the instructions that follow as a guide.

To use the Perspective Chart, list as may positive qualities as you think you possess. Following is a series of examples for each category that you can use as a guideline.

Personal qualities include honesty, fairness, open-mindedness, reliability and so forth. Strongest Skills may include verbal or writing skills, sizing up a situation, watercolor painting talent, listening skill, and others. Constructive Capabilities can include attentiveness to detail, good concentration, perseverance, and so forth. Finest Actions may include helping a friend in distress, landscaping your home, passing a difficult test, and others. Interests can include sports, socializing, wood carving, card playing, short story writing, coordinating charity drives, cooking. Desires can include comfortable home life, satisfying career, good sex life, improving your education, or any other desirable objective you have. Values can include economic stability, loyalty, family, freedom, and so forth. (Keep in mind that if, despite all your listed virtues, you still do not have that one thing in your life that you "must" have, you are about to sabotage yourself. Overfocusing on "missing assets" draws you away from self-acceptance and perpetuates misery.)

In detailing your list, cite at least thirty items, if possible, under each category. If you cannot think of that many at one sitting, return later. You can also ask friends to add what they know about you, and you can use their valid observations. Also, if you analyze each item, you will begin to see that each one suggests others you can add.

When you complete this exercise, you will have the beginnings of self-perspective. Used in conjunction with the concept of the pie outlined in Chapter 2, this exercise aids positive perspective.

Perspective Chart
(Positive Documentation)

Your Personal Qualities	Your Strongest Skills	Your Constructive Capabilities	Your Finest Actions	Your Interests	Your Desires	Your Values

chapter five
THE END OF DISCOMFORT DODGING

The discomfort dodger is like the person with a headache who doesn't want to get out of bed to get an aspirin. Her motive is to spare herself the hassle of moving, and she gets a worse headache for her lack of effort.

A discomfort-dodging pattern is an outgrowth of metaphorical thinking. The discomfort dodger perceives him- or herself as hampered by inaction. He sometimes feels close to breaking the rut pattern but just can't seem to turn the key in the lock of change. Thus, he is like a baseball pitcher who knows he can throw a ball, but believes that he cannot move his arm in a throwing arc.

The purpose of this chapter is to point out how to fearlessly pass through the portals of discomfort, and thus disrupt your rut.

Intolerance for Tension

When we think of people we know who cannot tolerate frustration, we ofter think of the hard-driving businessperson, always urgent, always demanding; the screaming parent who instantly howls when the children misbehave; the motorist stuck in traffic leaning on the horn; or anyone with a short fuse who blows up like a child with a temper tantrum. But these frustration reactions barely scratch the surface of intolerance for tension.

Through the work of Hans Selye (1956) on the general adaptation syndrome and Myer Friedman and Ray Rosenman, (1975) on
type A behavior, the problems of stress, urgency, and tension intolerance have been viewed as an important mental health
dynamic. Intolerance for tension is the basic dynamic in the fear-
depression-resignation syndrome. Indeed, intolerance for tension
is the thread that ties together all forms of the so-called neurotic
disorders. Considering the importance of stress tolerance for good
mental health, it is important to look at the problem of intolerance
for tension and discomfort dodging from many angles, which we
will do in this chapter and throughout this book.

Problem Magnification

Persons who have low tolerance for tension tend to overrespond to
circumstances where their goals are hindered. They also tend to
oversensitize themselves to almost any strain or tension. Mildly
unpleasant but normal variations in their biological condition, as
well as the normal and inevitable irritations of life, become magnified in the minds of the intolerant.

Sensitized individuals unfortunately preoccupy themselves
focusing on their tensions and intensify their stress by magnifying
the negatives. As Jerry Wine (1971) and Claire Weeks (1978) have
noted, this sensitization tendency is a major factor in anxiety, as
sensitized persons fear their own uncomfortable feelings.

One's Discomfort, Another's Challenge

Clearly, events that are stressful for one individual may be the
opposite for another. For example, Ernest and Harriet manage
bond portfolios at different commercial banks. Each one appraises
the jobs differently: Harriet views her work as challenging and
Ernest views his with uncertainty.

Stress is not something imposed on a person. For example,
Ernest's job at the bank does not cause him stress, Rather stress is a

reaction to his apperception of his job, which is largely a function of learning and a reflection of his temperament. Ernest's stress reflects a complex interaction between learning and temperament. Stress tolerance is variable. Some days we can tolerate more stress than we can on other days. In fact, there are some periods when we are faced with multiple stresses and our ceiling for the amount of frustration we can absorb is high. At other times, it takes little to set us off. This common-sense observation can be visualized by using the concept of the vulnerability glass (Figure 6).

The vulnerability glass looks like a normal-sized drinking glass. Imagine that its contents are vulnerabilities for stresses and tensions. A person with a nearly full glass is more likely to succumb to stress. That is because it takes little additional stress for the person's stress system to overflow.

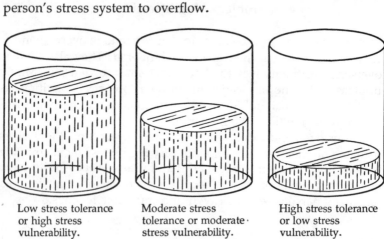

Low stress tolerance or high stress vulnerability.

Moderate stress tolerance or moderate stress vulnerability.

High stress tolerance or low stress vulnerability.

Figure 6

Thus, a person during a low stress tolerant period can "fly off the handle" on a slight provocation that most other people would let pass.

When a person's critical point is passed, he or she may have an anxiety reaction, slump into depression, act immaturely, feel immobilized, lash out, sulk, pout, or obsessively ruminate.

The stresses filling the glass can be physical: blood sugar imbalances, temporal mandibular joint dysfunction, mitral valve prolapse, hypothyroidism, viral infection, fatigue, hunger, adjustment to seasonal temperatures variation, humidity, pollen, air pollution, and so forth. The stresses can be psychological: time urgency, conflict, being "spread too thin," boring routine, multiple crises, and so forth. The stress can, of course, reflect both physical and psychological causes, which often play off each other, intensify each other, and threaten "overflow."

Feeling tense and irritable, a stressed person certainly would want to be rid of this discomfort, much like a person with a physical pain or annoying itch would want to deaden those sensations. Usually, however, there is no magical and immediate salve to ease physical and emotional tension. This is unfortunate because most people really don't want to experience discomfort. This is especially true of the discomfort of fear, depression, and other stressful, negative emotional states.

These sensations are like itches that seem to require scratching. And while there are some emotional itches one would wisely scratch, *how* one goes about scratching the itches determines if the underlying problem will be effectively treated or will worsen.

The Itch You Scratch

If you had an itchy spot on your arm, you would probably scratch it to get rid of the itchy feeling. Itches can be frustrating unless they are eased. However, if you have poison ivy, scratching will tend to exacerbate the problem. Therefore, you would normally choose to use a healing lotion to restrict the spread of the poison ivy and to reduce the itch. It may take longer for the lotion to ease the itch than scratching does, but you do this because you realize that:

- scratching the itch will cause it to itch more
- scratching the itch will spread the infection
- scratching the itch will increase the duration of the problem

So, to avoid long-term discomfort, you put up with the itch and live with your urge to scratch it. Experience has taught you that when it comes to poison ivy, it is better to manage the urge than to scratch.

It is easier for a person to stop the spread of poison ivy by managing the urge to scratch than for a threat-sensitive person to control an urge to overconsume food or alcohol if these or other compulsive indulgences temporarily ease the "tension itch." But easing the itch of tension by consumption is a mirage solution. The mental urge "I must consume now" provides short-term psychic pain relief and rarely allows for any long-term emotional gain. Thus, giving into the tension itch is like scratching poison ivy; one might get relief for a moment, but the itch goes on and spreads. And while the outcome of giving in to tension is often self-defeat, the intent is to spare oneself from discomfort, not to cause harm.

Treating the poison ivy itch with lotion helps the rash to go away within a predictable time-span. Poison ivy itches are, therefore, time limited and, thus, easier to endure. Because poison ivy is time limited and controllable, the suffering person will generally act in his or her best self-interest and avoid scratching. On the other hand, many psychological stresses and emotional discomforts seem to have unpredictable, perhaps "eternal" durations. But stresses and tensions, like poison ivy, really are time limited. If one is willing to endure the passage of time and seek productive solutions to deal with the stress, one is on the way to managing a discomfort problem. In contrast, a person who perceives personal discomfort as eternal and unendurable is likely to panic or feel helpless. And it is often this sense of helplessness to cope with inner tensions that tempts—indeed, impels—a person with a strong urge to avoid tension to scratch his or her psychological itch. The following case descriptions illustrate this principle.

Ginna, an obese adolescent female client, described a nightmare where she was helplessly trapped in a room filled with food. The food was piled high before her and blocked her exit. In her dream, she ate her way to the exit. As she passed through the exit, she entered another room. This room was also blocked by food.

Ginna's main psychological problems were reflected in her dream. She felt inadequate and was highly intolerant toward tension. Eating food was like a baby's pacifier. The purpose of eating was to feel calm, to get over feeling hopeless, avoid feelings of inadequacy, and smooth over tension. The impulse to binge, however, drove her more deeply into her rut. And at 100 pounds over her ideal weight, she also felt miserable about her shrinking social life.

Originally, Ginna's eating was a pacifier. Like a friend, eating sheltered her from inadequacy feelings and from fearing that she would fail at whatever she attempted. Her fears of failure grew out of experiencing failure when she was a young child with a perceptual-learning disability, which slowed her progress in learning to read. At the time her disability was acute, she ate to blanket her frustration; now, eating generalized as a pacifier to shelter her from inadequacy feelings generating out of her sense of inability to control her food addiction and her poor social life. No longer a "friend" that blocked the pain, eating became her problem. In the end, the pacifier became the whip instead of the salve.

Clearly, Ginna's pacifier accelerated her problems by drawing attention away from her real problem—learning how to overcome inadequacy feelings and tolerate tension. These problems were overshadowed by seemingly overpowering cravings to eat.

George, like Ginna, hated tension and had multiple malignant ways to "control" it. He was overweight, he chain smoked, and routinely abused alcohol. When he felt "nervous," he would wolf his food down, gulp beer "to get a quick buzz," and chain smoke. In his frantic scramble to avoid tension, he failed to taste the food he ate, the booze he drank or the cigarettes he smoked. Indeed, until I called this pattern to his attention, he was quite oblivious to his style of eating (wolfing), drinking (rapid gulping), and smoking (one cigarette would light the next). He was shocked when he realized how entrenched his avoidance pattern had become. Even though his goal was tension reduction, his outcome was the same as Ginna's—a continuous stream of unwanted tension. Like scratching poison ivy, George's problems spread and itched more.

Some people are more sophisticated than Ginna and George and will routinely use tranquilizers that they hope will become the emotional equivalent of poison ivy lotion, food, alcohol, or cigarettes. But tranquilizers, like other distractions, tend to seal over the problem of learning how to manage tension psychologically and may have side effects that include psychological and sometimes physical dependence. Thus, like using food and alcohol as pacifiers, drugs can add to the sources of tension or have only a palliative effect.

Drugs such as valium prescribed to alleviate tension at one time held the status of the "psychiatrist's stone"—the panacea to feeling good. The message conveyed was that tension is to be avoided and people need their medicine to feel good. Like ancient alchemists searching for the philosopher's stone (the magical substance to change baser metals to gold), those who seek the psychiatrist's stone seek to eliminate tension without changing conditions responsible for that tension.

Tension reduction may be desirable as getting rid of a frustrating itch is desirable. What the tension signifies and how it is to be dealt with, however, is as important as how the itch of poison ivy is managed. Thus, it is important to know what itch to scratch and what itch to leave alone.

Your Survival Instinct

Building tolerance for tension is a critical task to master on the pathway of breaking free from a rut. Indeed, building tension tolerance may prove your greatest challenge in your efforts to break loose.

Since tension is a normal condition for being alive, and thus cannot be avoided, those who seek to avoid all forms of tension are doomed from the start. The major question, therefore, is not whether you are going to be tense, but how you handle the tension.

Instinctively, we know that strong feelings of fear and discomfort often rightly signal a need to avoid circumstances that evoke those feelings. If you see an overwhelmingly powerful and menacing figure approaching, whom you rightly surmise intends to do you harm, it would be indeed peculiar if you did not feel fearful and have a strong urge to hightail it so that you can get out of harm's way. This survival instinct is strong.

If you put your hand into a bucket of scalding water, you would immediately withdraw it and would not put your other hand in. This reflexive withdrawal from pain is readily understood. The reaction is functional and adaptable. This same reaction can occur to psychic pain where, at the first hint of discomfort, anguish, or frustration, the person tries to squelch it in the hope that the feeling won't come back. But emotional pain is not like physical pain. Instead, it is more like a spring that pops up. If you sit on the spring to hold it down, you restrict yourself, and eventually the spring will cause you enough anguish that not only do you have the ruptured spring to contend with, but also the pain in your rump for sitting on it.

Like sitting on a spring, any form of holding onto a problem emotion to control it is likely to fail. To use another analogy, it is like trying to squeeze clay in your hand so as not to lose it, rather than gently molding it to the configuration you want.

People who "squeeze clay" or sit on "psychological springs" do so out of fear that their tensions will get out of control. The fear is that unless one is ever vigilant to boxing up tension, one will become an emotional basket case, become useless, and possibly lose one's identity. Paradoxically, this running from tension becomes self-inhibiting and creates "psychic pain." In this sad entanglement, one seems to be forever running from something rather than working toward something.

Behavioral Manifestations
of Tension Avoidance

Legitimate avoidance of physical pain can overgeneralize to avoidance of almost any form of discomfort. This avoidance tendency can get to the point where a person comes to fear any form of discomfort, and thereby creates the very discomfort that is feared.

The following cases illustrate the tendency to self-generate tension through futile self-protective efforts to control tensions. The futile efforts illustrated include demandingness, hostility, self-pity, and various forms of other self-protective manipulations. The cases are intended to represent symptoms of tension intolerance. They concern people with moderate emotional problems.

Each, however, may have elements in common with yours. After all, moderate emotional problems are extensions of mild problems, which are exaggerations of normal problems. The cases should raise your consciousness concerning the problem of intolerance for tensions.

Rita repeats a pattern of trying to be a good person and do what she considers right. She has a set of expectations, however, that other people should have extrasensory perception and read her mind, and likewise act in accordance with what she thinks is right. She becomes outraged when her expectations fail to be met, which, unfortunately for her, is quite often.

Unrealistically, Rita expects that the people at her office should act like a family, as should the members of the religious group she just joined. She finds it hard to believe that people at work or at the church would not call her periodically and inquire about how she is feeling. However, when a member of her actual family, such as her father, calls her to inquire how she is, Rita views that as meddling.

Because of unrealistic expectations, Rita experiences almost continuous discomfort. She hates feeling uncomfortable and attaches her problems to people—her employer, her fellow workers, her father, her brother, her neighbors. Presumably they are all at fault. Thus, she externalizes blame on others for internal problems that she has created. She sees hope for ridding herself of her discomfort as tightly tied to changing the "evil ways" of others. Rita's way of creating inner tension is essentially a demanding style.

Alice, like Rita, is intolerant of tension and self-generates the very tension of which she is intolerant. She also blames others. She goes beyond Rita's problem, however, by partially blaming her steady discomfort state on her teeth, body, and age. Her style is demandingness, hostility, and manipulativeness.

Alice's intolerance is attenuated by her sensitivity, which is such that she presents herself as a person needing to be treated with "kid gloves" lest she lash out. Since she is so vigilant to detecting what she considers "inconsiderations," people around her tend to walk on eggs. However, despite good intentions, inevitably someone will say or do something that Alice will upset herself about. Her pattern then is to interrogate them asking a series of leading questions, such as "Haven't I been considerate toward you?" Once the person has politely answered by admitting that Alice has not done anything wrong, she goes on to ask accusatory questions in a soft demanding tone, such as "Then why are you so unfair to me?" Typically, she snaps without waiting for an answer with angry statements, such as "I feel outraged by you," "I feel like hitting and kicking you." As might be surmised, Alice has no friends and few acquaintances with whom she is on speaking terms. Outraged, she wonders why people are not "giving" toward her and why they don't try to help make her life run more smoothly.

In addition to her people problems, Alice thinks she cannot stand having soft teeth because they cause her to make too many trips to the dentist. She dwells on her breasts sagging too much and believes that her breasts and her age of thirty are against her, preventing her from obtaining a good career and intelligent mate. Her real problem, howver, is attitudinal.

Carlo builds himself up by describing himself to others as supercapable. He is very frightened of feeling incompetent and anxious so his "build up" is compensatory self-sheltering. He thinks that if others view him as an amazing person, they will come to love, support, and rescue him from the normal daily pains of living. However, rather than being an amazing person, he projects himself as a precariously balanced, humpty-dumpty type character, and, like Alice, he is treated with kid gloves lest he shatter. But when people act overly gentle with him, Carlo gets the impression that he must be fragile and must need more protection; otherwise why would people act so cautiously with him?

Privately, Carlo whines and complains about his problems and tries to control others so that life will not prove uncomfortable. Thus, he manipulates himself and others to maintain the very uncomfortable rut he is in, which he strongly wishes he could be free from. Carlo's style is quiet demandingness, whining, self-pity, and manipulation.

Jack is the master of exotic excuses. For example, he hates to write term reports for his college courses, so he creates excuses to throw his professors off his trail until he can feel comfortable about completing the reports. He believes the normal discomfort and inconveniences inherent in term report writing simply should not be. Thus, he sees nothing amiss in telling professors that the reason his report will be late is due to:

1. Auto stolen with term paper in glove compartment.
2. Grandmother died and he had to handle funeral preparations.
3. Father had a nervous breakdown when his mother filed for divorce.
4. He was forced to take a full-time night job during the semester because of serious financial hardship.

Jack thinks his excuses are clever, and since they succeed most of the time—how many professors would fail a person if his grandmother just died?—he repeats the same pattern, avoids facing and living through his report writing tension, and thus digs himself deeper into his rut.

Rita, Alice, Rick, and Jack have a common problem; all find frustrations, fears, and other forms of tension intolerable. Their lives revolve around tension avoidance.

Discomfort dodging is not a realistic answer for Rita and her group of comfort-seeking cohorts. This tactic fails because the problems generating out of avoidance mount up, and with them comes more discomfort. This process readily advances to the point where the discomfort-avoiding person has double troubles—the original discomfort and his discomfort over his discomfort.

Time and Tension

When attention is on tension, the outcome is predictable. The person experiences him- or herself in the miserable "circle of sameness" called a rut. In this rut, the anguished person tends to be very much aware of the passage of time and the slowness of change. Thus, a person's perception of time infiltrates his or her sense of tension.

Alden Wessman (1973) conducted research suggesting that the way people experience and use time varies greatly. Some people are inclined to use time effectively and feel a sense of mastery, purposefulness, and efficiency. Those who fail to manage time tend to experience themselves as harassed, apprehensive, tense, goal-less, lacking in commitment, disorganized, inefficient, and discouraged.

Heinz Werner (1957) said it well when he noted that pathology is a blending of time, event, and self where the involved person loses the ability to order and differentiate what is important. The person who blends event, time, *tension* and self often urgently tries to change the event or to escape tension by forcing time to pass swiftly. The result of his efforts is that time drags and he experiences an intensification of discomfort and insecurity.

Self-Concept and Tension Tolerance

Low stress tolerance and inferiority concepts tend to be related. Where you find one factor, you will likely find the other. Although there is no law that says stress tolerance problems and inferiority concept problems need to coexist, low stress tolerance is generally accompanied by feelings of insecurity.

One need not feel inferior to be intolerant to tension, but it is quite rare to meet a person who thinks badly of himself and downs himself who is not also a person who has ducked one form of tension or another: discomfort-dodging tendencies often are taken as negative documentations for ineptitude. It is quite likely that self doubts often develop from this discomfort dodging process and feed this process.

The expanded formulation that includes this feedback process is shown in Figure 7.

Figure 7   Self-Doubt Discomfort-Dodging Model

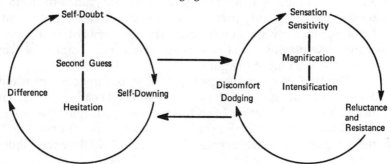

As can be seen in figure 7, a person can get tied up in psychological underwear when self-doubts and discomfort-dodging tendencies play off each other.

A self-doubting person hung up on second guessing and self-downing will feel tense. He will also tend to view himself as unable to absorb potential frustrations outside of his usual routine. Thus, he will see his vulnerability glass nearly full and he will try to protect himself from an overflow. By avoiding potential tension points, he thinks he can maintain equilibrium. But change itself is often viewed as a tension point, so he narrows his range of activities to accommodate his wish to avoid tension. Soon the routine of tension avoidance lends to monotony without a real abatement of tension.

As shown in Figure 7, *Discomfort Dodging* model, the discomfort-dodging person anticipates feeling tense, intensifies the sensation, and resists this feeling through discomfort dodging.

Weakening either the self-doubt or discomfort-dodging sequence or the transaction points between the two systems paves the way for new opportunity and new emotional muscle building.

Breaking the Doubt-Discomfort Cycle

George Ainslie (1975) proposed that people who exhibit difficulty controlling their impulses often go for short-term conterfeit solutions. These solutions he terms "specious reward." He sees people who go for specious rewards as doing so because their perceptions of the consequences of impulsive actions are distorted. Although impulsive action may get a short-term gain in the form of tension relief, it hardly prepares one to learn to delay gratification for a significantly greater reward. Specious reward is, in other words, like playing chess and moving your pieces rapidly so you can get to the end of the game.

The label of specious rewards is new, but the concept is old. Sigmund Freud spoke of the pleasure principle early in the twentieth century. Operating from the pleasure principle, the person would move toward the line of least resistance without necessarily reflecting on the consequences. Albert Ellis (1962) described short-term hedonism or goofing tendencies. A person with goofing tendencies goes for expedient rather than effective solutions to a problem.

A person is impulsive when he or she goes for specious rewards to avoid tension. A person boxed into a rut is also inclined to go for what will provide immediate gratification even though he or she substitutes a lesser for a greater reward.

A person in a rut often goes for specious rewards when she avoids risks and opportunity because she might feel initially uncomfortable. The young man at a party who approaches a woman he is confident will talk with him, rather than approach the woman he is really interested in, is opting for a specious reward.

Clearly, there are conditions where it is important to think before acting. Conditions that put long-term gain in conflict with short-term gain are conditions that require thought. Sometimes what you must do is explain to yourself what your nonimpulsive purposes and goals are.

Donald Meichenbaum (1974) streamlined a system for helping people who opt for specious rewards to operate more reflectively. What he suggests is that you explain to yourself out loud what you think is best for you to do, then whisper the same explanation, then think the explanation silently to yourself. This process will slow down your conceptual tempo, allow you to develop a more realistic perspective, and increase your chances for effective action. This approach certainly will help when you are considering:

- bingeing to anesthestize tension;
- touching a new paint job because you hoped that it dried sooner than expected;
- purchasing material that you don't really want because you will have to wait several days or weeks for what you do want;
- displacing your aggression onto someone who won't or can't respond;
- picking vegetables from your garden before they are ready;
- considering how your immediate actions will affect your future, and so forth.

Clearly, at times it is wise to act without too much thinking, and to follow your inclination. If you see a person you would like to meet at a party, why hesitate? If you are playing a game of softball and the ball is hit at you, you let your reflexes go into action. If you feel like taking a cool shower on a warm day, what is there to hesitate about? If you think your lawn needs mowing and you have the time to do it, why not get started?

Rethinking, and reviewing actions that are best handled rapidly reflect needless inhibition. Indeed, if you can handle routines that do not require a great deal of thought without second guessing or hesitations, you are likely to experience much less strain and enjoy more gain.

Rethinking generally is a result of habit and a reaction to sensations of discomfort. Some people are ergophobic, that is, fearful of making an effort. Because they associate effort with strain, what appears to require effort is avoided. This effort aversion (ergophobia) is often a function of misreading bodily sensations by interpreting them as saying one is too tired to act or the task must be too difficult. So, if you think washing the dishes is too tough, and you think that you don't have the energy to wash them, ask yourself if someone paid you $1000 for doing the dishes, or if you could have sex with your ideal sex partner right after doing the dishes, could you find the energy? Chances are you would. Thus, you have to be alert for the "inner con" that you don't have the energy when you do have the energy.

Low Frustration Tolerance Language

Persons intolerant of tension develop a communication system that reflects and perpetrates their discomfort. The system consists of low frustration tolerance language, words, and gestures. The language is toned with strain and stress. It is important to recognize this language and eliminate it because it serves only to support a negative outlook. It consists of a vocabulary of terms and phrases that reflect distress, woefulness, urgency, squeamishness, shock, and ineptitude. Some examples follow.

1. Distress phrases—I don't feel good, I'm nervous, I'm having a breakdown, I feel like I'm falling apart, how will I ever manage?

The distress phrases suggest that circumstances are beyond control and one is helpless. This is clearly muddled thinking because these statements are not facts. They are descriptive of their own effects.

2. Woe phrases—I always ruin things for myself, poor me, I'm a real loser. Woe phrases suggest resignation. They also suggest a refusal to take responsibility for one's own life. More importantly, they are a futile plea for pity.

3. Urgency phrases—I must have what I want when I want it, I can't stand feeling this way any longer. I must get better right away, I've got to get finished now. Urgency phrases reflect a demand language. This language is filled with imperatives, such as shoulds, oughts, musts, got to's, and other terms that convey a sense of urgency. Ninety percent of the time, these imperatives falsify the urgency of a situation.

4. Squeamishness terms and phrases—disgusting, ugly, revolting, sickening, nauseous, hate it. These phrases are subjective perceptions, taken for fact because the feeling supports the idea. They mostly reflect an oversensitive reaction and a tendency to over generalize.

5. Shock terms—horrible, awful, ghastly, frightful. Shock terms convey a sense of catastrophe. They are often too loosely used and reflect sloppy thinking.

6. Ineptitude phrases—I'm so helpless, I can't control anything, I have no skills. Ineptitude phrases convey a sense of weakness and, like woe phrases, reflect an abdication of responsibility.

Numerous words and expressions convey an intolerance for tension and a sense of suffering. Some, however, suggest relief, such as *whew*, which normally implies that one had faced a discomfort. The word and accompanying emotive expression, however, reflect a relief from a self-inflicted discomfort originally built by talking forebodingly to oneself. Sighing and grunting also reflect mentally generated tension.

Gestures, like low frustration words and phrases, also convey intolerance. The most common gestures are pouting, sulking, frowning, and sullenness.

Low frustration tolerance words, phrases, and gestures reflect a self-defeating coping style. These communications reflect and create tension, and because they are attached to stress situations, they also evoke power to create stress.

Make up a list of the low frustration tolerance phrases you find yourself using. Convert these phrases to more objective ones. Examples follow.

Low Frustration Tolerance Phrase	Objective phrase
1. I feel like I'm falling to pieces.	1. I'm not thinking clearly and will need to pause and reflect to determine what my problem is.
2. This situation is awful; I can't stand it.	2. I don't like what I see, but I'll certainly live through this.
3. Woe is me, I can't do anything correctly.	3. It's unfortunate that I'm not performing well; now what can I do to do better?

In the future, when you catch yourself engaging in the low frustration tolerance phrase, follow this sequence:

1. Repeat the phrase four times.
2. After the fourth repetition, say *stop*.
3. Repeat the new objective phrase to yourself four times.
4. Act on the basis of the new phase.

The purpose of repeating the low frustration phrase is to defuse its impact by putting it under voluntary control. The purpose of the word *stop* is to associate "stop" with the low frustration tolerance (LFT) phrase. Stop is then used as a bridge between the LFT phrase and the new objective phase. With repeated practice of this system, you increase your chances of thinking *stop* after a spontaneous LFT utterance and then shifting to an objective outlook.

III

GETTING OUT BY BANISHING FEAR

Some people avoid their fears by avoiding change, trying to live their lives within the narrow confines of a self-created "comfort zone." In this zone, the person plays it safe. There are few risks, but neither are there many opportunities.

Comparable to a sanctuary a person erects to protect him- or herself against a coming storm, the comfort zone may do its protective job. But the trade offs one makes for living in this comfort zone are costly. The costs are boredom, restraint, and *fear*. So, in reality, the comfort zone becomes like a guardless prison. And the longer one stays in this "sanctuary," the more strained one feels.

People who become entangled in this comfort zone soon discover that they are really in a stagnant zone, but they psychologically fear the thought of getting out. Psychological fear is an outgrowth of self-doubts and intolerance for tension. It is an ego and discomfort dodging problem where the psychologically afflicted person anticipates emotional danger outside of his comfort zone, doubts he will be able to cope with that danger, and intimidates himself by fearing the onset of the sensation of fear.

Obviously, a person who is fearful will tend to avoid change and thereby will condemn him- or herself to follow the pattern of the seemingly endless circle of sameness we term a rut. Dissatisfied for remaining in the rut and yet fearful of change, this person is on the horns of a dilemma of his or her own making.

Part III addresses the issue of how to recognize and cope with psychological fear. Chapter 6 introduces the concept of fear, describes its characteristics, discusses its forms, identifies how people come to think fearful thoughts, and provides a general approach for eliminating fear. Chapter 7 introduces the rational-emotive approach for countering fearful thoughts. Powerful self-questioning methods are described along with a system to get involved in counter-rut problem-solving behavioral activities. In Chapter 8, psychological fear is countered by behavior therapy strategies. An innovative "cluster hierarchy" method is described to provide the self-helper with a powerful way to use behavior therapy to counter fear. This cluster hierarchy approach is designed to give the self-helper an orderly, systematic, and logical method to break from his or her rut pattern. Chapter 9 introduces psycho-regulation training methods geared to aid the reader to deal with tension and to optimize his or her efforts in order to break the barriers of fear and perform better at what he or she wants to do. Combining relaxation with mobilization methods, psycho-regulation provides powerful self-help possibilities.

Part III is a pivotal section. Fear is emphasized because a person who learns to master fear has moved far in mastering him- or herself. Furthermore, as will become clear, fear is a symptom of self-doubts and tension intolerance.

chapter six
KNOWING YOUR FEAR

Fear can be a reaction to a possible danger. A monkey who has never seen a snake appears startled and tries to escape. A cat scurries away at a strange sound. A wild horse gets jumpy on first entering a new pasture. A person sees a large shadowy figure moving out of the darkness and feels afraid. Indeed, fear of the unknown is a reaction common to most mammals.

However, the reaction of fear is not limited to possible danger or the threat of real danger. People can be afraid of their dreams, harmless animals, *even themselves*. Fears that do not pose an actual danger are psychological fears.

Chronic psychological fear is frequently indicated as a major source of psychological and physical health problems. It is pivotal to maintaining a rut and can lead to a depressed state if the fear victim resigns him- or herself to this state. For these reasons, it is essential to know psychological fear as an enemy and to know how to dispatch it.

This chapter is designed to help you identify and diagnose your fears. Following the educational description is a basic framework for countering psychological fears. This framework can stand on its own, but it also lays the groundwork for the more sophisticated counter-fear systems that follow.

Characteristics of Fear

George has trouble falling asleep nights. He worries whether he will soon be fired, if he can still attract friends, and if he will pass the upcoming bar examination. Carol is uptight around people and finds it difficult to engage in small talk. She feels lonely much of the time, but finds herself "too much of a stiff" to relate comfortably with people. Wilton feels edgy when he contemplates talking to fellow employees over lunch hour. He fears that he will not be able to participate in the conversation, that he will get uptight, and might not be able to hold down his lunch. Bonnie panics at the thought of being trapped. She avoids parties, department stores, grocery stores, and other places where she might be stuck—automobiles, buses, trains, airplanes.

Although each person's circumstances and symptoms differ, George, Carol, Wilton, and Bonnie all suffer from psychological fear. In each instance, the fearful person dwells on *possible* threats to "self-esteem" and thus suffers from anticipatory dread.

A psychological fear is one that comes from *threat*, not real danger. The threat is to self-worth or emotional stability. It is largely derived from misconceptions and false contingencies, such as that one's sense of personal security depends on success, control, and the approval of others. For example, the person who believes approval, worth, and personal security are one and the same craves affection and approval and thinks he or she must have it from everyone, including such unknown persons as bellhops, taxi drivers, or local politicians.

In contrast, *real* fear is both a signal of and a reaction to natural danger. An eighteen-wheel truck thundering toward you is a well-understood natural danger. As you see the truck bearing down on you, your body goes into emotional high gear and you blaze a retreat from the pathway of the truck. Like fear of an oncoming truck, fear of the unknown is a natural reaction to a novel but potentially risky situation. A person traveling to a new country, in which he or she does not understand the language or customs, may initially be apprehensive. The newcomer studies the foreign land with cautious apprehensiveness until he or she becomes assured that there is no danger.

Individual Reactions to Danger

When endangered or threatened, people respond differently to the same circumstance. This principle of individual differences is demonstrated in an experiment described by Gregory Raiport (1980). It illustrates the reactions that people can have to *anticipated danger*. The experiment was conducted by the Soviet military, and it was designed to evoke fear in naive military participants and yield data about Pavlovian theories of brain functioning: there are only two major reactions of the nervous system, excitation and inhibition. Under stress, only a few people are capable of resisting either extreme.

In the experiment, trucks of soldiers are transported to a barren and arid desert in one of the Asian Soviet states. The trucks depart, leaving the soldiers behind. A sergeant has an attache case containing brochures, which are distributed to the soldiers. The brochure reads: "Comrades! You are located in a zone of an A-bomb explosion, which is due in 30 minutes. In defense of the motherland, scientists must investigate the effects of radiation on human beings. There is almost no chance that any of you will survive; but you must be proud to give your lives for our great country!"

The troops exhibit different "fear" reactions. Some frantically race around, cursing and swearing. Some remain frozen in their tracks like rabbits caught in the beam of an automobile headlight. About twenty percent remain calm and continue reading the brochure to the last page, where they learn that there is to be no explosion and they are part of an experiment.

So, in the experimental circumstances designed to evoke reactions to anticipated danger, the Pavlovian theory was supported. Furthermore, it seems that the groups could be psychologically classified on the basis of their reactions—impulsive, reflective, and repressive. In addition, the experiment suggests that those who were able to monitor their level of arousal by taking a reflective "let's wait and see" attitude adapted to the circumstances and functioned most effectively.

The Yerkes-Dodson Law provides additional data to explain the Russian "experiments." This law says that there is an optimal level of arousal important for effective functioning. If you are either

89

under- or overaroused, predictably you will do less well. Thus, fear, frustration, or any other strong emotional arousal can be functional to coping if the feeling provides the impetus for action and is not disorganizing. Figure 8 shows the familiar inverted U-shaped curve that describes the Yerkes-Dodson Law.

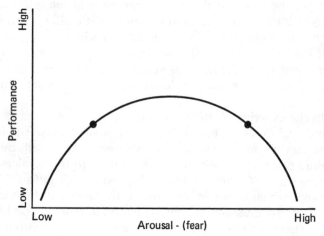

Figure 8

The distance between the two dots on the curve represents the optimal combination of arousal and performance. As can be seen, at certain levels, fear can be a facilitator. Doubtless, the twenty percent of the Russian soldiers who did not panic were able to operate in an optimal range of thinking and acting. Those who did panic or froze became overly aroused, and thus became disorganized. So, in danger and threat situations, a person's level of fear can vary from mild to severe. In the milder level, fear may well be highly functional, if it results in increased vigilance, alertness, and bodily preparedness.

When Fear Persists

Mild fear reactions (existing for short interludes) attached to legitimate real fear can be functional. When fear is persistent and intense, however, it has many unpleasant psychological and health-disrupting side effects. Persistent psychological fear disrupts the person's ability to functionally organize his or her behavior and promotes what Robert White (1964) refers to as a "visceral storm," which causes a wide range of baffling physical symptoms.

Tragically, the vast majority of deleterious psychological and physical symptoms are due to adopting *faulty assumptions* by thoughtlessly accepting them as fact, reindoctrinating oneself about the perils of the assumed danger, and thus suffering at one's own hands. Much will be said in this book about this faulty indoctrination process and how to counter it.

Following is a partial list of the psychological and physiological symptoms that are *possible* consequences of chronic psychological fear.

A. *Psychological Symptoms*
  1. Work-a-holism: burying oneself in activities to keep busy and to avoid fear sensations.
  2. Difficulty making friends.
  3. Shyness.
  4. Hypersensitivity.
  5. Problem avoidance.
  6. Withholding expression of feeling or emotional liability.
  7. Lack of confidence.
  8. Constant apprehensiveness.
  9. Approval seeking.
  10. Perfectionism.
  11. Success avoidance.
  12. Avoidance of *possible* (not necessarily *probable*) failure situations.
  13. Phobic or strong irrational avoidance of normally harmless situations (going out of doors, heights, airplane travel, small animals, dirt).
  14. Thoughts of going crazy.
  15. Pressure of speech where words flow like water flows over Niagara Falls.
  16. Problems with attention and concentration.
  17. Stammering.
  18. Compulsions, such as *having* to recheck the stove numerous times to be sure the gas is off, or any other needlessly repetitive activity.
  19. Obsessions, repetitive and unwanted thoughts.

20. Procrastination.
21. Difficulty in experiencing pleasure.
22. Nightmares.
23. Worry.
24. Loss of spontaneity.
25. Inflexibility; approach problems in same way.
26. Disruption of orderly mental processes.
27. Impulsiveness.
28. Intolerances.
29. Uncertainty.
30. Indecisiveness.

B. *Physical Symptoms*
  1. Mental *fatigue* (neurasthenia).
  2. Numbness.
  3. Sleep disorders, particular problems in falling asleep.
  4. Frequent urination.
  5. Twitches, tics, and jerking.
  6. Conversion symptoms, such as pseudo blindness, deafness, or paralysis, that seem real but are not.
  7. Panic reaction syndrome: heart palpitations, shortness of breath, dizziness, sweating, blushing, muscular constrictions, coldness, disorganization of thinking.
  8. Reduced resistance to stress.
  9. Diarrhea.
  10. Gastrointestinal disorders.
  11. Headache.
  12. Nausea.

The stresses and strains of fear can create havoc on the body. Indeed, the lowered resistance of your system after a prolonged bout with fear increases your susceptibility to more fear and more unpleasant body systems. For example, peptic ulcers, gastritis, and other forms of the so-called psychosomatic reaction are thought to be symptomatic of prolonged stress.

Hans Selye (1956) pointed out that continuous stress (and psychological fear is certainly a possible source of continuous stress!) causes actual physical damage to the nervous system, which in some cases is irreversible. Sometimes rest is offered as an antidote for stress. Rest by itself, however, does not restore the system to a healthy state. Learning how to cope with stress is infinitely more helpful and provides the person with the option to "rest." Face it, it is hard to rest when you feel stressed.

With increases in psychological fear come an increase in disruption of organized thinking and behaving and the reduction of the nervous system's ability to adapt to new and different stresses. Thus, it is hard to "rest" under such disruptive conditions. Repressive defenses emerging under disruptive conditions only add to the stress. And when a person's focused attention is away from coping and on to defending, there is an increased likelihood of the tension continuing.

It is understandable that a person who suffers from persistent psychological fears, and who is not tuned into the psychological cause of that fear, would fixate on psychological or physical *symptoms* and blame the symptoms for his or her tension.

One of the more difficult tasks in life is the task of knowing and understanding yourself. Indeed, it is difficult to be objective when you feel physical pain. For example, one person who was entrapped in a psychosomatic circle was Damon. Prior to entering therapy, Damon spent over $100,000 in medical bills trying to trace the physical causes for his highly elevated white blood count, chronic headaches, gastrointestinal disorders, neck pain, slipped discs, and so forth. He felt racked with pain for over five years. And his symptoms were real. When I first met with Damon, it did not take long to determine that he would make the neurotic "insect" character in Franz Kafka's *The Metamorphosis* look like he sat on the throne of self-actualization. Damon had an exceedingly negative, woefully inadequate self-image. He was riddled with fearful thoughts. His problem was that he was ignorant of the impact of his psyche on his soma, was bewildered and confused by his physical symptoms, and never stopped to think about how he was thinking about himself; how his gross lack of confidence, chronic hostility and panic level fears were producing enormous body strain and regular systematic breakdowns. And with each new physical symptom, he panicked more because he believed his whole body was going to ruin and that he was too weak and helpless to do anything about it.

It was a long hard battle for Damon first to admit that he was the architect of his own stress and then to, step-by-step, counter his fear by promoting clear thinking habits. But counter it he did, and in the process he earned the reward of experiencing a marked reduction in physical symptoms. Moreover, he achieved a more organized and pleasurable "psychological" existence. It was a happy day for Damon and for his insurance company when he learned to manage his fears.

After Fright

After fright is another of the many faces of fear. In after fright, a person may have gone through a dangerous situation, such as surviving an auto accident. John, for example, was a passenger in an auto when it hit a tree. After the accident, he was driven home unharmed. In the following weeks, however, he became increasingly apprehensive about riding in an automobile. At the point when he first came to see me, he was unable to ride in a car and nearly panicked when he thought of one. In addition, his fear *generalized* to buses, trains, and other forms of transportation.

This after fright reaction has been discussed by K. Diven (1937) who described how fear sometimes increases with the passage of time even when the person is not exposed continuously to the danger. It is almost as though some fears require time to incubate before they rise. Diven also pointed out how fears have a tendency to generalize.

One fear that may generalize is the fear of the unknown. Fearing one's own bodily sensations is a special form of fear of the unknown. A person who feels tense sensations and does not understand their cause can panic by making him- or herself afraid of the sensation.

Credibility of Fear

Psychological fear is not completely irrational. A fear of heights, for instance, has a basis in reality. One *could* fall and get injured. A person who is in good health but imagines an oncoming heart attack may have a muscle contraction or painful spasm that is misinterpreted as a heart attack. Such powerful self-suggestions can start a flood of symptoms, including light-headedness, weakness, and so on, which appear to give credibility to the "danger." For example, few would fault those Soviet troops whose nervous systems responded to the presumed threat of mass destruction with excitation or inhibition; the *anticipated* danger seemed authentic enough!

The physical results of real or psychological fear, particularly protracted fear, are often real, not imaginary. Fatigue, gastritus, or headache are *real*. Merely passing such psychosomatic symptoms off as caused by mental dribble and suggesting that one get one's mind off those thoughts can only serve to exacerbate rather than help the problem.

Fearfulness: A Mirror of Superstitions and Faulty Evaluations

Psychological fear is an anticipation of future weakness. The psychologically fearful person *predicts* emotional disaster because she thinks she is too inept or weak to manage or cope. In short, psychological fear is an affliction of the imagination where mental monsters are created and the person humbles herself and trembles at the very thought of her own creations. Often she does not recognize her own handiwork. Instead, she concentrates on the ailments it creates.

The mental monsters can reflect serious apprehensiveness about one's physical or mental well-being, as when the psychologically fearful person fears he or she has cancer, may have a heart attack or might go crazy. The fear can be focused on possible external events, as when a person thinks an acquaintance might reject him, he will fail a test, will appear out of control, or would seem stupid in the eyes of others. Clearly, a person who creates more than his or her share of these mental monsters curtails his or her activities.

Wendel Johnson in *People in Quandaries* (1946) gives us a framework for understanding how people make themselves psychologically fearful. He believes that psychologically fearful people are superstitious and/or victimize themselves by adopting and maintaining fearsome but false *evaluations*. This same position is supported by Albert Ellis (1962), Aaron Beck (1967, 1976), Arnold Lazarus (1971, 1976), Michael Mahoney (1974), and other cognitive-behavioral or rational-emotive therapists and writers.

Superstitious Fears

Ernst Cassaire (1946) sees the human myth-making tendency as a reflection of creative imagination. It is portrayed through storytelling and art. It reflects the intuitive side of our personality. According to split-brain theorists, it may well be the workings of the right hemisphere of the brain translated through the logic and language of the left hemisphere.

Through the ages, people have frightened themselves over their own supernatural mythological inventions. They have created such characters as powerful Zeus, Thor, Count Dracula, and a wide assortment of hobgoblins. To counter these mental inventions, they invent other forces: ragweed to ward off vampires, placing a knife in a bucket of water outside the door to destroy a marauding devil. Presumably the devil sees the knife in his reflection and dies of fright.

The creation of supernatural powers is part of the history of human myth-making. People have historically invented myths to describe their way of life and to entertain and explain a natural phenomena that otherwise seemed incomprehensible.

The myth is an intuitive explanation that applies a type of logic to the inexplicable *to quell fears of the unknown*. For example, people who lived in the age of the ancient Greek city-states often invented gods to explain the feared forces of nature, which they were unable otherwise to comprehend. For example, many ancient Greeks found it reassuring to think that Zeus, "the father of all gods," displayed his anger by showering the earth with thunder balls (lightning). The ancients invented the myth partially because they had no natural explanation for the creation of lightning.

Myths that were invented to quell uncertainty and the fear of the unknown became like a two-edged sword. Although the myth might quell the nagging fears of uncertainty and the omnipresent fears of the unknown, it also could become the source of yet another fear—*fear of the uncontrollable force*. Thus, some particularly frightening myths became like a nightmare or activating source of terror. For instance, a storm that seemed to rage out of control, with high velocity, whipping winds, drenching rainfall, and flashing lightning, could heighten the fears of those who believed in Zeus; they saw this terrifying god as uncontrollable in his rage and unpredictably ready to destroy. Now, not only did those frightened believers in Zeus have the actual storm to contend with, but the vision of an angry, unpredictable, omnipotent god loomed even more terrifying.

Oversensitive self-doubters often fall into the same trap as the ancient Greeks who believed in capricious, all-powerful gods. They fabricate myths to explain their oversensitivity, inferiority feelings, and groundless fears. Unable to understand their self-doubts, inferiority feelings, and at the same time fearful of being overwhelmed by this mental state, many externalize their problems. For example, portraying others as critical, spying, and negating is an externalized explanation for one's distress. Externalization becomes a major problem as the person moves further from a rational solution to his or her problems. Now the person must contend with a second "external" problem that potentiates the original inferiority. Indeed, as can be seen, superstitious solutions to quell fears of the unknown are about as effective as drinking 100-proof bourbon to stop a nasty wound from bleeding.

Evaluative Fears

Evaluative fears are *status fears.*. They are artificial fears that reflect threat to one's self-esteem. They are derived from the emphasis in Western culture on achievement, status, success, and the avoidance of failure. They grow out of the belief that self-worth is tied to achievement. More importantly, they grow out of the belief that one should be like one's idealized self, flawless in every respect. Thus, loss of self-esteem occurs when a disparity appears between how one is supposed to be and actual behavior.

Evaluative fear is most pronounced in "ego" survival where the goal is to preserve the integrity of the "idealized self." The idealized self is that part of our conceptual system that represents what we think we *should* be and how others *should* view us; in other words, our "image." For example, a person suffering from perfectionism problems suffers because he believes he needs to maintain a flawless image. As this person perceives danger to his image because of a possible "inadequate" performance, he experiences "performance fear."

There is a more common and possibly more self-defeating form of threat than performance fear; it is discomfort fear. When discomfort is viewed as threatening, a person suffering discomfort fears will tend to avoid situations that might be uncomfortable.

Psychological fears such as ego fears and discomfort fears are the fabrics of ruts. Because each of these fears is so unpleasant, a psychologically fearful person will do almost anything to block them. But the attempt to try to block psychological fear heightens self-doubts and discomfort fears.

The hypochondriac readily falls victim to this pattern. Magnifying the importance of minor physical symptoms, he convinces himself that he has serious medical problems and needs treatment. Sensitized to the slightest physical variation, he converts credible minor symptoms into a major medical problem. Absorbed in his medical problems and fearful of poor health, he avoids acting to get out from his rut until he is certain he is well. This person is really in a rut as his life revolves around his self-created "medical" disorder. This medical revolving door leads to more self-doubts and discomfort because, as he ruminates on his "helpless condition," he becomes more sensitized to his body sensations.

Countering Imaginary Fears

Psychological fear is imaginary fear built on superstition and faulty evaluations. It is what John Dollard (1942) calls "foolish fear," which he believes can be combated by "self-study."

The focus in this section is on a simple straightforward assault against imaginary fears. The plan involves five steps:

1. Problem analysis.
2. Sensation detection.

3. Action planning.
4. Behavioral action.
5. Evaluation.

Since psychological fear can include numerous symptoms and reflect individual differences, it would be practically impossible to apply this five-step counterfear system to all possible types of fear. Instead, the program represents an *approach* you can use to cope with your psychological fear. It is an approach that is, therefore, adaptable to your course of self-study.

Problem Analysis

In analyzing your psychological fears, break your problem down into its constituent parts so that you better know what it is that you have to deal with.

As part of your fear analysis, it is often helpful to write down your thoughts about your fears, even the random thoughts that seem tangentially related. John Dollard (1942) suggests that a person who feels fearful would be wise to write down his or her thoughts, particularly those *sentences* that seem to blend with fear. Once the fear sentences are written out, one has greater freedom to objectively re-evaluate his or her thinking because the visual display of the fear-inducing thoughts makes them contradictable.

Tom Williams (1923) wrote in *Dread and Besetting Fears* that when a particular feature of a new experience is believed to be threatening, the whole situation is regarded as a threat. He says that when " . . . we think of it (the situation) studiously, in a scientific spirit, with a view to penetrating its meaning, and understanding its causes, one would cease to be afraid because one would exorcise the bogy which is always the real cause of fear."

Williams suggest breaking down a fear situation into its components. This strategy is well suited for *self-assertion* situations, such as applying for a pay raise, meeting new people, traveling to unusual places, expressing your opinions, and other conditions that you might normally fear.

When you employ this breakdown approach, you examine the event you are fearful of and determine specifically what it is that you fear. Is it a fear of rejection? If so, in what way are you likely to be rejected? What would you have to do to bring the rejection upon yourself? Is it a fear that you might appear choked and blocked, and thus look foolish? If so, examine *what* is so frightening that you dare not risk expressing yourself.

In playing the role of the scientist, look for the positives in a fear situation as well as what you fear. What is it that you are not afraid of? What are the benefits for acting to cope with the fear? This positive appraisal of a psychological fear situation allows you more accurately to direct your efforts toward building on the positive elements. Indeed, inherent in each "feared" condition are hidden opportunities, including the opportunity to dispel your fear, build your confidence, tolerate tension, get experience, and build action skills.

Edward Cowles (1941) suggests that some elements in a fear situation are more powerful than others. In your analysis of a fear situation, it would pay to determine what fear symptoms or ideas are the weakest elements in the pattern. For example, perhaps you feel dizzy when you feel afraid and dizziness is the least of your concern. If you can accept the dizziness and not preoccupy yourself with it, you might better be able to proceed to deal with the intense mental suggestions that produce the visceral storm that contributes to the dizziness.

In summary, the problem analysis of your fear requires that you think like a scientist to assess the elements inherent in your fears.

Sensation Detection

If psychological fear did not feel so uncomfortable, there would be no need to be concerned about the sensation. However, it is the dread of fear sensations (discomfort fears) that drives many to distract themselves, block the feeling, or unwittingly create false attributions to explain what is happening.

Fear can be exacerbated when a person defines the sensation as mysterious or of unknown origins, and panics when he or she does not comprehend the sensation. In fearfully contemplating this mysterious sensation, thoughts and sensations become intermingled, and the victim of the psychosomatic entanglement creates all sorts of illusions to explain the sensation, including that he or she must be going crazy. As this sad progression advances, the person fatigues, becomes increasingly vulnerable to negative thinking, and the process intensifies. Part of this intensification is a function of false prognostications that the mysterious fear sensation cannot be controlled, might last forever or might lead to a subjective loss of self (psychological annihilation).

Acceptance of a fear sensation is difficult because the sensation may seem uncontrollable and inescapable. After all, who wants to feel tense forever? So, first of all, one would be wise to accept a fearful sensation as a *time-limited sensation* and as tolerable. This acceptance is realistic compared to giving oneself mental dribble such as "I have endured this feeling for too long; I must get rid of it now because I can tolerate it no longer." Chances are you will continue to tolerate it no matter how much you harp at yourself to get rid of it. So, if the sensation is there, accept it, and try to understand what your body is telling you. And as you do so, keep in mind that acceptance does not equal pleasure. You can accept a feeling even though you don't like it.

Clearly, if a person were not afraid of uncomfortable fear sensations, he would be better able to read the signal his body is giving him and then to decide what the signal means and what action, if any, he might want to take. The signal could mean he is fatigued, ducking his problems, coming down with a virus, victimizing himself with irrational thinking, or there simply may not be a clear reason for the sensation, and he will simply have to live temporarily with the mystery.

To assist this process of acceptance of the fear sensation, you can use a technique suggested by Victor Frankl (1975) called *paradoxical intention*. Using paradoxical intention, you focus your full attention onto the fear sensations and try your darndest to intensify them. Typically, the sensation weakens for the same reason that such sensations intensify when you try not to pay attention to them or try to snuff them out. You experience a paradoxical effect; you get the opposite of what you expect.

Fear sensations can be managed by a technique I call *mind migration*. In mind migration, you identify where the sensation is localized in your body and change the location. If the sensation is localized in your shoulders, try to shift it to your calf. If the sensations is in your "head" transfer it to your right biceps. You can even try to generalize a localized sensation by spreading it throughout your body.

Sensation acceptance, paradoxical intention, or mind migration techniques are helpful because you can see that the sensation is tolerable, and, therefore, you are less likely to victimize yourself by urgently insisting that the sensation go away.

Once you can accept the sensation, however miserable you might feel, you are better positioned to engage in action planning.

Action Planning

Once you have identified a specific fear that you want to deal with, and have analyzed the parameters to your problem, the time has come for action planning. For action planning, you can use a simple TATG system. TATG stands for Task, Approach, Time, Generalization. In using the TATG approach, you define your *task*—asking for a pay raise. Next, you define your *approach* by specifying the steps you will take to accomplish the task: identify what you are afraid of about the task; identify what you are not afraid of about the task; reevaluate your fearful assumptions; devise ways to take advantage of the positives in the situation. *Time* refers to specifying when you will take action. *Generalization* refers to identifying similar situations you are fearful of, identifying common components, and determining how you can employ what you learn in your initial target task to help in these similar situations.

Behavioral Action

Fear situations can be faced and action plans enacted simply by *directing your muscles to do the work your plan outlines.* Put your muscles through their paces. Fight against inhibiting feelings by allowing your muscles to *act.*

Sometimes, there is no easy way to proceed behaviorally against fear other than compelling yourself into some form of action. If the action you have planned is realistic (you will tackle the weakest of your symptoms *or* take actions that are in your capability of readily enacting), then what is required is putting your body through the paces.

Evaluation

Any scientist worth his or her salt evaluates the outcome of his or her experiments and uses the results to create new experiments. The goal of this experimental evaluation process is to advance knowledge and build skills. The same principle applies to experiments planned to disrupt psychological fear patterns. By objectively evaluating your counterfear performance, the strengths and weakness can be identified. Strengths can be used to advance your program. Weakness can be addressed and eliminated. The following criteria can serve to help you evaluate your counterfear program:

- Have I accurately analyzed what it is in a fear situation I specifically fear?
- Have I assessed what makes that "specific" situation threatening?
- Have I accurately analyzed what it is about the fear situation that is pleasant?
- Have I assessed what makes that pleasant aspect pleasant?
- Have I developed a workable plan for coping with my fear?
- Have I organized my plan according to workable steps, defined when and where I will act, and clearly laid out how I will begin?
- Have I used the feedback from my actions to improve upon my plan and to creat a more effective way of organizing my actions?
- Have I persisted in this creative process until I have mastered my fear?

chapter seven
COPING RATIONALLY WITH FEAR RUTS

The poet Rilke (1934) cautioned that patience in addressing questions often provides the answers. He suggests living the question and "perhaps you will gradually, without noticing it, live along some distant day into the answer.'

Rilke's view of solving a problem by living the problem is addressed in this chapter on the application of rational-emotive therapy (RET) principles to solving problems that provoke fear. In the rational-emotive system, many questions are raised and targeted toward rousting your rut pattern by disrupting self-doubts and tension intolerances. Uttering pat answers to questions that are raised, however, may only result in boxing yourself in an intellectualized web of self-deception. Instead, the purpose of the RET system is to serve as a tool to help you open up and live freely. To succeed in using the rational-emotive system, you have to live the questions raised by the system.

Strategies for Change

Albert Ellis and I (1979) pointed out in *Overcoming Procrastination* that a person lives in three main ways: cognitively, emotively, and behaviorally. The three main ways are transactional, and so a person's thinking reciprocally intertwines with his or her emoting and behaving.

The implications of these observations is that if you want to break down the mental barriers of fear and wrench free from your rut, you will have to attack the problem as you would any behavior pattern you want to change:

1. You have to train yourself to think differently about yourself and your situation.
2. You have to act differently and more effectively.
3. You need to possess "real" desire to change.

To help this process you can use a simple, effective, rational-emotive therapy (RET) method pioneered by Albert Ellis to counter your fear. To use the system you have to know it, so this chapter will help you to understand the RET method.

The Rational-Emotive System

William James (in Allport, G., 1937) gives an example of four men who visit Paris, a businessman, a politician, an artist, and a playboy. On this trip, each will see, hear, and remember Paris in entirely different ways. Each person's expectations, motivations, and interests guide him to seek different experiences and to act differently.

The four men James speaks of think differently about the Paris experience. Each feels and acts differently because each perceives the situation in different terms. If the businessman thought, for example, that Paris was overflowing with murderers and thieves, he might fear being robbed or injured. Thus, as he entered Paris, he might display extreme caution and limit his activities. Furthermore, his anticipations of confronting a thief might tighten his body with fear.

People who think differently feel and act differently from each other. Unlike the businessperson who upsets himself by *believing* Paris is full of thieves, most visitors to Paris are delighted with the city and find cause for enjoyment, not alarm.

Rational-emotive mental health strategies are built on the theory that emotional upset, like the businessman's upset, is primarily caused by a person's negative and erroneous beliefs. The rational-emotive position maintains that how one feels and acts is a result of what one perceives and how one thinks.

RET emphasizes emotional and behavioral change. Its uniqueness, however, is its emphasis on cognitive change (changing your thinking). The central objective of the system is on altering ideas, beliefs, or attitudes that result in dysfunctional emotions like fear and dysfunctional behavior patterns like a rut.

Basic Assumptions

The foundation of rational-emotive philosophy is grounded in the philosophy of stoic philosopher Epictetus and his student, Marcus Aurelius. This 2000-year-old philosophy states that it is not so much the events in peoples' lives that cause them to feel as they do as much as it is the meaning they ascribe to those events. In this view, context is of minor importance. Instead, great emphasis is placed on acceptance of reality and passive resignation to the seemingly unalterable events of life.

The rational-emotive philosophy similarly holds that there are virtually no realistic justifications for people to make themselves emotionally upset over life's circumstances. This view, unfortunately, can be misinterpreted to mean that there is virtually no reason for a person to feel intensely and passionately about anything.

On this point, rational-emotive philosophy sharply deviates from the philosophy of the ancient stoics. The stoics abjured any strong emotion. They believed strong emotional expression to be detrimental. Rational-emotive views specify that there are innumerable basic emotions, such as sadness, happiness, regret, and determination, that are normal and that can be appropriately intense. To deny their expression is to deny reality. However, certain other dysfunctional emotions, such as psychological fear, are unnecessary and can be changed.

Emotional Skill Building

The rational-emotive system is geared to reduce "negatives": irrational thinking, unnecessary emotional overreactions, and malfunctional behaviors. The system also emphasizes the importance of going after what you want in life.

Rational-emotive mental health systems place emphasis on *teaching* people coping skills. The system's practitioners follow the advice of Tom Williams (1923) and use *persuasive* and *educational* methods to provide their clients with coping strategies to counter negative, irrational, emotionally disturbing ideas and philosophies.

The rational-emotive system is ideally suited for disrupting psychological fear. It is designed to promote straight thinking, appropriate emotionality, and effective problem-solving skills. Once mastered, the system will prove a valuable tool in your counter-rut armament.

A-B-C's of Rational-Emotive Therapy

The rational emotive position is similar to the position of Gordon Allport (1937): (1) we live our lives, in part according to our *conscious* interests, values, plans, and intensions . . . (2) the cognitive and emotive processes in personality become fused into an integral urge, and (3) a person's symptoms . . . . . . can be handled better by re-education than by reliving.

Albert Ellis (1962) notes that most emotionally disturbing attitudes and beliefs are fully conscious or easily can be made so. His approach is an awareness-action one because he emphasizes helping people to develop realistic rational *awareness* of their own self-defeating ideas and values and *awareness* of action methods to counter these malignant cognitions; he also emphasizes persuading people to take positive-corrective *action* to change.

The RET system provides a straightforward approach to diagnose psychological fear and to conceptually, emotively, and behaviorally disrupt it along with the rut patterns it motivates. In the

A-B-C's of the RET system, the *A* stands for activating events, the *B* for beliefs about those events, and *C* for the emotional consequences. According to the system, it is the activating event, *A*, plus *B*, the belief about the event, that results in *C*, the consequences or outcome. In other words, A + B = C.

Activating events (*A*) are external or internal. External events happen outside of yourself. They range from positive (receiving a desired gift from a friend) through neutral (buying milk at the grocery store) to negative (receiving a failing grade on an important examination). Internal events occur within yourself and also range in impact from positive to negative. They include the pleasant anticipation of an upcoming wedding, neutral self-reminders of what to buy at the grocery store, and negative internal events such as nightmares and obsessive, unrelenting, disturbing, worrysome thoughts and peculiar and unpleasant body sensations.

If the belief about the event (*B*) results in an emotional reaction, it is an *emotive cognition* or what is sometimes called a "hot cognition." Thinking that you love a person and feeling a surge of warmth and happiness when you see him or her is an emotive cognition. A nonemotive, or "cold," cognition would be like unemotionally glancing at your green living room rug. The emotional consequences (*C*) are the result of a person's thinking. Powerful suggestions can result in emotional consequences. For example, anticipating victory in an upcoming marathon race could stimulate *excitement*.

Rational and Irrational Beliefs

Some interpretation of events (or beliefs) lead to emotions that seem appropriate. For example, a person denied a desired salary increase would rightly feel frustrated, particularly if the denial hindered his or her economic goals. But the person who thinks that not getting a pay raise is part of a conspiracy by hostile Martian interplanetary intruders is thinking irrationally. This second person's terror is certainly inappropriate because his or her "hostile Martian" premise is unrealistic. We can legitimately conclude, therefore, that the first person has an adaptive outlook and the second person's outlook is irrational and paranoid. However, as will be shown, this rational-irrational discrimination is not always readily seen.

Beliefs can range from rational, realistic, and adaptable to irrational, unrealistic, dysfunctional, and painfully self-defeating. In his A-B-C model, Ellis (1962), therefore, distinguishes between beliefs that are rational and beliefs that are irrational.

Interpretations that hold together logically and result in appropriate emotional and behavioral reactions are rational beliefs. Rational thinking is based on fact and reflects sensitivity as well as objectivity. It is usually associated with compassion and concern as well as normally occuring negative emotions such as frustration.

Irrational functioning typically reflects unrealistic, overgeneralized, conjectural thinking based on faulty assumptions. Beliefs that are interwoven with psychological fear, depression, hostility, or inhibition are called irrational beliefs. They hinder satisfaction in living and promote unnecessary stress and anguish. Irrational beliefs are like surplus mental baggage that depletes energy. This surplus mental baggage is like carrying suntan lotion and bathing suits to the North Pole instead of thermal clothing.

A second way in which rational and irrational thinking can be discriminated is through the following five-point rational thinking criteria modified from the original formulations of Maxie Maultsby (1975). Does your thinking and acting help you to

1. Act productively and creatively in your life?
2. Foster positive relationships with people who are significant to you in your life?
3. Feel free of persistent emotional distress such as fear and depression?
4. Develop skills and knowledge important to advancing important goals?
5. Lead a happier, more satisfying life?

If the idea fails to meet at least three of the five criteria, chances are it is irrational.

The third approach to discriminating between rational and irrational thinking is Ellis's worth-based definition: if thinking results in a generalized condemnation of self or others, it is irrational. So, thinking is irrational if it

1. is clearly crazy, such as thinking that Martian spies are watching one;
2. is overgeneralized and illogical;
3. fails to meet three of the five criteria for rational thinking;
4. is a reflection of a wholesale condemnation of self or others.

We all live with irrational beliefs every day, even the psychologically healthiest among us. This surplus mental baggage is unnecessary to carry, but most of us can live with it in small doses. Irrational beliefs create serious problems, however, when they recur, distract, are painful, and distort reality.

Both rational thinking and emoting and irrational thinking and emoting can and often do coexist. Dominancy of one over the other will determine whether one operates optimally or falls into a rut.

Diminishing Erroneous Thinking

Many people are not in touch with their thinking. A psychologically fearful person in the midst of a fear reaction, for example, can scarcely draw attention from his or her fearful feelings. Yet, to arrest the fear requires stopping and putting thought in slow motion, much like one would slow down the speed of a movie film.

Before you can cope with the irrational mental influences in your life, you have to be able to recognize and admit to them. Once accomplished, you have taken two major steps: you have made yourself accountable for your own distress and you have identified the major element in psychological fear—erroneous thinking. Once your erroneous thoughts are recognized, you have the opportunity to bring your outlook in alignment with reality. Once recognized, irrational or erroneous thinking can be subjected to reality testing and you can see what your options are to modify your thinking, feeling, and behavior. In Albert Ellis's system, recognition of *how* your thinking affects your feelings and actions is a critical *awareness*. It is *insight number one*—if I feel emotionally disturbed over a situation, I am causing my own emotional disturbance. Insight number one is instrumental to *insight number two*: if I don't like reacting as I do, I had better act to change my outlook and my actions.

As anyone knows who has tried to identify and correct his or her own erroneous thinking, the task is tricky. Oftentimes some of our erroneous concepts are so well practiced and so familiar as to feel natural.

Rational Analysis
of a Psychological Fear

To assist this thinking-recognition process, let us look at Craig's case, which illustrates the irrational basis for a person's psychological fears and how he countered them.

Craig's complaint when he entered therapy was that he felt tense and depressed. He had a sense of "going nowhere in my life." Married four years, he had one child and had worked steadily for the same company for six years. He was happy with his family and job, but could not understand why he felt as he did.

The following therapeutic dialogue reveals both his fears and the perfectionistic life-style pattern basic to his rut. The dialogue is typical of the *problem identification* phase of rational-emotive therapy. The questions directed toward Craig are designed to identify and clarify the conceptual basis for his fears.

As you review the therapeutic dialogue, note that the questions I ask Craig are designed to pin down the psychological and behavioral specifics of his problem. This is done to develop an understanding of his problem in preparation to better help him recognize his irrational thinking pattern and to prepare him for insight number one.

Bill: Craig, can you tell me what you feel most bothered by today?
Craig: There's a lot to choose from, but I guess what's bothering me most is a report I'm going to have to present on how to upgrade the efficiency of our company's communication system. I'm worried quite a bit about that talk.
Bill: What kind of worrisome thoughts are you having about the talk?
Craig: I'm afraid I'm going to bungle it.
Bill: How are you going to bungle the talk?
Craig: I'm bound to make some stupid error and make a fool out of myself.
Bill: What type of error do you anticipate making?

Craig: I don't know. I'm just afraid I'll forget to include something signifi-cant and get badly criticized. I'm worried sick about that. I feel so upset about giving that damned talk, I think about it all the time. I have trouble sleeping. I can't get it off my mind.

Bill: Who are the people you'll be talking to?

Craig: The people in my unit.

Bill: How many are in the unit?

Craig: Seven including me.

Bill: Have you spoken before this group before?

Craig: Yes, about three times.

Bill: And how did your previous three talks go over?

Craig: All right. My boss made a notation in my last evaluation that the talks were informative and highly helpful.

Bill: Did anyone criticize you?

Craig: Actually, no.

Bill: Are you more prepared or less prepared for the upcoming talk than for the other three?

Craig: About the same.

Bill: Then is there anything in particular about this talk that makes you think it will flop?

Craig: I don't know. I just have a feeling it will.

Bill: Did you have the same feeling for the last three talks?
(Pause)

Craig: Come to think of it, I did.

Bill: Your "feeling," as you've expressed it, seems to boil down to: if I did an incompetent investigation or had gaps in my presentation, I would be criticized and that would make me some kind of fool. I must avoid making a mistake. The picture I am getting is that you think this way whenever you have to give a talk.

Craig: That's right. I can't afford to goof. My colleagues would see me as an incompetent. I don't think I could stand myself.

Bill: Sounds to me like you're tying your worth as a person to the star of success. You'll be okay if you achieve the star, but you are a worth-less lout if you don't. That, incidently, is a very perfectionistic attitude: "I must be absolutely sure I've covered all bases." Perfec-tionism is an attitude. Simply stated, perfectionism involves estab-lishing a standard, insisting on meeting the standard, and failing yourself as a person if you don't do what you *insist* you must do! That perfectionistic attitude is a prime catalyst for the tension you feel.

This session served to uncover the tip of a very large perfectionistic iceberg, for as we proceeded, Craig presented a lengthy list of situations in which he *feared failure*. Chief among his failure fears were: sexually disappointing his wife, whom he assumed (without evidence) expected him to be a "superstud"; ineptly rearing his child because he had not read enough books on child-rearing (the ten books he read he considered too few); and disappointing his friends because he assumed they wanted him to be permanently "up" and lighthearted. With this perfectionistic attitude, it is little wonder that Craig felt immobilized and in a rut!

The psychological portrait that Craig sketched of himself was of a person tied up in psychological knots, trying valiantly to be perfect to avoid threat to his self-esteem. So much of his energy went into this perfectionistic pursuit that it was little wonder he felt tense; he feared to make a mistake lest he become unravelled.

Achieving the perfectionism he sought was a hopeless quest. So, in addition to fear, Craig felt depressed because he could not achieve perfection.

The basis underlying Craig's psychological fears was a self-definition that he was a person with unacceptable deficiencies. To compensate for them, he thought he had to be perfect. Indeed, in the back of his mind, he believed that if he were perfect he would be average (after all, isn't everyone perfect?), and thus, acceptable. Interestingly, he discounted other people's foibles as understandable. Since he was unacceptable, his errors were unacceptable.

Once Craig's tension was tied to erroneous perfectionistic thinking, he clearly saw that he had assembled a set of impossible standards that if met, would make him Mr. Perfect. Since they could not be met, he could see that he would continually feel like a failure as long as he *insisted* on making no mistakes.

To untangle himself from his psychological knot, Craig had to dispute the erroneous assumption that his emotional survival depended on perfect conduct and behavior. He had to fight the irrational conclusion that he was inadequate and unacceptable as a person if his ideals were not met.

Disputing Irrational Thinking

It is certainly helpful to understand what one is doing to oneself to cause an emotional hangup. Helpful awareness, however, does not proceed beyond the joys of self-revelation *unless* awareness leads to constructive actions.

One highly constructive action involves *disputing* and disposing of fear-induced psychological barriers that block progress. This
process of disputing and disposing of mental myths involves: (1)
framing and answering questions that provide a rational analysis of
your problems, and (2) engaging in actions that counter erroneous
ideas.

A-B-C-D-E System

So far, we have considered the A-B-C's of rational-emotive
therapy. The next phase is called the disputational phase. Albert
Ellis's rational-emotive system is an A-B-C-D-E system. The *D*
stands for disputation of irrational ideas. The *E* stands for new
cognitive and behavioral effects, which are the results of effective
disputation. The following rational self-help form outlines the
structure of the A-B-C-D-E system.

D—Disputation

To *dispute* his erroneous assumptions and irrational conclusions,
Craig first used self-questioning techniques to undermine his erroneous beliefs. The questions he employed were self-confronting.
They fall into two categories: inquiry and strategy questions. Following is a brief description of each type:

- *Inquiry* questions are designed to generate *objective explanations.*
- *Strategy* questions are designed to help identify workable action plans
  to counter self-defeating thinking and acting.

Both inquiry and strategy questions are framed as follows:

- The question is specific; it is a *what, how, when,* or *where* question
  designed to evoke concrete answers.
- The question is open-ended; it can accommodate more than one
  answer.
- The question is scientific; it requires an objective answer.
- The question can be designed to obtain a realistic explanation.
- Why and *if-then* questions are admissible if they lead to realistic ex-
  planations.

Craig directly confronted his perfectionistic beliefs about his unit presentation. He disputed his irrational beliefs by asking inquiring and strategy planning questions. The following illustrates Craig's questions and the answers from this disputational phase of the A-B-C-D-E sequence. The sequence is divided into two sections: inquiry questions and strategy questions.

Inquiry Questions

1. *What* makes my acceptability as a person depend upon maintaining a lifelong practice of exhibiting only perfect performances? *Answer*: There is no universal law that compels me or anyone else to act perfectly. I can certainly accept myself, enjoy my progress, and improve my performances, even if I never become absolutely perfect.

2, If I can accept fallibility and errors on the part of others, then *what* stops me from accepting my own fallibility and errors? *Answer*: It is grandiose to expect myself to be perfect. There certainly is nothing to stop me, except myself, from forgiving my human failings. Furthermore, I need not continue to ascribe to the myth of perfection, even though I have long been an advocate of the system.

3. If my goal is to be perfect so that I can feel secure and to obtain self-acceptance, *what* is the likelihood that I will succeed? *Answer*: The goal is impossible to achieve because it mandates behavior that is impossible. Working for quality by doing the best I can is highly preferable to insisting on perfection. Maintaining a life script that being an imperfect person is being a "nothing" person detracts from doing the best I can, leads to self-tyranny, and leads to more and more impossible requirements, demands, should, oughts, and musts.

4. Even if I don't make an adequate presentation, *how* does an inadequate performance render me an inadequate person? *Answer*: An inadequate performance means I failed to express my point of view skilfully. That performance is but one of many I have performed or will perform. So, my worth as a person can hardly be based on that performance alone. Indeed, even if I've had a con-

sistent string of 1,000 public speaking performance failures, those failures would strongly indicate that either public speaking is not for me or I am repeating a correctable error(s), which I need to recognize and counter. However, even if my public speaking talents are nil, or I have failed to recognize a constant error, this performance does not represent or symbolize the rest of me and wipe out the numerous other traits, qualities, and talents I possess.

These inquiry questions helped Craig to counter his perfectionism, accept himself, and defuse his panic over the upcoming presentation to his unit members. The questions were not designed to make him feel exuberant or comfortable prior to delivering his communication systems talk. Thus, they are not *feel good* solutions to alleviate normal discomforts. Neither are they psychological "hex signs" guaranteed to ward off disastrous performances. Honest answers to legitimate questions can, however, reduce the risk of weak performances due to psychological fears. This is because if time is expended in preparation compared to "worry work," the likelihood of success increases.

Strategy Questions

1. *What* are the steps I can take to counter my fear of making a presentation to my unit? *Answer*: My primary fear is a performance fear. Although I might legitimately convince myself that my personal security and worth are not on trial, I still want to make an effective presentation. Perhaps I would wisely begin by gathering facts about communication systems, identifying facts relevant to my company's situation, interpreting the facts, organizing them, and rehearsing the presentation.

2. *What* is inherently positive in the upcoming presentation that I can expand and/or build upon? *Answer*: There is a genuine interest in communication systems among members of my unit. Their interest and knowledge can be drawn on in the course of the presentation so as to involve them and enrich the presentation.

3. *How* can I assure that I will follow through on my plans and not succumb to the resistance of fear? *Answer*: By making a list of steps, scheduling time for each and keeping to my schedule.

The purpose behind Craig's *rational analysis* using inquiry and strategy questions was to help him to develop a method to defuse his anticipatory fears about his unit presentation. A rational analysis will probe reality and promote objectivity. Properly executed, it will suggest legitimate answers that run counter to mental myths that block pathways to personal advancement.

A Criteria For Helpful Questions

In self-help efforts to create rational questions, there is a risk that questions can be devised resulting in an analysis that adds to an irrational thinking pattern. "Iatrogenic" questions that "sneak" by disguised as rational probes, for example, need to be uncovered and eliminated. Iatrogenic questions are intended to be helpful, but end up causing more harm than good. Following are illustrations of iatrogenic questions and their revisions:

1. *Iatrogenic question:* What's wrong with me that I don't change?
   Revision: How do I stop myself from changing "x" behavior?
2. *Iatrogenic question:* Shouldn't things be easy for me? Haven't I been a good person and tried hard?
   Revision: What do I think is difficult? *What* makes the task difficult? *How* can I "step off" the problem and attack it step by step?

The reasons that the above iatrogenic questions require revision are that they:

1. Do not meet the four criteria for objective questions listed on page 110.
2. Have self-defeating answers built into their structure: the first question implies one is inferior; question two implies that one poorly tolerates tension and feels sorry for oneself.
3. Are overgeneralized, personalized, self-defeating, and framed to heighten tension rather than probe reality.

The questions you frame in your rational inquiry need to be objective questions if you are to probe for realistic answers and avoid answers that are overly generalized, personalized, and self-defeating. Rational-emotive mental health systems involve the use of a comprehensive array of cognitive restructuring and behavioral techniques. Objective self-questioning is the cognitive restructuring phase. The prominent behavioral method is the behavioral activity assignment.

Behavioral Action

Behavioral activities are direct learning experiences that can be employed to counter a rut pattern. The behavior assignment blends with the disputational phase of the RET sequence, works against erroneous concepts, helps promote self-knowledge and counterrut behavior skills.

To be effective, the behavior assignment needs to meet the following minimum criteria:

1. It is directly relevant to the problem.
2. It is purposeful in that carrying out the assignment holds clear promise of helping disrupt the problem pattern.
3. It is constructive because it does not needlessly create problems for others or accentuate the problem it was designed to alleviate.

Let's use the earlier case involving Craig as an example for a behavioral assignment. Because Craig had multiple fears, his assignments could be varied. However, multiple fears are not simultaneously eliminated. Thus, Craig concentrated first on his most pressing fear.

Craig's most pressing problem was his upcoming communications talk where he *sensed failure* if his talk was imperfect. With trepidation, Craig agreed that as part of this counter-perfectionism strategy (and also counter-rut strategy) he would introduce a controversy in his talk. He would talk about the topic of why people resist the development of more effective communication systems. He decided to include this section because he believed that presenting a controversial topic would heighten the risk that his talk might generate some disagreement.

Understandably, Craig was uncomfortable about his assignment. He realized, however, that sooner or later he would have to directly confront his fears.

The *planned* behavior assignment made it possible for Craig to pick his own time and place to behaviorally confront his fears. Although he could wait for a natural opportunity to spontaneously confront his fears, his behavior assignment put the reigns of change directly in his hands.

Craig followed through on his behavior assignment. He made his presentation. As expected, his talk created controversy. It lead to a lively discussion that involved questions he could not answer. However, rather than criticize him, his group joined with him in developing a modified communication system that actually served to advance his original thinking.

The Results of New
Questions and Actions

In using the system of rational analysis to dispute irrational thinking and by engaging in behavioral assignments, Craig created a new cognitive-behavior *effect*. It resulted from his self-questioning, where he convinced himself that:

1. His total worth was not tied to his public speaking performance.
2. He would do the best he could in preparing for and in making his presentation; if his best was not adequate enough to suit his audience, too bad!

The behavioral assignment resulted in the following behavioral and cognitive *effects*:

1. He developed skill in fielding questions.
2. He developed a more realistic perspective by seeing that his colleagues contributed to his presentation and were not against him as he thought.
3. He could take a risk without a *guarantee* of success.
4. He felt greater self-confidence and ability to tolerate the uncomfortable by facing his psychological fears.

Clearly, Craig advanced in breaking free from the perfectionistic restraints that pushed him into a constricted circle of actions.

Devising Your Rational Strategies

Figure 9 outlines a rational-emotive, self-help, counterfear approach. It is intended to provide you with a structured procedure to contest your psychological fear and get out of your rut.

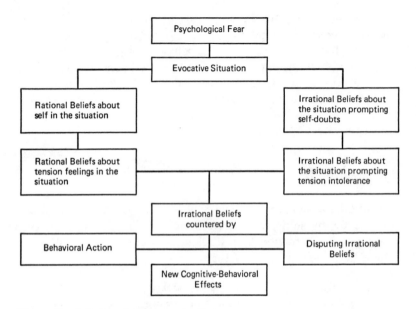

Figure 9   A Rational Counter-rut System

To begin this charting approach, specify a target psychological fear you want to counter. For example, if you are in a rut because you are afraid to meet new friends and would like to change that, you would write "interpersonal fear" as the title under psychological fear.

Next, specify the conditions that primarily tend to evoke your fear reaction. For example, the primary evocative conditions might be at club meetings—bridge club, Lions club, and so forth.

Phase three requires that you identify both rational and irrational beliefs about the situation.

An analysis of rational responses to the evocative situation is illustrated by the following:

- A rational belief about yourself in the "situation" might be that if you want to make friends at club meetings you had better learn to get over your fear of the meetings.
- A rational belief about tension in the situation might be the idea that you will probably feel initially uncomfortable in social situations, and that is just too bad.

An analysis of the irrational responses to the evocative situation is illustrated by the following:

- An irrational belief about yourself in the situation might be: "I'm afraid I'll be criticized and lose face because I won't know what to say at the club meeting."
- An irrational belief causing discomfort fears could include fears of being helpless or fears of being uptight. These discomfort fears reflect egocentric concerns about one's feelings and are likely to be expressed in low frustration tolerance language such as "I'm afraid that I won't be able to *bear* the tension of attending the party."

The purpose of this analysis is to separate the rational from irrational components to the fear-rut problem. More importantly, its purpose is to separate ego from discomfort fears so that these fears can be more readily conquered. The following table on Separating Fears provides an abbreviated example of this process.

Charting Section

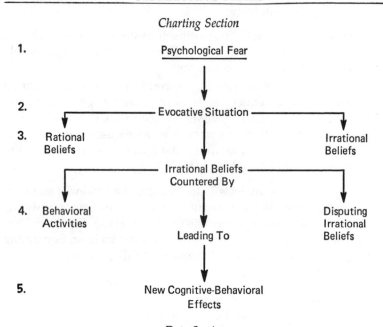

1. Psychological Fear

2. Evocative Situation

3. Rational Beliefs — Irrational Beliefs

Irrational Beliefs Countered By

4. Behavioral Activities — Disputing Irrational Beliefs

Leading To

5. New Cognitive-Behavioral Effects

Data Section

1. Psychological fear: interpersonal fears.
2. Evocative situation: clubs or parties; get uptight at mere suggestion of social gathering.
3. Rational beliefs: would not want to feel uncomfortable at social gathering. Irrational beliefs: afraid people will see I'm uptight; my feelings will get out of hand and I'll freeze and that would be awful; I'm helpless to change. Basic fear: self-doubts, downing, difference, tension intolerances.
4. Forcing myself to go to bridge club; challenging ideas that disaster is eminent at the club; questioning what is so bad about feeling uncomfortable; why discomfort will result in catastrophe.
5. Acceptance of discomfort, increased social skills, heightened self-confidence.

chapter eight
OVERCOMING FEAR WITH SYSTEMATIC DESENSITIZATION

Charlie the chipmunk trembled in his den hidden under the protective umbrella of a huge fallen oak tree. He trembled because the children had come back with their sticks and stones to drive him from his little home. "Perhaps," he thought, "they will not see me and will soon tire of this nasty game they play." And sure enough, when Charlie failed to appear, the youngsters ran off to amuse themselves chasing a local cat.

The next few days, all Charlie could think of were the staring, laughing faces of the monster children who came to torment him, capture him, and who knows what else!

Charlie knew he would have to move his den. The children would be back and would keep coming back. They were relentless.

As he waited to gather the energy to move, his little body was racked with strain and his mind raced full of thoughts of the danger of finding a new den. As he thought of his plight, the children returned, went through their ritual search, and left.

Once again Charlie vowed to leave. But his body felt weakened and he could scarcely do more than hope to spring free. He was trapped between the jaws of mental and physical strain. Because of his fear, Charlie was in a worry-filled rut.

Fearful thinking can evoke muscular tension and visceral reactions in humans as well: (1) increased parasympathetic nervous system activation, which involves an increased output of stress hormones such as adrenaline, and (2) decreased sympathetic nervous system functioning in areas normally associated with relaxation. Muscular tension and autonomic adrenal reactions contribute to unpleasant body tension, which can be the stimulus for more fearful thinking. Muscular relaxation can eliminate a vicious cycle where tension stimulated by fearful thinking stimulates fearful thinking. In other words, it is unlikely that you will experience psychological fear if fearful thoughts are not running through your mind and your body feels *calm*. It is also unlikely that you will remain in a rut when your mind and body are free from fearful stresses.

To help you (and Charlie) develop relaxation skills, this chapter describes a proven muscular relaxation method. Once you have mastered it, you can further apply this relaxation skill as part of a program to counter fearful mental images and to take action to get out of your rut.

An Introduction
to Systematic
Desensitization

A muscular relaxation program is part of the systematic desensitization approach pioneered by behavior therapist Joseph Wolpe. The method is designed to disrupt psychological fear. The procedure *desensitizes* the person to the fear image and eliminates the fear sensations associated with that image.

Joseph Wolpe (1969) believes that a fear habit can be deconditioned through systematic desensitization, which is based on his theory of reciprocal inhibition. The concept of reciprocal inhibition is easily described. The idea is that you cannot be fully relaxed and fearful at the same time: relaxation inhibits the effects of fearful images and thoughts. Wolpe's emotional reconditioning, therefore, involves countering fear-provoking thoughts and images with relaxation to allow the relaxation response to dominate. In other words, psychological fear is reduced by developing relaxation responses that compete with the fear and replace or inhibit it.

Systematic desensitization, the method that Wolpe uses to produce reciprocal inhibition of anxiety, is an extensively researched, excellent counterfear approach. An unexciting method to learn and apply, it has potential effectiveness high enough to more than compensate for its format.

Systematic desensitization combines relaxation methods with imagination. You first learn a muscle relaxation method that involves contracting and relaxing major muscle groups. Then, in a relaxed state, you imagine a mild example of what you fear. When you can think of the example and do not feel tense, you envision a second example, slightly more fearsome than the first. These examples are predetermined and are arranged in a hierarchy that ranks fear-image situations from high to low intensity. For exam-

ple, a person afraid to eat in a public restaurant may include in his
or her hierarchy:

1. sitting at a table near the door in a small restaurant with a few customers present and ordering a cup of coffee;
2. sitting at a counter near the door in a small restaurant with a few
   customers present and ordering a cup of coffee;
3. opening the door of a small familiar restaurant;
4. walking by a small familiar restaurant;
5. looking at a color photo of a small restaurant;
6. looking at a restaurant newspaper advertisement.

If the end goal is to drink a cup of coffee in a small restaurant, the
desensitization process continues until the person can fearlessly
visualize drinking the cup of coffee in that small restaurant. Once
the person has progressed through the hierarchy and has visualized the experience without fear, he or she gets actively involved
in the experience. This involvement is called *in-vivo* desensitization
because the action involves facing the actual fear situation in real
life circumstances.

Systematic desensitization is structured to allow you to proceed in a graduated pace from the lowest to highest fear-provoking
situations. This approach helps you to build confidence as each
challenge is met.

The success rate of systematic desensitization is quite high
when used by a skilled therapist and understandably lower when
used by the self-helper.

Let us see how you can apply this approach to reduce your
psychological fear. The training approach is divided into two sections. The first part describes a muscular relaxation technique,
adopted from the work of Wolpe, which is based on the relaxation
techniques of Edmund Jacobson (1934). The second part describes
how to construct and use a behavioral hierarchy.

Muscular Relaxation

Muscular relaxation is chosen here as the specific relaxation
method for this desensitization exercise because it is traditionally

used in such exercises and it is simple to master. (Wolpe, however, uses imagery techniques as well as other methods to induce relaxation.) The goals of the muscular relaxation exercise are to learn to isolate, contract, and relax major striated muscle groups; make a distinction between relaxed and tensed muscles; and induce a state of deep relaxation.

To begin, find a comfortable spot where you are unlikely to be distracted. Position yourself comfortably, either sitting in an easy chair or lying on your back. Then involve yourself in a contraction-relaxation cycle with each muscle group. The contraction-relaxation cycle follows this sequence: increase tension of the target muscle for approximately five seconds, and then allow five seconds to slowly release the tensions until, at the fifth second, the muscle is fully relaxed. Following are the muscle groups and instructions:

- Tighten your hands by making them into fists; then loosen your hands and let them go limp.
- Tighten, then loosen your forearms.
- Tighten, then loosen your biceps.
- Tighten, then loosen your triceps.
- Shrug your shoulders to tighten them; then loosen them.
- Stretch your neck muscles by pulling your head back; then let your neck muscles go loose.
- Stretch your neck muscles by pulling your head forward until it touches your chest; then let your neck muscles go loose.
- Wrinkle up your forehead; then let your forehead go loose and limp.
- Make a grin like a cheshire cat; let your cheeks go loose and limp.
- Make a deep frown by tightening your lips downward; then let them go loose and limp.
- Tighten your jaw; then let it go loose and limp.
- Close your eyes until they are tight; then release the tension.
- Press your tongue against the roof of your mouth; then release the tension.
- Arch your back to make it feel tense; then relax your back muscle by releasing the tension.
- Tighten your chest muscles; then release the tension.
- Push your stomach out (like a potbelly); then relax the tension.

- Pull your stomach in toward your backbone; then let it return to a comfortable state.
- Tighten your buttocks; release the tension.
- Tighten your thighs; relax the tension.
- Tighten your calf muscles by pointing your toes forward, release the tension.
- Tighten your shin muscles by pointing your toes up; then release the tension.

When you begin to practice muscular relaxation, first try to get the feel for the sequence and to become familiar with each muscle group. Once you are comfortable with the procedure and feel that you know the steps well, add the following: as you are tightening each muscle group, slowly breathe in fully so that your lungs are filled at precisely the point your muscle is most tense. Then release your breath until you have emptied your lungs at the point your muscle is relaxed.

Once you have mastered this second step, you are ready for the third: recite the word *relax* to yourself as you tense, then relax each muscle group. This is done so that you associate the word *relax* with the bodily sensation of relaxation. As you breathe in, think *reeeeeee*, and as you breathe out, *laxxxxxx*. Time the cadence so that it coordinates with your breathing; *reeeeeee* as you breathe in, *laxxxxxxx* as you breathe out.

The relaxation procedure is accomplished in three stages. Stage one is relaxing muscle groups in a pattern that represents a flow from hands to head down to toes. Stage two combines the flow with deep breathing. Stage three coordinates the flow and breathing with the word *relax*.

As you practice relaxing each muscle group, your bodily tension should decrease. Eventually you will be able to feel relaxed over your entire body. This relaxed state is accomplished by letting yourself go further and further each time you practice the relaxation sequence. Although you might believe you are letting yourself go as much as possible in your initial efforts, experience will teach you that some of your muscular fibers in each muscle group remain slightly tense. With repeated practice, however, those additional fibers will respond.

Typically, practice this procedure fifteen minutes in the morning and fifteen minutes in the late afternoon (however, practice anytime you wish). In a few weeks, you may think yourself into a state of relaxation within a few minutes just by concentrating on the word *relax*, concentrating on relaxing your muscles, and by breathing deeply.

Behavioral Hierarchy Building

Behavioral hierarchy building, the next phase of systematic desensitization, is simply identifying situations that typically evoke fear and arranging them in order from high to low. You can do this with any situation you fear: fear of small turtles, fear of flying in an airplane, fear of closed-in places, fear of heights, fear of open spaces, and so on. In hierarchy building, fears are organized under specific themes. If you are afraid of a turtle, open spaces, closed spaces, public speaking, or eating in public restaurants, each fear is treated separately.

Not all situations when you are fearful provoke the same intensity of feeling. For example, if you had a turtle phobia and you were in a museum and saw a small stuffed turtle in a glass display case, you might hardly react at all. However, if you saw a turtle meandering toward you in the grass near your house, you might react with strong fear. So, a second part of behavioral hierarchy building involves the concept that thematically related fear situations can evoke reactions different in intensity.

Fears can be graded in intensity. Fear of losing consciousness while eating alone in a public restaurant, for example, may be more frightening than fainting in your living room with a kindly and medically competent friend present.

In hierarchy building, you make a list of circumstances that evoke fear. Next, you organize these fear situations from high to low intensity by rating situations from one hundred to nearly zero. The highest situation is the most frightening possible (for example, loss of consciousness while eating alone in a public restaurant); the lowest is the least frightening (reading that someone you don't know felt faint while walking with friends near a medical complex).

Subjective Units of Fear

Your desensitization program could be defeated if large gaps exist between items in your heirarchy. These gaps would resemble a ladder with too many rungs missing to allow the climber to reach his or her destination. To correct this potential problem a subjective units of fear index will be used. This index is used rather than the subjective units of disturbance index recommended by Joseph Wolpe. I prefer to use the subjective units of fear index for this exercise because the concept of fear has already been used in this book and the reader is now familiar with it. So, since a distressing and uncomfortable sensation is present, the reader can invent situations that would tend to draw these feelings out that could serve as the missing rungs on the fear ladder. In the world of behavioral experiences there are many possible areas that tie to what you feel fearfully uncomfortable about. You won't have to look very far in order to find uncomfortably fearful situations.

Although discomfort is appropriate when contending with trying circumstances, there will be no need to accept discomfort in the imagery exercise when your hierarchy items are paired with relaxation. Here your goal is to imagine the condition and *do so relaxed*.

The assumption behind the subjective units of fear is that people can discriminate between conditions that produce more or less fear. The SUF system assures that each hierarchy situation is less fearful than the one before it, as it is more fearsome than the item that follows it. In other words, if the most frightening item on the hierarchy is rated at 100 SUF, item two should produce approximately 90 SUF, and item three 80 SUF. Since the systematic desensitization approach is like walking up a staircase, you may have to invent items to assure that the SUF between items are roughly equivalent.

There is no specific number of items you will need to construct, but chances are that your hierarchy will be insufficient if you have fewer than ten items and will be overextended if you have more than twenty items. In summary, traditional hierarchy building involves:

1. identifying the fear you wish to counter;
2. identifying situations related to the fear;
3. organizing the situations according to intensity;
4. assuring that hierarchy situation differences are relative in intensity;
5. creating new items to fill in gaps if the relative difference between items is disproportional to adjacent item(s).

Using the Cluster System

Based on the above guidelines some readers could create good hierarchies and use them in conjunction with relaxation exercises. But most people lack experience in hierarchy building and will have problems developing an effective hierarchy from scratch. Therefore, I have developed a *Behavioral Cluster Hierarchy System* to simplify the development of behavioral hierarchies and to improve the quality of home-developed systems. The Cluster System increases assurance that the items will tend to be relative in fear-provoking intensity.

An example is sometimes worth pages of "how-to" description, so the following is a model Behavioral Hierarchy Cluster System. The example is structured to illustrate the steps in cluster hierarchy building.

The Cluster System was successfully used by Tom, a young man who was afraid of eating in public restaurants. Tom was in a social rut partially because he kept putting off luncheon and dinner engagements with friends and potential friends. As he did so, he came to feel more and more isolated and deeper into a rut. He wanted to overcome this fear, and his first step was, therefore, to define major types of restaurants he feared.

The three major types of restaurants that Tom feared where classified as formal, family, and fast food. Next, he organized them according to their relative intensity. His prior experience taught him that he was most uncomfortable eating in formal restaurants (privately owned, exclusive-type establishments). He was less afraid of eating in chains of "family-type" restaurants. He was least afraid of eating in fast food restaurants (such as McDonald's).

In the first phase of cluster hierarchy development, the major fear situations are defined. Tom delineated three general fear conditions relating to type of eating establishment. In this first phase of development of your cluster hierarchy, you should

1. identify your target fear;
2. select two or three general conditions that can evoke that fear;
3. arrange these two or three conditions according to intensity, the most fearful first, the second most fearful, and so forth.

The next step in cluster hierarchy building is to develop a listing of ancillary conditions that can be used to add specifics to your program. For example, the size of a restaurant, the location, whether stationary or rotating, or whether it is highly illiminated or dark are possible ancillary conditions.

The primary condition-ancillary conditions provide an orderly way to cluster fear-arousing situations. The distinction is like the difference between a topic sentence and supporting sentences. Thus, the distinction between a primary and ancillary condition is a logical and practical distinction. For example, it makes more sense to talk about fear of eating in a fast food restaurant (primary) that is nearly empty (ancillary) than fear of a nearly empty situation in a fast food restaurant.

In Tom's analysis of ancillary conditions, the number of people in the restaurant and how close to the door his table was were major ancillary conditions that contributed to his fears. For example, when Tom thought about getting a McDonald's hamburger with few people in the restaurant, he felt less tense than when he imagined buying a burger at a busy time of day. His greatest fear was eating at Chaucer's Saucer (a formal-type restaurant) when the restaurant was crowded and when he would be seated far from the door. These major ancillary conditions were identified and categorized as follows:

Ancillary Conditions	*High to Low Intensity of Fear*
1. *People Conditions*	
a. crowded	high
b. semifilled	medium
c. almost empty	low

2. *Proximity Conditions*
   a. far from exit   high
   b. middle of restaurant   medium
   c. close to exit   low

In setting up *your* ancillary conditions

1. identify the general ancillary conditions that contribute to your fears in each of the primary conditions;
2. break each general category down into high, medium, and low intensity conditions;
3. order your general ancillary conditions from high to low in intensity;
4. create a chart for your primary and ancillary conditions so that you can have a visual display of how your program is organized to assure that it logically fits. Figure 10 is a Full Behavior Cluster Hierarchy.

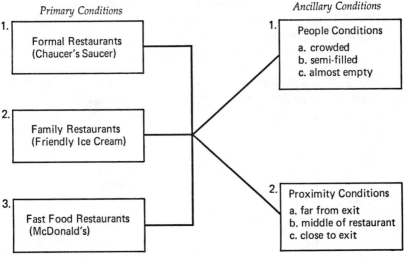

Figure 10   Full Behavior Cluster Hierarchy

When Tom developed his hierarchy, he detailed his conditions as concretely as he could. It is important when you create *your* system to make it as "lifelike" as possible. It will do little good to imagine eating at The Sign of the Dragon restaurant in Hong Kong if you never plan to go to Hong Kong. It is better to include specific restaurants in your hierarchy, like Chaucer's Saucer, located in your area.

Adding specifics to your hierarchy clarifies your target actions. Thus, if you are trying to overcome fear of meeting strangers at cocktail parties (xenophobia), specify the cocktail parties you plan to attend. If you are afraid of speaking in front of small groups of associates, be clear about the conditions by naming situations. If there is a specific restaurant you are fearful of entering, state that restaurant's name.

In devising your cluster hierarchy, the principle of Occam's razor (the law of parsimony) holds: avoid complex tactics when simple ones will do; avoid abstractions when concrete references will do. The goal is to simplify by concretizing.

The Behavioral Cluster Hierarchy is implemented through use of a card system. Each primary provocative condition is written on a separate 3" × 5" card and numbered in order of intensity. Each ancillary topic condition is written on a separate card. The items under that topic are ordered and numbered according to intensity.

Once the primary and ancillary conditions are defined and relaxation mastered, tackling the problem is systematic and straightforward. The cards are laid out in a logical order. Tom's system (Figure 11) is used to illustrate this ordering.

Figure 11   Tom's Cluster Hierarchy System

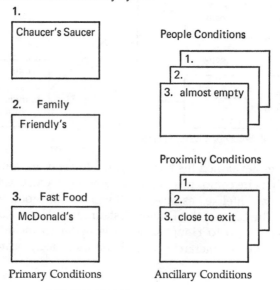

Primary Conditions   Ancillary Conditions

The system is called the Cluster System because the cards are combined so that the *least* frightening provocative condition is aligned with the *least* frightening of *each* of the two *ancillary conditions*. For example:

1. Tom began by taking fast food restaurants as his target task because it was the *least* feared condition. He took the card labeled Fast Food, McDonald's on Quick Avenue.

2. Tom took the least fearful people condition and proximity condition card and aligned them with the fast food restaurant condition.

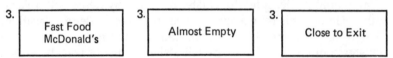

3. | Fast Food McDonald's   3. | Almost Empty   3. | Close to Exit

Following is the completed sequence of steps that Tom followed for McDonald's restaurant. They are the same for Friendly Ice Cream and Chaucer's Saucer: all that changes is the restaurant classification.

FAST FOOD HIERARCHY—McDonald's Restaurant

1. Nearly empty near the door.
2. Semifilled, near the door.
3. Crowded, near the door,
4. Nearly empty, middle area.
5. Semifilled, middle area.
6. Crowded, middle area.
7. Nearly empty, far from exit.
8. Semifilled, far from door.
9. Crowded, far from door.

In Tom's hierarchy, distance from the door was more frightening than crowd size. Thus, the proximity variable gains prominence over the crowd size variable.

Once you have advanced this far in building your cluster hierarchy, before proceeding check to determine that your cluster conditions are relative in subjective units of fear (SUF). If they are not, you may have to break down your ancillary conditions into smaller units. For example, the "people condition" on Tom's cluster system might be broken down into numbers: fewer than five, five to ten, ten to twenty, twenty to forty, forty to eighty, eighty to 120, and more than 120. Although this breakdown results in extra steps, they are steps worth taking if you are intent on overcoming your fear. Sometimes it pays to overextend.

Generally, adjustments will not be necessary as the structure of the cluster hierarchy automatically equates for fear intensity because of the way items are clustered *and* because of the natural repetition built into the system: the ancillary items are repeated with each of the primary items. Thus, there is a built-in practice effect that offers overlearning possibilities and "new" learning stability.

Pairing the Cluster with Relaxation

Tom paired his least fearful cluster of hierarchy items with relaxation.[1] He did this by placing himself in a deep state of relaxation. When he felt completely relaxed, he imagined the least fearsome cluster combination. When he felt a slight tinge of fear, he closed off the image and concentrated on relaxing. Once again in a state of deep relaxation, Tom reactivated the least fearful cluster combination until he felt completely relaxed imagining himself, for example, at McDonald's near the door when the restaurant was nearly empty.

When Tom felt relaxed with the image of being at McDonald's, he actually went there when the restaurant was nearly empty and ordered his food from the counter position nearest the door. He repeated the experiment several days until he felt confident: *then* he concentrated on the next most fearful condition, McDonald's restaurant, semifilled, closed to exit. He practiced imagining eating at McDonald's under such conditions until he felt relaxed with the image.

Tom repeated the relaxation-imagery-action procedure until he could eat without fear in crowded formal restaurants far from the restaurant exit.

It was not necessary for Tom to carry each hierarchy item out in action. Sometimes it is impractical to do so. Instead, he carried

[1]Sometimes relaxation can be intensified by resting in a warm tub of water and imagining your hierarchy items. If you use this procedure, you would follow the normal coordination of muscle relaxation, breathing, and word *relax* while in the tub. In addition, Edward Cowles (1941) recommends placing a cold towel behind your neck; this will add to a sense of deep muscular relaxation.

out, in action, the first, middle, and last steps in each primary condition. For example, with McDonald's hierarchy, he entered the restaurant when it was nearly empty and stayed near the door; he entered the restaurant when it was semicrowded and got served from the middle counter and sat in the middle area; he entered the restaurant when it was crowded, got served from the farthest counter, and sat in the corner farthest from the door. However, you may decide to initiate action several times at each step in your hierarchy of challenges. This is certainly appropriate because as you progress, you learn about yourself, build confidence, and build tolerance for tension, which is, after all, the underlying intent of the Cluster System.

The Cluster System is individually paced. Your pacing depends on your desire for change, the intensity of the fear you are confronting, and how generalized the fear is.

The lapse of time for Tom to complete his program was ninety days. Although ninety days may seem a long time, it really was quite short in comparison with the seven years Tom had suffered with his restaurant phobia.

In summary, the approach to getting out of fear ruts by using the Behavioral Cluster Hierarchy is:

1. Identify primary provocative fear condition (restaurants).
2. Identify variants of that condition, which evoke high, medium, and low levels of anxiety (formal, family, fast food) and give specific examples (such as Chaucer's Saucer).
3. Identify specific ancillary conditions that support the major fear conditions (number of people present, distance from door).
4. Break down the ancillary conditions into high, medium, and low intensity areas (filled, semifilled, nearly empty, far from door, middle of restaurant, close to door).
5. Take the least fearsome provocative fear condition and the least fearsome condition in each ancillary category and combine them to describe the condition you are least afraid of.
6. Put yourself in a state of relaxation.
7. Take the least fearful situation and imagine yourself in that situation.
8. Revert to relaxation at the first sign of tension.
9. Repeat relaxation-cluster pairing until you can fearlessly imagine yourself in the cluster situation.

10. Move to next cluster and repeat the sequence.
11. Behaviorally test out clusters as appropriate.

The Cluster System
and Interpersonal Fears

The Behavioral Cluster Hierarchy System can be used to confront interpersonal fears that lead to interpersonal ruts. For purposes of illustration, we will use Wendy's case. Wendy wanted to date attractive men, but she was fearful of approaching them. She saw herself in quite a rut because it seemed to her that the men she was disinclined toward were the ones who wanted to date her. She believed her social life had stalled out, and she wanted to change her situation. Her goal was to initiate contacts with attractive males.

Her objective was ultimately to develop a relationship with a man she cared for. She determined that she would employ the Behavioral Cluster Hierarchy technique to help her overcome her fear of introducing herself to attractive males under the primary conditions of:

1. Formal social event: Martha's wedding
2. Informal social: intermission at the summer series concert, Redrock's singles bar, oceanside at the seashore.
3. Nonsocial: Wuldo Museum, Somerset Park, Sears Department Store.

The major ancillary conditions:

Attractiveness of Person
1. high: very intelligent, good sense of humor, common values, handsome appearance.
2. above average: same as above, but a little less.
3. acceptable: same as above, but less.

Using the relaxation-cluster pairing, Wendy began by imagining herself approaching an "acceptable-looking" person at her friend Martha's wedding and introducing herself. When she felt fear-free with that image, she imagined approaching an above-average person at Martha's wedding and introducing herself. To add realism, she cut out pictures from magazines that provided her with a visual image of each class of attractiveness, and she used them as part of her ancillary condition.

In the area of interpersonal anxiety, the conjured image of a situation is rarely like the actual one. Furthermore, unless you are expecting to see a specific person, you will have to be flexible in translating your imagery into real life circumstances. However, there are certain conditions over which you are likely to have some degree of control. Introducing yourself is a condition over which you have a potentially large measure of control.

Wendy mentally role-played under relaxed conditions. In her mental role-playing, she limited her fantasies to introducing herself. The introduction she could control; what happened beyond introductory remarks would have to be played by ear.

In overcoming interpersonal anxiety situations, the relaxation-imagery-action approach has its limitations. In real life situations, the limitation is that you cannot control another person's response after you have introduced yourself: he or she may slowly or abruptly move away, or the person could show extraordinary interest in you too soon. You might also find that you are more confident in approaching a highly attractive person after you have been turned down by the less attractive. After all, beauty is in the eye of the beholder, so you may fare better with the person who appears more attractive.

The Cluster Hierarchy
and Public Speaking Fears

The next example deals with public speaking anxiety, chosen because: (1) fear of speaking in front of groups is common, and (2) many people are in ruts because they have not overcome this problem (as a result they socially restrict themselves and restrict themselves on the job).

A primary provocative condition in public speaking anxiety is audience response: specifically, fear of criticism. There are multiple causes for public speaking anxiety, so for purposes of this exercise, we will identify fear of audience response as our target concern.

Audience response can be divided into three main categories: critical, open-minded, supportive. These three factors will comprise our primary provocative condition category. Common ancillary conditions include audience size, preparation, and types of questions the audience might ask. The following is a breakdown of three ancillary conditions.

1. Group Size
   a. large
   b. moderate
   c. small
2. Preparation
   a. minimum preparation with notes available
   b. free structure: off the cuff
   c. prepared written speech
3. Questions
   a. practical, long explanation required
   b. practical explanation required
   c. practical single-word answer required

The sequencing for the public speaking anxiety problem would be:

Primary Conditions	Ancillary Conditions

3. Speaking before a critical group	3. Audience Size
	  3. large
	  2. medium
	  1. small

2. Speaking before an open-minded group	2. Preparation
	  3. minimum
	  2. free structure, off the cuff
	  1. prepared written speech

1. Speaking before a supportive group	1. Question Types
	  3. practical, long explanation
	  2. practical, short explanation
	  1. practical, single-word answer

It is helpful to specify the types of groups you would speak before, such as critical—Wolfe Club members; open-minded—fellow employees in the packaging department; supportive—students I instruct in gardening. It would be helpful to fix on the topic you would talk about, such as "How to Get Out of a Rut." It would also be helpful to create examples of questions you might anticipate. For example, if you were to talk on the topic of "How to Get Out of a Rut," you may want to anticipate the questions you might be asked, such as: Isn't there a fast and easy solution that requires only a little effort?

Public speaking fears before large formal groups or small informal groups of colleagues cover a range of ancillary possibilities. Possible additional conditions include importance of message and length of time available for presentation. Although it is quite impossible to cover each public speaking contingency, if in the process of working through your hierarchy, you discover a major ancillary condition, which if not included would virtually wreck your chances for success, by all means develop it in high, medium, and low intensity conditions. However, try not to go overboard with ancillary conditions. Usually, one to three general ancillary conditions are sufficient.

Summary of the Behavioral Hierarchy Cluster

The behavioral hierarchy cluster system has many applications for the self-helper seeking a structured and orderly approach to contending with his or her fears. Figure 12 summarizes the approach

Figure 12   Cluster Approach Summary

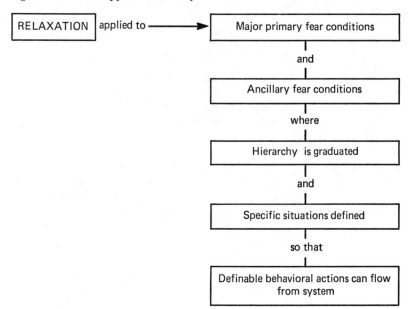

so that the general framework can be clearly visualized and thus more readily adapted to the conditions for which you would choose to employ it.

The ISA System

Once you have mastered rational-emotive principles and systematic desensitization the ISA—Idea, Sensation, Action System—can be used as a guideline for dealing with fear ideas and fear sensations and for improving problem-solving activities. Figure 13 illustrates this approach.

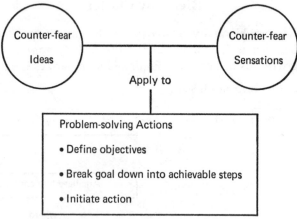

Figure 13   ISA System

The ISA System is designed to counter dysfunctional ideas and sensations and leave, as a by-product, an improved psychological outlook and physical state. In this improved psycho-biological environment, the person is better able to solve problems and break from his or her rut.

Fear ideas can be countered by any psychological system that fosters objective thinking: cognitive problem-solving methods, reattribution methods, education, constructive feedback, good old-fashioned common sense, and rational-emotive principles.

Fear sensations can be dealt with by meditation, stretch exercises, physical exercise, biofeedback, whirlpool baths, yoga, positive imagery training, a good night's sleep, pleasant music, antianxiety medication, autogenic training, acceptance of the sensation, and relaxation.

Fear reduction methods can be used in combination. Since no two people are alike, one person's approach may not be effective for the next person. So, one will simply have to experiment until he or she discovers the right combination to counter fear thinking and counter fear and sensations. Whatever combination works best, however, needs to be practiced regularly to be mastered.

The ISA System is reciprocal. An improvement in countering fear ideas should reduce fear (stress) sensations; a reduction in stress sensations should reduce stressful thinking. Developing skill in problem solving should reduce stress thinking and sensations. The implications of this reciprocal process are that cognitive coping skills and tension-sensation reduction skills can be applied to help solve problems previously fearfully avoided.

chapter nine
MOBILIZING FOR OPTIMAL PERFORMANCE

In George Lucas's movie production of *The Empire Strikes Back*, a band of escaping rebel warriors are engaged in a life-and-death struggle against the seemingly overpowering warriors of the evil Empire. The Empire warriors pursue the rebels throughout the universe in order to destroy them. In an attempt to defeat the Empire, a rebel warrior, Luke Skywalker, is guided in the use of an omni-directional power that can be used constructively or destructively. This power is called the "Force" and its secrets are taught by an 800-year-old Jedi teacher named Yoda.

The Empire Strikes Back tells the story of the struggle between the constructive and destructive sides of humanity. It tells of the ways people can mobilize their resources to survive and triumph. The "message" in the movie has been transmitted in many stories throughout history, even in the less romanticized tales such as Bram Stoker's *Dracula*. In the story, Count Dracula, the deadly "human" vampire, uses supernatural powers and the experience of the ages to triumph over his victims. Those who finally subdue and destroy the evil Count succeed by deriving knowledge from books that tell of the vampire's vulnerability, and they use this knowledge to destroy him.

The Empire Strikes Back and *Dracula* are stories of construction versus destruction. In a sense, such stories symbolize struggles that exist within each of us. We all have energy, power, capacities, and talents. Sometimes we subvert these energies to inhibit our own progress. Negatively charged, our personal powers can emerge as fears and energize the very rut from which we strongly desire to be free. Like the "Force" of Yoda, our inner powers are omni-directional. They can be used to construct and create as well as to fuel our inhibitions, energize our fears, and produce our ruts.

To constructively use the "force" within us could be the result of a single decision to confront our fears at their most vulnerable points. The decision is to challenge one of the greatest of our enemies within—that enemy generated when we energize negative forces of psychological fear by self-doubts, self-criticisms, and self-flagellation, or by thoughts of helplessness, or by imaginary dangers to our self-image.

Do not be deceived. A decision to disengage from an internal push-pull struggle of the mind against itself is empty without a commitment to act. A decision by itself will not make something happen. It simply reflects a direction for actions, and is of little value unless there is a committment to action.

Negatives and Positives

Fear is freezing and restricting. You cannot be both emotionally frozen as well as relaxed and spontaneous. Continual tension due to fearful thoughts counters your potential to actualize your abilities. To break free of the self-imposed bonds of manufactured fears requires acting against the negative. But this is only half the story: to move forward and to enjoy life requires recognizing and calling upon strengths and abilities. The preparation for moving forward requires positive thinking and positive action. Such emphasis on the positives increases the likelihood that you will

1. reduce destructive effects of stress;
2. bring out dormant potentials.

Positive thinking in conjunction with relaxation can crowd fearful thinking into the corners of your consciousness. Once fearful thinking is cornered, your positive thoughts, creative potential, and constructive inclinations are free to wander over the great expanse of your mind.

Psycho-regulation training is a method that can be adopted to heighten your positive potential. It is used to counter fear by helping you to concentrate your attention and actions on positive construction and creative pursuits. Clearly, it is hard to be creatively and constructively absorbed in living and simultaneously feel fearful.

Psycho-Regulation Training

Psycho-regulation training is a psychotherapy system popularized by Berlin psychiatrist J. H. Schultz (1969) who labeled the system "autogenic training" to describe a self-employed hypnotic process. The technique had its origins in Germany around the turn of the twentieth century and was first described by Oskar Vogt (1897). and Korbinran Broadman (1902).

The psycho-regulation system has been used to treat a variety of psychosomatic conditions, such as peptic ulcer, hypertension, and migraine headache. It has also been used successfully in helping people overcome their psychological fears.

Soviet psychologists use psycho-regulation training as part of a program to "psych" up athletes in order to maximize their potential. These psychologists devise individualized approaches using psycho-regulation training that enables the athlete to draw upon his or her best resources to achieve an optimal performance state (OPS) in competition.

Psycho-regulation training, like systematic desensitization, involves a relaxation phase and an action phase. The relaxation phase involves reciting self-suggestive phrases to create a state of relaxation.

After learning and practicing the suggestive phrases, you advance to the next step; you create a mental atmosphere to energize yourself. This mobilization phase is a natural outgrowth of the clear-minded state of relaxation. The objective of the mobilization phase is to prepare yourself to operate at your best. These suggestive phrases help to activate your sympathetic nervous system and increase blood flow, stamina, energy, and so forth.

The mobilization phase parallels systematic desensitization. It requires that you use your imagination to create a past experience when you were performing at your peak. This optimal performance state becomes translated into a series of phrases involving key word stimuli that intellectually and emotionally remind you of a peak performance you experienced.

The psycho-regulation system described here is based on Gregory Raiport's (1980) adaptation of the work by Schultz. Raiport was a sports psychologist for the Russian Olympic team. Since his emigration to the United States, he has worked with American athletes to assist them to reach optimal performance states through psycho-regulation training. These techniques, found useful by American athletes, have been effectively employed with shyness problems and other inhibiting fears. They have also been helpful to persons not inhibited by fears, but who normally restrict the use of their potential.

Psycho-regulation training is a system that requires active participation by the person desiring help. Once the skills are developed, psycho-regulation becomes a self-directed process.

Psycho-regulation training includes the steps of:

| Relaxation | Mobilization | Action |

This sequencing is similar to the sequencing of systematic desensitization (Chapter 8). Psycho-regulation, however, varies from systematic desensitization in two respects. In psycho-regulation training, there are *two* imagination phases; desensitization only has one (imaginary fear situations). Systematic desensitization is employed to directly *counter* fear. Psycho-regulation training is employed to directly *accentuate* positive potentials. Both systems, however, aim to free people from inhibiting restraints. In the final analysis, both serve to accentuate positive strivings.

Mental Preparation

Preparation is important for the successful use of psycho-regulation training to: (1) learn to think with a relaxed mind, and (2) learn to mobilize to achieve positive goals. The following describes the mental attitude that makes psycho-regulation techniques work.

When you consciously try to force yourself to feel a certain way, you are almost certain to defeat your intent. You have about as good a chance of forcing a feeling as forcing yourself not to think of a pink elephant if someone instructs you definitely not to think of a pink elephant. Under such conditions, your best chance of not thinking of a pink elephant is not to concern yourself if you *do* think of a pink elephant. The same "passive" mental attitude essential to get rid of the "pink elephant" is employed in the popular biofeedback method that helps train people to attain the alpha-brain wave state, a brain wave pattern associated with relaxation and clear-mindedness.

Biofeedback works in this way: a person is hooked up to an electroencephalograph unit that reads brain wave patterns. The mechanism has a feedback device that alerts him or her by sound or light when the brain waves are at alpha frequency. By associating the signal with the alpha state, the person learns to recognize or bring on this state at will. But, to succeed, it is important that the person assume a posture of "passive volition," which is an attitude that if one achieves alpha, fine, if not, too bad. It is an attitude of *desiring*, but not *demanding* the state. This same alpha state can be achieved through the successful application of the relaxation phase of psycho-regulation relaxation training.

Psycho-Regulation Training
Relaxation Exercise

You will have to master two imagery systems to be able to use psycho-regulation methods effectively to break free of your rut. Each system relies heavily on the evocative power of words. One series of words evokes relaxation, the other mobilization. The following describes the power of words and their use in creating relaxation.

In psycho-regulation training, words are viewed as possessing evocative powers. They can conjure up recollections and images that can influence bodily states. For example, if I ask you to think of a drop from a ripe juicy lemon splashing against your tongue, can you feel your mouth watering? Does the thought of being immersed in a tub of warm bubbly water stir a reaction?

Words can stir images and reactions. Ivan Pavlov noted that words are our secondary signaling system: they can symbolize the real thing and evoke a fractional reaction to that thing. For example, words can stir pleasurable and positive feelings, such as when a person you love says that he or she loves you, too. The relaxation phase of psycho-regulation training draws on the power of your own words to evoke relaxing images.

In the relaxation training phase, there are five stages of practice that build on the evocative power of words and images: word experimentation, weight sensation association, relaxation phrases, coordinated breathing, and relaxation intensification.

In the word experimentation stage, you test the power of your words to evoke desired emotional and physical reactions. For example, think of the word *heavy*, and imagine your body feeling very, very heavy. Soon you will begin to feel the sensations of heaviness when you think the word *heavy*, much as the word *relax* in the desensitization exercise in Chapter 8 became associated with a state of muscular relaxation.

In stage two, lie down on your back and place a heavy pillow on your right arm. Make sure your body is comfortable and in a relaxed position. Then close your eyes and concentrate your attention on the heaviness of your right arm. While you are concentrating on the weight of the pillow resting on your arm, repeat the phrase "my arm feels heavy." Repeat this exercise a few times for several days until you feel comfortable and relaxed with the exercise.

In stage three, you will add to your power of self-relaxation by using relaxation phrases that include the word *heavy*. In this stage, you will no longer need the pillow. As part of this stage, you will repeat four phrases that have been carefully developed to facilitate the relaxation process. To initiate the practice in this stage, first position yourself comfortably, preferably on your back with outstretched arms and palms down. Close your eyes and repeat these relaxation phrases slowly and silently to yourself while concentrating on the sensations they suggest.

My right arm is becoming heavy (repeat four times before reciting the next phrase).

Both my arms are becoming heavy (repeat four times).

My legs are becoming heavy (repeat three times).

I am resting (repeat four times).

Once you have practiced and memorized the phrases, the next stage is to coordinate your breathing with the relaxation phrases. When you recite the words that are in italics, such as I am resting, breathe in fully, then exhale as you repeat the remainder of the phrase. After repeating each phrase, pause several seconds before starting the next. Repeat this coordination procedure for each of the four phrases.

After you master coordinated breathing, proceed to stage five, which involves deepening the relaxation response by learning to produce a warm feeling all over your body. This is accomplished by taking a shower and adjusting the water so that it is warm and comfortable. Step out of the way of the water and let it flow only over your arms. Close your eyes and repeat slowly "my arms are warm." Try this for several consecutive days. When you have associated the word *warm* with the warm sensations of the water, think the word *warm* after each relaxation phrase. You do this to conjure up the image of the sensation of the warm shower to deepen your state of relaxation.

The deep state of relaxation this exercise produces makes it possible to restore your energy when you feel the need to recharge. It will help you feel refreshed and rested.

In summary, the main stages in psycho-regulation relaxation training are:

1. Word experimentation.
2. Practice with stimulus term *heavy* with pillow on right arm with thought "heavy."
3. Practice with relaxation phrases.
4. Practice with relaxation phrases and coordinated breathing.
5. Practice with stimulus term *warm* in conjunction with warm shower, and practice use of term *warm* between relaxation phrases.

Psycho-Regulation Training
Mobilization Exercise

Abraham Maslow (1974) describes the self-actualized person as possessing the following qualities:

Creativity and inventiveness.
Problem-centered in approach.
Accurate reality perceptions.
Accepting self and others.
Autonomous.
Spontaneous and natural.
Experiencing a sense of unity with life and the universe.
Ethical.
Unprejudiced.

This person is, as Carl Rogers (1961) would say, open to experience. By being open to experience, the self-actualized person has many peak experiences.

A peak experience, as Maslow notes, is a very personal happening that you experience as a sense of unity with your surroundings and peace with yourself. For example, flying your own airplane high in a crystal-clear midnight sky and glancing down on the shadowy world, then up at the sky, could be like an "oceanic" or peak experience where you feel as one with the universe. Being on the same wavelength while communicating with a person you love, then feeling a warm sense of unity with that person could also be a peak experience. An explosive action where you have lifted more weight than you thought you could is an optimal performance peak experience.

In the mobilization training exercise, the energy of a peak or optimal performance state is recaptured. To re-experience that burst of energy requires learning a psycho-regulation mobilization imagery method. This method is similar in form to relaxation imagery training. Its content, however, is developed from your memories and your words.

A mobilizing series of phrases can evoke dormant strengths and can activate optimal performances. To create these phrases requires tapping your memory for peak optimal performance experiences. Optimal performance memories are the wellspring for the mobilizing phrases you employ to optimize your performance. An optimal performance experience need be only a brief evaluation-free moment when your efforts were concentrated and highly effective. For example, one of my peak performance experiences occurred at an amusement park. I was engaged in trying to shoot out a red star on a sheet of newsprint paper with a rapid-fire, air-powered pellet gun. If I succeeded, I got a prize. I became so engrossed in the process that the pellet gun became an extension of my thoughts and I concentrated on clustering the pellets to the tip of the points of the star. Then my concentration was on blasting the star out by clustering the final volleys at the center of the star; purpose—to blow the star out as a unit.

My efforts were successful and I won a stuffed panda as a prize. As I was told later, the concession owner was busily trying to distract me as I was shooting, but I was too absorbed in the experience to notice.

A series of phrases I might use to reconstruct that experience are

my eyes are fixed on the target;
my thoughts and movements of the pellets are one;
I am directing the pellets to the target;
I am absorbed in the movements of my actions.

When I think those phrases, I can reconstruct the feeling of the experience.

Another peak performance occurred when I was a high school senior at the city track championship. One of the events I was competing in was the javelin. I had just taken a cold shower prior to entering the field and when the time came to compete, I recall running with the javelin in hand to the throw mark. My pace was flowing, smooth, solid and ever-quickening. The javelin moved forward from under my arm in circular motion, and with a smoothness of power, my arm and javelin arched forward; at the perfect moment the javelin left my fingertips to soar along a flight pattern that gave me victory in that event.

I broke no city field and track record in the javelin that day, but my throw was fifteen feet farther than I had ever thrown the javelin

before, and the throw was the winning throw.
The phrases I think of when I recall that event are

I am gaining momentum;
my body movements are becoming coordinated;
the javelin and I are one;
I feel a release of power in my actions.

When I think of these phrases, I can reconstruct the experience.

A peak performance need not end in victory. For example, once I met with the two chief administrators at a clinic where I was employed. As it turned out, the purpose of the meeting was to place limits on my actions, and so two successful projects I initiated were removed from my command. I recall clearly expressing my views with a strong sense of truth ringing in my words. To no avail. However, I expressed my ideas without hesitation and regret. To me, this was a peak performance.

A similar experience occurred when I was an expert witness in a child custody case. I stated my position clearly. The position I took ran counter to prevailing precedents, and the case was lost for the moment. However, it has subsequently been appealed to the state supreme court. While I feel happy about the appeal, I feel a deep sense of satisfaction that I expressed what was important.

The last two examples are illustrations of losses despite best efforts. In defeat, however, I still felt a sense of victory. It is this sense of victory I recall; I was true to myself and expressed the truth I had seen. From both experiences I create a series of recollective phrases:

I am in harmony with myself.
I am expressing my thoughts clearly.
My truth is in my words.
My words and I are one.

These phrases reflect the spirit of two experiences when I lost, yet won.

Clearly, optimal performance need not be earth-shattering. All an experience requires to qualify as an optimal performance is that: (1) you are acting congruently, (2) you are absorbed in the experience, and (3) you are not evaluating the experience as you are absorbed in it.

Although there is no requirement that you need exactly four phrases to jog your memory of a "peak" experience, four phrases should be sufficient to capture the spirit of that experience. To begin to develop your self-catalyzing phrases, try to recall a positive experience that meets the criteria of

> congruence;
> self-absorbing;
> evaluation-free.

This experience could be one where you

> swam farther than you thought you could;
> became engrossed in the act of skiing down a slope;
> were able to envision a concept, like freedom, in an exciting new way;
> spoke to a friend and experienced a strong sense of mutual understanding;
> wrote a poem that said what you wanted said;
> solved a difficult puzzle;
> saw the configuration of and meaning of events, which enabled you to make accurate predictions (for example, group of stocks poised to advance in the stock market).

Try to reconstruct this experience by remembering a physical sensation you associate with it. Perhaps you felt a sensation of smoothness and rhythm as you swam, a cool breeze against your cheek, and a surge of energy as you skied, or a light-heartedness when you envisioned a new meaning for "freedom." Fix this sensation in your mind and write down key words or phrases to describe it. You will later use these words and phrases in constructing your mobilization phrases.

Next, try to recall emotional sensations you had during your experience. Perhaps you felt a sense of emotional warmth toward your friend, ecstasy when you wrote your poem, peacefulness when you solved the puzzle, or tranquil and excited when you saw the configuration. Fix these emotions in your mind and write down key words and phrases to describe them.

Now, combine key physical and emotional words into phrases that help you recall the event. Try to keep each phrase short (six words per phrase or less) and limit the total number of phrases to four.

Even with the use of these guidelines, there is no perfect step-by-step formula to recreate the experience to put yourself into the mood of the experience. The important point in constructing your phrases is to make them positive and "flow". Following are two more illustrations of optimal performance phrases you can use as models.

The next series of phrases illustrates word-phrase stimuli that Susan, an opera singer, devised to create an optimal performance experience.

> I am singing well and strongly.
> I am projecting fantastically.
> I am immersed in my singing.
> My voice and I are one.

The following series of phrases was developed by Bert, a business executive:

> I am charged with energy.
> I am feeling tingly.
> My energy is seeking expression.
> I am acting with confidence.

Once you have created your phrases, your next step is to use them in combination with the psycho-regulation relaxation. So, you would begin the sequence by using the relaxation phrases.

> *My right arm is* becoming heavy (repeat four times).
> *Both my arms* are becoming heavy (repeat four times).
> *My legs are* becoming heavy (repeat three times).
> *I am* resting (repeat four times).

Use these phrases in conjunction with breathing sequence and the word *warm*. (Of course, when you are able to self-induce a state of deep relaxation by thinking the words *warm* and *heavy*, you need not regularly repeat the sequence. Periodically, it would be wise to complete the entire sequence, however, to maintain the connection between the stimulus words *warm* and *heavy* and the sensations of relaxation.)

Once you have achieved a state of relaxation, shift to the mobilization phase. Repeat each phrase and coordinate your breathing with your mobilization phrases. Bart's phrases serve as an illustration.

> *I am* charged with energy (four times).
> *I am* feeling tingly (four times).
> *My energy* is seeking expression (three times).
> *I am acting* with confidence (four times).

Breathe in, repeating the words in italics and exhale while thinking the remaining words of the phrase. At the completion of each phrase, think the word *energy*.

Coordination of Relaxation and Mobilization

The intent of relaxation and mobilization is different. One is to create a peaceful state, the other, an energized state.

Both systems are equally important. Relaxation lays the foundation for the energizing phase by helping you to clear your mind of worries and troubles. It also helps you to clear your mind of desirable distractions, such as thinking about an upcoming exciting event like going on vacation.

Mobilization builds on the relaxation platform. This platforming is important. Gregory Raiport has noted that distracting thoughts can threaten productivity and performance. You cannot, in other words, be swamped with mental distractors and simultaneously optimize your performance. So, if you step into your mobilization phase with your mind free of distracting thoughts, you will be better prepared to act.

Developing a distraction-free state is rare. Intrusive thoughts are bound to invade your consciousness when they are least wanted. This is true even for a person highly skilled in psycho-regulation. When the inevitable occurs, rather than struggle to rid yourself of distractors, let them flow and trail off on their own while you reattend to the task of repeating relaxing and mobilizing phrases. As we know from biofeedback research, passive rather than active volition will better allow you to achieve the state you desire.

So, when you drift off into the past or future, all you have to remember is that your task of the moment is to allow yourself to generate relaxation and mobilization sensations through repeating your phrases in coordination with breathing and stimulus terms.

Set Goals and Use Psycho-Regulation

A. H. Overstreet (1925) noted that everyone has a large number of habit systems: work habits (accuracy, slovenliness), bodily habits (cleanliness), moral habits (honesty, reliability), emotional habits (sympathy, nearness), and so forth. So, in the goal-setting stage, it is wise to specify habits or qualities you want to develop to supplant those you dislike, even for short-term limited goals. Following are examples of limited goals:

> Phone the person you were fearful of asking for a date.
> Tackle that writing project you have put aside.
> Reignite that exercise program you have abandoned.
> Express affaction to that important person in your life.
> Speak up at that party where past experience would predict you would be a "wallflower."
> Read that article you wanted to get into.

A Bidirectional Approach to Harness Your Strengths

Systematic desensitization and psycho-regulation training branch in two directions. Systematic desensitization counters negative images that evoke fear. Psycho-regulation creates positive mental images for purposes of optimizing performance. Both methods are correctly geared to help the user to build confidence and build problem-solving action skills. Used conjunctively, they form a bidirectional approach.

Each system is used independently of the other. However, because systematic desensitization and psycho-regulation training have common elements, a bidirectional approach can be structured to obtain the best from each system.

Systematic desensitization and psycho-regulation training can easily be contrasted to reveal common elements (see the Comparison Chart, Figure 14).

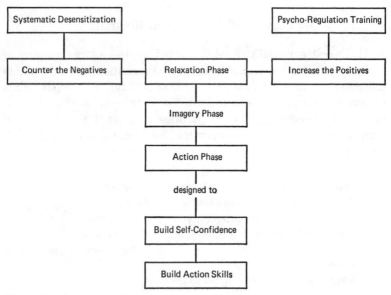

Figure 14   Comparison Chart

The major difference between the two systems is the method of achieving relaxation and the directions in which your efforts are focused. Systematic desensitization counters negatives; psycho-regulation training increases positives. Each system, however, involves relaxation, preparation for action through imagination, and constructive actions.

The Convergence

Once you have mastered behavior hierarchy building using the Cluster System and have mastered relaxation and mobilization strategies, systematic desensitization and psycho-regulation training can be put together in a bidirectional system to potentiate self-help efforts.

The bidirectional system can be used to confront your fears. The system can also be used to directly advance your positive intents. Let's use Sam's case to illustrate this procedure.

Sam was an account executive for a large brokerage house. In the early years of his career, he carefully researched his stock recommendations and made a point to establish client contacts through the usual methods of "cold calling" and making customer contacts through community organizations. As a result of his efforts, he developed a solid client base and enjoyed a steady income. Then he glided on past accomplishments.

As he glided, Sam began to slip deeper and deeper into a rut. His old clients repeated their "same old stories" and he followed the same old stocks. His work life became increasingly humdrum.

When Sam first embarked on his brokerage career, he felt a sense of enthusiasm and dedication. He worked hard and rightly deserved the success that resulted. Rising success was met with diminishing effort, however, and so Sam "plateaued." As he did, his work seemed unappealing, dull and bland. As he heard himself talk to his clients, he sensed a resounding hollowness in his tone. He felt the absence of his earlier sparkle of enthusiasm. Despite efforts to induce a false exuberance to his clients, he could not block out the lack of enthusiasm from himself. Furthermore, he found himself eagerly awaiting his retirement. The thought that he was going through the job motions while awaiting retirement caused Sam to jar himself out of his complancency, and he sought help to break his unhappy pattern.

What proved the solution to Sam's complacency problem was simple and straightforward. Working with me, he developed a bidirectional tactic that provided a structured pathway out from his growing rut. The bidirectional approach involved applying psycho-regulation methods to cluster hierarchy activities. The specific steps included

- establishing goals;
- creating mobilization phrases to be used with standard psycho-regulation relaxation phrases;
- cluster hierarchy development;
- mental rehearsal;
- behavior implementation.

Sam defined his goal as increasing stock sales 30 percent in the up-coming year compared to the prior twelve months. Together we constructed a chart that logically outlined the steps needed to achieve the goal (Figure 15).

Figure 15

The sales dimension to Sam's plan was telescoped to include in-vestment advisement to old and new accounts who could profit from long-term growth investments. This was the dimension that would be dealt with using the bidirectional approach.

Sales to end product users was Sam's tension point. However, since his general level of fear was low, the sales phase mainly served the purpose of reactivating his interest in performing effectively. It provided him with a way of logically approaching selling to customers with different resources and interests.

The second step involved the creation of four optimal performance mobilization phrases. To establish these phrases, he followed the usual methods and concentrated on work-related peak experiences.

Sam's analysis revealed that peak performance periods occurred after a lengthy period of personal in-depth research. The research centered on developing a basis for predicting market trends. It also centered on developing predictions concerning specific stock groups and how they would perform in his predicted market conditions. These peak performance periods reflected profound satisfaction that he had made his best effort. He was frequently reinforced for his efforts when his predictions proved accurate.

From past peak performance experiences, Sam created the following mobilization phrases:

I am working comfortably and steadily.
I am absorbed in the intricacies of my work.
I am becoming excited about my predictions.
I feel a lightness in mind and body.

Then he practiced using them until they produced the desired result.

The third step involved the development of a cluster hierarchy. The hierarchy was developed in the usual manner of establishing primary and secondary conditions. The primary conditions were defined as type of accounts (new and established). The secondary conditions concerned sales considerations: sales resistance, financial resources of the client, and client sophistication. Sam's cluster hierarchy included direct action steps—sales sequencing. This step was added because it represented the action steps that Sam intended to take.

As is typical in cluster hierarchy development, Sam developed a series of cards that included each of the above categories.

In sequencing this project, he imagined himself applying his research knowledge first with established accounts: high financial resources, low financial sophistication, and low sales resistance individuals. His goal: to provide these accounts with a suitable investment plan.

In his mental rehearsal sequence, he included closing sales. He began with established accounts that were low in sophistication, high in financial resources, and low on sales resistance. He ran through the sales sequence with this type of account, then he behaviorally applied his plan. He continued this sequence through his most difficult cluster of new sales-resistant, sophisticated accounts with low financial resources.

Sam was systematic in the application of his system. He diligently applied relaxation-mobilization to his cluster hierarchies through mental rehearsal, and then applied relaxation-mobilization sequences just prior to each behavioral enactment. Using this process, Sam not only succeeded in breaking out of his career rut, but he also shattered his prior performance records. He received as an additional bonus a dividend of gratitude from his accounts who financially profited from his comprehensive and detailed analysis of the market and timely updating of information as financial conditions changed. The structure he employed is shown in Figure 16.

Figure 16

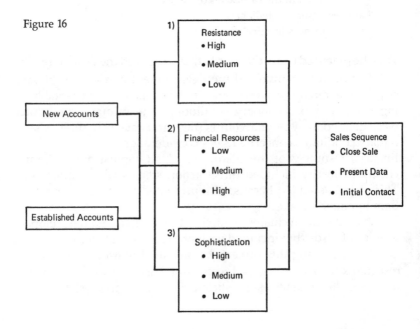

This bidirectional method can be applied to a variety of projects, such as:

> Upgrading an athletic skill, such as tennis
> Improving teaching competency.
> Building self-confidence.
> Increasing sexual pleasure.
> Advancing up the corporate ladder.
> Improving listening skills.

In each project, the method is adapted to provide a functional structure you can use to further your goals by getting yourself out of your rut.

IV

UP FROM DEPRESSIVE RUTS

In the fourth century B.C., Hippocrates, known as the father of medicine, wrote that he thought depression was physically caused by a bodily (cardinal) humor he termed "black bile." Aretious, in the second century A.D., wrote that he thought the black bile theory was wrong and that depression was a psychological problem. In his writings, Aretious described many of the psychological symptoms of depression that we observe today.

The physical versus psychological camps are still in conflict over what causes depression. Today, depression is viewed as genetic or the consequence of a biochemical accident; *or* the result of pressures of daily living, and thus psychological. Undoubtedly, either view is correct depending on the individual case.

Clearly, a person who feels and acts depressed is in a rut. But, for some forms of depression, the fact of being in a rut is academic, such as severe forms where the depressed person suffers from a biochemical imbalance, is morbidly incapacitated, unable to function, and suffers major perceptual and cognitive distortions that frequently render him or her out of contact with reality. This person definitely requires professional help.

Depression in moderately severe forms also ought to be professionally treated. Moderate depressions are those with persistant *vegetative symptoms*, such as headache, diarrhea, constipation, loss of appetite, and sleep disturbances (early morning awakening or oversleeping); persistant *behavioral symptoms*, such as social withdrawal, failure to maintain reasonable personal hygiene, failure to dress attractively; and persistant *psychological symptoms*, such as suicidal preoccupations, impulsive self-defeating thoughts (to leave a recently satisfying career or pull out of a recently satisfying intimate relationship), guilt, worthlessness, helplessness, and hopelessness. Fortunately, most depressed people are not so severely incapacitated, *nor do they have to look forward to such severe incapacitations*.

In this section, we will consider *psychological depression* and ruts. Here, depression is not just of academic interest, but often is synonymous with a rut. So, if you feel depressed much of the time, chances are you are in a depressive rut and need to deal with your depression to get yourself out of your rut. Happily, there are many ways to disrupt a psychological depression. The very nature of the depressive process, however, makes it difficult to see what these counter-depression routes might be. Part IV is designed to be like a flashlight in a dark room of depression. Once the room is illuminated, the mysterious places can be seen, as can many routes from a depressive rut. Once you have come to understand psychological fear and learn how to counter it, getting out of a psychological depressive rut can be accomplished.

Both psychological fear and psychological depression grow from self doubts, tension intolerances, and a sense of helplessness to control one's destiny. But a person who is psychologically fearful believes that *something* of danger to his or her ego integrity is around the corner and cannot be stopped. The person who is depressed believes that there is *nothing* around the corner except for misery that he or she cannot stop. But psychological depression is manufactured depression; it *can* be stopped!

In Part IV, three chapters address the matter of the depressive rut. Chapter 10 is intentionally educational and diagnostic. To deal effectively with depression requires that you recognize what psychological depression is and discriminate between mood, sadness, grief, and depression; and that you know the forms of depression most closely associated with a rut. Chapter 11 concerns correcting depressive thinking patterns and builds on the rational-emotive theory described in Chapter 7 to accomplish this objective. Chapter 12 describes behavioral strategies to break a depressive rut.

chapter ten
DEPRESSIVE RUTS

━━

When the gates holding back self-doubts are sprung open, the rush of depressive negative thoughts is like a polluted river, which floods and swamps the plain of reason and soaks its way into the grounds of objectivity, turning it into humorless mental mud.

American psychologist and philosopher William James wrote of a "law" of depression. To James (1892) a depressed person:

> . . . is filled through and through with intensely *painful emotions* about himself. He is threatened, he is guilty, he is doomed, he is annihilated, he is lost. His mind is fixed as if in a cramp on those feelings of his own situation . . . His associative processes, to use the technical phrase, are inhibited; and his ideas stand stock-still, *shut up in their own monotonous function of reiterating inwardly the fact of the man's desperate state.*

James knew psychological depression well, inspired by hopeless thoughts and negative, debasing self-preoccupations. Although he observed many people who felt depressed, his best resource was himself. William James suffered many bouts of depression and became an expert in coping with it.

Pessimism and helplessness, prominent signs of psychological depression, exist because a depressed person feels *helpless* to control the events in his or her life, not only for today, but for tomorrow and for tomorrow's tomorrow. Depression, when it persists, continues because a person doubts he or she will ever stop being helpless and thinks that the future is, therefore, out of his or her control.

Although many people are in ruts because they feel too swamped with pessimistic thoughts to be otherwise, still others mask their depressions from themselves by engaging in diversionary activities. Thus, William James's description of depression is not always so obvious to the person running from his or her depression. Indeed, a rut may be the person's mask for the depression he or she seeks to ignore.

In the remainder of this chapter, various forms of depression are described to help raise readers' consciousness of their importance in the dynamic picture of what constitutes a rut. Some of the forms that depression takes are more easily masked than are others. First, however, let us take a look at moods and sadness, sometimes confused with depression.

Moods and Depression

A mood is simply a prevailing emotion or attitude, such as an angry mood, a sad mood, a happy mood, or a depressed mood. Moods are usually short-lived.

Practically everyone from time to time gets into depressive moods. What distinguishes a depressive mood from a depression is persistence. A depressive mood can last for hours or days; a depression can last for weeks, months, even years.

The mechanism triggering a mood is probably physiological: a brief hormonal disbalance; a flip-flop in blood sugar level, body reactions to barometric changes and so forth. Conceivably, people can easily live with such temporary bodily stress and discomfort; many do.

The somatic mechanisms that promote unpleasant moods feel similar to the somatic sensations accompanying depressive thoughts. Because the feelings and depressive thoughts have previously been associated, the occurrence of similar somatic sensations can remind the person of depressing situations. This mild somatic state of tension and arousal can become an activating cue for recalling a negative event. That in turn, activates self-depressing thoughts about that event, thus giving direction to the mood. This reverse-conditioning process works like most associations one makes with the events in daily living; when you feel hungry, you think of food; when you hear the word *black*, you might associate the word *white*. In depressive moods, the process works as shown in the tables following.

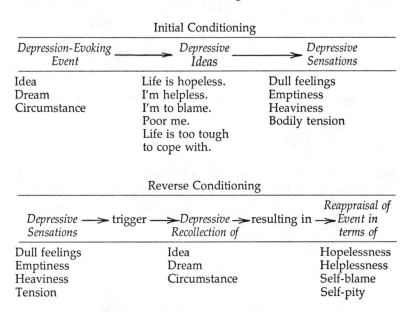

Initial Conditioning

Depression-Evoking Event	→ Depressive Ideas →	Depressive Sensations
Idea	Life is hopeless.	Dull feelings
Dream	I'm helpless.	Emptiness
Circumstance	I'm to blame.	Heaviness
	Poor me.	Bodily tension
	Life is too tough to cope with.	

Reverse Conditioning

Depressive Sensations	→ trigger →	Depressive Recollection of	→ resulting in →	Reappraisal of Event in terms of
Dull feelings		Idea		Hopelessness
Emptiness		Dream		Helplessness
Heaviness		Circumstance		Self-blame
Tension				Self-pity

A physical sensation that feels like a depressive sensation can stimulate a depressive flow of thought due to conditioning. This same sensation can trigger a depressive flow of thought for yet a second reason. Sometimes a person habitually seeks to find causes for unpleasant physical sensations. When causes are not readily apparent, he or she attributes causation to some external event or unconscious motive that probably has nothing to do with the mood. For example, the person who embarks on a psychological witch hunt seeking an answer often creates a pseudo-explanation, such as I feel depressed because: "Jane doesn't love me anymore,"

"My boss doesn't like my reports," "I'm too overworked," "I don't have enough fun," or "Dan's nasty manner is to blame."

Inaccurate attributions magnified out of proportion block true awareness and lead to needless upset. Mary, for example, was driving in her automobile one day. She had been traveling several hours and periodically stopped to have coffee to stay awake. The combination of coffee, empty stomach, and the long trip heightened Mary's vulnerability to stress, and soon she began to think about Carl, a fellow student in her advanced biology course. She recalled how Carl had challenged her interpretation of an experiment, and she began first to feel humiliated, then angry (How could he dare do that to me?), and finally depressed. She felt depressed because she inaccurately concluded that she

1. Was incompetent because she did not ably defend her position;
2. Would never be able to express herself properly;
3. Was a real fool;
4. Was without hope.

Mary thought she had found the explanation for her sensations. But hours later, after a meal and a good night's sleep, the event disappeared from her mind and she felt like her old self again. These thoughts and feelings did not return until she once again felt fatigued several weeks later. When they returned this time, Mary recognized that her agitated thinking was a reflection of her fatigue, and she rested instead of needlessly upsetting herself.

Sadness, Grief, and Depression

Edward Garcia (1977) describes sadness as a bittersweet experience; it is bitter because one has experienced a loss and the loss is distressing, and it is sweet because fond memories remain.

Sadness is highly personal. What might appear sad to one person, such as watching a delightful summer come to an end, might be viewed with glee by another who looks forward to the crisp cool air of autumn and to viewing the colorful fall leaves in the New England mountains. Sadness is an unhappy feeling that differs from depression in that the vision of hopelessness and waves of self-blame are not present in sadness, even though the saddened person may be helpless to change what he or she is saddened over.

Grief is a more intense reaction to a loss, such as the death of a close family member or friend. It is a deep sorrow. In purest form, grief is an emotion free of anger and self-blame.

Both sadness and grief are emotions that need to be lived out because they are normal reactions to a loss, are appropriate for the situation, and have a limited life-span. Squelching them creates a sense of unreality.

Ennui

The depressed state that generates from a rut is called ennui, a depression that grows out of boredom. It is characterized by a sense of dull indifference.

Ennui is like a reinfection agent. Growing out of boredom, it leads to more boredom and indifference. Mental indifference, complacency, and ennui are forged into a unit of blandness where the affected person stares blankly at the world and looks without care upon him- or herself.

This form of depression is common. It is seen in occupational stress situations. It is seen in the homemaker with no outside interests, who repeats a never-ending cleaning ritual, suffers from a sense of dullness, and reads romance magazines as a substitute for active participation in the vital events of life. It is seen in the masses of humanity who, like lemmings, rush to the sea of their own destruction by restricting their lives to the point of boredom.

Ennui is like a lightly destructive veil that softly laces the lives of those who adhere to the principle of maintaining an unwaveringly monotonous routine. Thoroughout this work, ennui is rarely labeled but often described.

Apathetic Depression

A person who believes he or she cannot muster the energy to make desired changes is a prime candidate for *apathetic depression*.

Apathetically depressed people scale down the pace of life and withdraw as much as possible from what they construe to be insurmountable conflicts and challenges. The apathetically depressed person characteristically "plays it safe" and tries to insulate him- or herself from change through inaction. Indeed, this person appears *allergic to change* and seems to dull vitality and blunt interests in the service of what Gardner Murphy (1958) refers to as *canalization*: seeking to maintain the familiar.

Tony, for example, is apathetically depressed. He regularly goes to work, engages in family activities, participates in a local environmental group, but does so without enthusiasm. He goes through the paces of life like an automaton and characteristically feels numbed. He does what is expected, but derives little in the way of satisfaction from his actions.

The pathway of apathetic depression expands on its own momentum because the apathetically depressed person sees *change* as his or her "virtual focus" for distress, when in reality the "virtual focus" is his or her sense of being able to cope.

Apathetic depression are productivity thiefs. They are like conversion demons that sap productive energy and transfer this energy to thoughtless routines.

Apathetic depressions persist unless circumstances force change or one creates circumstances that can cause change. Delineation of personal goals, objectives, and concrete steps to attain them is a self-created circumstance that is instrumental in energizing from an apathetic depression.

Our Focus:
Psychological Depression

A mild psychological depression is largely self-induced depression primarily caused by erroneous ideas and irrational conclusions. These ideas and conclusions reflect pessimism, worthlessness, and tension intolerances. Suicide is not seriously contemplated, even though suicidal thoughts may be present.

In its milder forms, depression is characterized by preoccupations with thoughts of hopelessness, helplessness, and self-pity. Sexual interests may be suppressed, and other activities that formerly brought satisfaction are experienced as bland and joyless. Most importantly, the person experiences a low grade sense of dullness, discomfort, sluggishness, and fear. He may complain of headaches or not having enough energy. He is prone to spend time and money looking for a physical cause for his psychological problems. Under these conditions, he is clearly in a rut.

Mild depression like other forms of depression can be *reactive*; precipitated by events such as a divorce, a lost pet, retirement, relocation to a new area, loss of a job, rejection by a friend, physical disability, and so forth. Mild depression also can be *autonomous* and reflect chronic self-doubts.

The mildly depressed person is in a conceptual rut of her own making, but is often very naive about how she keeps her depressive feeling flowing. She fails to recognize how she fires up her dull depressive feelings with thoughts of her own sense of hopelessness and helplessness. Despite the fluidity of these "monotonous" depressive restraints, the flood of depressive thoughts can be interrupted, the bound energy constructively channeled, and the depression disrupted.

Psychological depression is the result of an organized flow of pessimistic self-statements, concepts, and images. The organization is like a layer cake. It allows for interchanges between the ideational layers of the cake (see Figure 17).

Figure 17

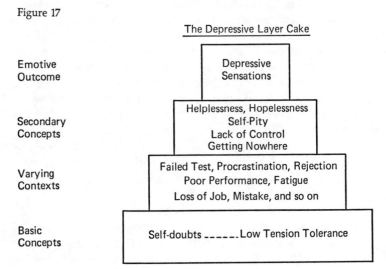

The Depressive Layer Cake

Emotive Outcome	Depressive Sensations
Secondary Concepts	Helplessness, Hopelessness Self-Pity Lack of Control Getting Nowhere
Varying Contexts	Failed Test, Procrastination, Rejection Poor Performance, Fatigue Loss of Job, Mistake, and so on
Basic Concepts	Self-doubts ------ Low Tension Tolerance

According to the concept of the layer cake, the psychologically depressed person views life through the eye of one who lacks worth and ability to tolerate stress. Therefore, inconveniences and setbacks take on heightened meaning. For example, if a depressed person performs poorly, he is more likely to magnify the significance of the event and think worse of himself for his performance. And, although the context for self-depressing thoughts varies, the primary and secondary concepts that stir up the emotional juices remain remarkably the same: helplessness, hopelessness, self-pity, self-doubts, low tension tolerance, and so forth. These conceptually instigated emotional juices are the depressive sensations.

Mild psychological depression is like a chameleon: symptoms change as mental outlook changes. The distress signal waxes and wanes like a summer storm; the mildly depressed person can feel fine at one moment, as his mind drifts away from self-depressing thoughts, then the next moment he feels down as his negative outlook once again erupts and dominates the mental scene.

This description of mild depression portrays the natural history of many mild depressive states. The mildly depressed person who accepts these bewildering fluctuations, and focuses on solving the basic problems leading to this symptom, is likely to break free from the depressive rut sooner. So at the very least, what mildly depressed people need to do is objectively recognize and encounter the erroneous foundations to their mild depression, and stop thinking that temporary respites or pits are permanent.

Clearly, many readers will not feel so oppressed by the full weight of this depressive layer cake as to be immobilized by it. Nevertheless, Chapter 11 is built around the assumption that the reader is laboring under the weight of most of these depressing ideas. The rationale for this position is that if the reader knows how to take an organized approach to deal with more extreme self-depressing thoughts, this knowledge can be used as part of an intervention strategy to disrupt a depressive thinking process before it gains momentum.

It is estimated that 80 percent of the population have *at least* one or two major bouts with depression in the course of their lifetimes. Thus, a heavy emphasis on basic counter-depression techniques is in order as a tool to fight this unfortunate emotional state. Depressing thinking organized around basic and secondary concepts can be disrupted and replaced with an objective nondepressed organization of thought. Chapter 11 describes how you can do just that.

chapter eleven
UP FROM
DOWN UNDER

In recent years, cognitive approaches to help people overcome depressive thinking have proved effective. These cognitive methods developed out of ego psychology and were refined by rational-emotive and cognitive theorists.

The Cognitive View

The ego psychology view is that a person feels depressed because he or she establishes a goal that he or she is helpless to achieve, then suffers a loss of self-worth because of this failure. Rational-emotive therapists moved forward with this theory and defined depression as a consequence of *interpreting* one's life circumstances as negative, oneself as a worthless person, and one's future as bleak and hopeless. In addition, the rational-emotive view emphasizes that people who feel depressed continuously reindoctrinate themselves with *pessimistic self-statements*, such as "life is hopeless," "I'm so worthless," and "poor me." Aaron Beck's (1976) cognitive theory of depression builds on the ego psychology approach and bears considerable resemblance to Albert Ellis's (1962) rational-emotive approach. The cognitive view is that people depress themselves because they view themselves as helpless to change, and thus their situation is hopeless.

Helplessness and hopelessness are pivotal to Beck's *depressive triad*. In this triad of thought, the depressed person thinks the world presents *too many obstacles* that hinder his or her goals, feels *helpless* to overcome these obstacles, and gives up when he or she thinks there is *no hope* of ever controlling his or her future destiny. Fortunately, the work of the ego psychologists and rational-emotive and cognitive theories have provided powerful methods that are now available to use to develop skill in breaking free from depressive ideas.

Recognizing Depressive Thinking

Mild depression is a special variation of the self-doubt-tension-avoidance syndrome that complicates life in many unpleasant ways. The following describes the primary and secondary self-doubt-downing-tension-avoidance ideas inherent in depression.

Primary Classification

1. *Self-doubts.* The depressed person perceives him- or herself as lacking confidence, bound to fail, and unable to render good decisions. The person believes that he or she is unable to fulfill expectations.

2. *Low tension tolerance.* The depressed person views the process of change as uncomfortable, current circumstances as unbearable, the need for comfort as a top priority, and the need for protection against hurts and failures as critical.

Secondary Classification

1. *Unfavorable comparisons.* The depressed person thinks others are more capable, have more fun, are better adjusted, are more zestful, and are able to meet reasonable standards. He or she often worries about what others think.

2. *Helplessness.* The depressed person thinks he *cannot* change the uncomfortableness of his condition or circumstances are beyond control.

3. *Pessimism*. The depressed person thinks life will not get better, her situation is hopeless, and life in general is just crummy.

4. *Self-pity*. The depressed person feels sorry for herself. She thinks in "woe is poor me" terms, construes herself as brave in the face of uncontrollable adversity, and thinks her struggle for survival is noble since she carries on despite torment and mental anguish.

5. *Self-blame*. The depressed person downs himself for his helplessness and inability to overcome incontrollable circumstances, or for faults, or for inabilities to render good decisions, or for inabilities to stop the rush of frustrating negative thinking, or for failing to enjoy a happy fulfilling life.

A psychologically depressed person is likely to construe life and him- or herself in at least a few of the following ways:

1. My situation is hopeless.
2. I am helpless to do anything about it.
3. I can't tolerate these lousy feelings.
4. Poor me, why do I always have to suffer?
5. I'm so unworthy.
6. I'm to blame.
7. I'm not like other people (I'm hopelessly different).

There are contradictions between a few of these seven depressive constructions that appear paradoxical. For example, the depressed person will think he or she is helpless to control circumstances, yet is self-blaming for not controlling those circumstances.

The Self-Blame
Uncontrollability Paradox

Inherent in the self-blame-hopelessness scenario is what A. Abrahamson and H. Sackein (1977) refer to as the paradox in depression: helplessness and self-blame. People who are depressed blame themselves for outcomes over which they claim no control. Obviously, this is quite irrational if taken on face value. Either one has control and is capable, or one has no control and is not culpable. However, helplessness and self-blame are not so paradoxical considering that many depressives blame themselves for their helplessness because they "should" have been able to assert control. And it is this expectant "should" that requires evaluation if the paradox is to be understood and disrupted.

This apparent contradiction is not paradoxical, and indeed is logical, if one starts with a faulty premise that he or she is basically worthless. Operating with such a premise, the person may well view circumstances as uncontrollable, but simultaneously blame him- or herself for having the sort of emotional problems that block progress. The person compares himself to others whom he thinks can better manage themselves. In essence, the depressed person may blame himself for being different and presents himself as different because he thinks and acts despondently.

Most depressed people do not identify and evaluate the hopelessness-helplessness blame paradox. Instead, they continue to blame themselves for their problems and believe they are helpless to change. And, seeing circumstances as hopeless, they make no connection between hopeless thoughts and inhibited actions. Indeed, helplessness, self-blame, and inhibited actions become one and the same. For example, a "helpless" self-blamer may think: "I don't know how to use my potential" or "I'm at fault for wasting my time and not acting to change my life when opportunities were available." And as the person blames herself, she sits in her rut and fails to act.

Gilbert Ryle (1954) observed that many "paradoxes" like helpless and self-blame are word games, not real paradoxes. They are mental dilemmas. In my view, they are fraudulent paradoxes that bring unnecessary pain. They are concepts that are shredded together, but need to be considered separately.

Abraham Low (1950) points out another contradiction that must be clarified. According to Low, helplessness and hopelessness are not the same. One can legitimately declare him- or herself helpless. For example, one cannot stop a thought from racing through one's mind. However, declaring one's situation as hopeless (believing the thought will never stop) is unrealistic and inappropriate. The hopeless judgment requires a prognostication that an emotionally distressed person is not qualified to make.

To place the hopeless-helplessness-self-blame paradoxes in perspective can be aided by this question: if circumstances are out of my control, how am I blameworthy? The conclusion is that either one does have a chance for making change and had better stop blaming himself and start to change, or one is not to blame for uncontrollable circumstances, so he had better graciously accept the unchangeable and stop blaming himself.

Sometimes the apparent contradiction is negatively resolved. A person who blames herself because she cannot control her destiny sometimes claims she is *inherently* damaged. If a person thinks that "bad genes" or "biochemical disbalances" are to blame for such things as an inability to form positive, productive work habits, then the person has backed him- or herself into a depressing mental prison. True, one's biology does set limitations; however, psychological limitations can be as great because of the depressed person's needlessly complicated, "logic tight," irrational system of thinking.

Depressive Susceptibility

Some people are more susceptible to stress than are others. At least one manifestation of stress is depression, as Figure 18 shows.

People who are subject to the ball and chain of depression are overly susceptible to negative thoughts or unpleasant sensations. A. Davids (1956), for example, has shown that college students who are pessimistic and distrusting tend to learn and to remember a larger number of gloomy sounding words than their nonpessimistic peers. Even if one does not normally think gloomy thoughts, sometimes exposure to negative-sounding statements can negatively influence one's mood. Emmett Veltens (1968) scientifically demonstrated this effect by exposing people to both depressive and uplifting statements. His experiments show that people exposed to positive and uplifting statements typically feel uplifted, and people exposed to negative depressive statements typically feel their moods depressed. The fact that his mood induction method has a mood-changing effect indicates that people are susceptible to the "emotional" suggestions implied in both the uplifting and depressing statements. Velten's report that people's emo-

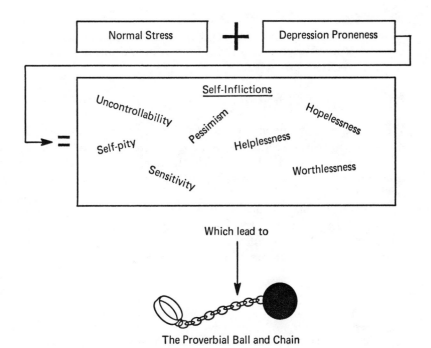

Figure 18

tions are influenced by suggestion finds considerable support in the work of Magna Arnold, (1960), Richard Lazarus (1966), and the collaborative research of Stanley Schacter and Jerome Singer (1962). These investigators found that emotions are not thoughtless experiences. Quite the contrary, when a person is emoting, his or her emotions reflect his or her thinking.

Depressed persons harboring emotionally disturbing thinking patterns victimize themselves with pessimistic assumptions and negative overgeneralizations. This tendency, Albert Ellis (1962) believes, is exhibited by the depressed person when he or she adopts pessimistic *assumptions* that lead to depressed feelings. Ellis sees depressive distress as tied to the depressed person's human tendencies to develop highly prejudiced, negative, irrational thinking.

Aaron Beck (1967) has amplified Ellis's view. In his work with depressed people, Beck points to their tendency to look at the dark side of the street. His data indicate that the depressed person has a tendency to distort and magnify the importance of negative circumstances and then act as though such distortions are real and uncontrollably oppressive.

Dealing with Psychological Depression

William James's nineteenth-century writings on depression anticipated the thinking of contemporary cognitive-behavioral therapists who came to see that negative thinking laced with self-debasements and extreme pessimism are one and the same as depression.

Because of his practical inclinations, James pointed to pathways to change. Some of his trial-breaking ideas were the precursor of contemporary counterdepression strategies. Specifically, he pointed to the importance of emotional freedom as the pathway from depression:

> If namely, we wish our train of ideation and volition to be copious and varied and effective, we must form the habit of freeing them from the inhibitive influence of reflection upon them of egoistic preoccupations about their results. Such a habit, like other habits, can be formed.

The concepts and suggested activities in the remainder of this chapter are designed to break the depressive thinking habit and *get up from down under* by forming objective thinking habits and assertive behavioral actions.

A Rational Approach to Psychological Depression

When you feel depressed, you probably feel quite unfriendly toward yourself. But you can learn to be your own best friend by learning to counter self-defeating depressive thoughts. You can do this by developing and using a rational-emotive, problem-solving approach called *systematic rational desensitization*.

Systematic rational desensitization interfaces the behavior hierarchy system of Joseph Wolpe (discussed in Chapter 8) with the cognitive restructuring approach of rational-emotive therapist Albert Ellis. I developed and lectured about this system at the Institute for Rational Emotive Psychotherapy in 1970 and described it in a 1975 publication. It has proven highly helpful for many people who suffered from psychological depression, as well as various forms of fears and guilt.

In systematic rational desensitization, upsetting ideas are identified and ordered in a hierarchy instead of imaginary situations as in classical systematic desensitization. In using the systematic rational desensitization approach, you first identify situations about which you depress yourself. The situation you consider your top priority is dealt with first. Next, you set up your hierarchy system by identifying your depressing and inhibiting thoughts about that situation. Then you order your thoughts according to their impact in the same manner as imaginary situations were ordered in the desensitization exercises described in chapter 8. (Sometimes the thoughts cannot be hierarchically ordered, and instead are ordered according to the sequence in which they appeared.) Lastly you apply rational restructuring methods to counter those depressing thoughts and to think straight.

Prior to employing this approach, you should skim over the instructions, review the case examples, then reread the instructions with the intent of setting up your own rational desensitization program. Using this review-performance sequence, you can acquire a good overview and a logical framework for starting to implement the system.

The Program

The systematic rational desensitization system is established by doing the following:

1. *Identify the major situations about which you depress yourself,* and state them thematically.
2. *Prioritize the situations in order of their significance.*
3. *Start with your top priority only and:*
   a. obtain paper that can serve as worksheets
   b. list the priority problem on the worksheet

   c. cite specific activating situations that can be categorized under the heading of your priority problem. For example, if your priority is interpersonal relations, your activating or trigger situations might be group meetings, family gatherings, and so forth. These trigger problems represent specific situations you depress yourself about. For purposes of this analysis, initially limit yourself to between three and five activating trigger events.

   d. list each activating situation on a separate sheet using the following format:

Activating event: _____

Ideas about the event: _____

_____

_____

_____

   e. List your ideas or beliefs about each situation separately. In this phase, do not try to censure your thinking; write down your thoughts as they flow out.

When you have reached point "e" in the preceding outline, you are ready to move to phase two. This is an evaluation phase where you verify whether the ideas you have listed are depressing. In addition to the criteria for rational and irrational thinking cited in Chapter 7, you can use a direct comparison between the thoughts you have identified as depressing against the primary and secondary depressing ideas listed earlier in this chapter. If the idea matches, chances are it is a depressing idea.

In the third phase, you order your thoughts for each idea according to intensity; apply a subjective unit of depression scale (SUD) to "objectify" this process. On a separate worksheet, list depressing ideas from high to low in impact. Try to limit yourself to no more than ten ideas that do not overlap each other. When you complete this phase, you will have your thoughts organized according to intensity. At this point in your analysis you should have:

   1. Separate worksheets for each depressing activating event listed under your priority problem area.

   2. A separate listing of ten or fewer depressing ideas for each of the activating events, ordered according to their depressing impact.

As you look over your separate lists, you will probably see that each has similar as well as different ideas. Similar ideas may appear for each situation, but not uncommonly the ordering of ideas in each category may differ. In a systematic rational desensitization program, regularities as well as irregularities across separate themes are not unusual.

Now you are ready for phase four, which requires that you make up a rational desensitization form chart for each activating event, as shown below.

Rational Desensitization Form

Activating Event	Ideas about Event	Rational Self-Help Questions	Results

To use this form, state the activating event in the column labeled Activating Event. Then list each of the depressing ideas you have about the event, beginning in order of highest to lowest intensity.

Phase five is the employment of rational self-help questions to each isolated depressing idea. The examples of what constitutes a rational question cited in Chapter 7 can be helpful in formulating these questions. The case example at the close of this chapter provides a concrete example to illustrate relevant questions.

To structure this rational-desensitization program, you:

1. First concentrate your efforts on the least depressively noxious idea on your rational restructuring hierarchy of beliefs.

2. Write down your answer(s) to the question(s) you have targeted toward the "weakest link" in the chain of self-depressing ideas.

3. Check your answer(s) against the *five criteria for rational thinking*. If the answer(s) meet the criteria, they should be credible answers. See Chapter 7 for list of criteria.

4. Repeatedly raise and answer the designated rational question(s) that are designed to counter that self-depressing thought. Keep challenging the self-depressing idea until you have neutralized its depressive impact. Then move to the next statement on the hierarchy.

Feel free to use any evidence, including ideas and concepts described earlier or later in this book, to add to your questions to counter each depressive thought.

Avoid blaming yourself if you cannot work through the system "quickly enough." Success is measured in percentage gains, not necessarily in a quick problem reversal. The important goal of the exercise is to learn an *approach* that can be applied to coping with depressing ideas and that can *prevent* depressing ideas from emerging or recurring.

You can use the systematic rational restructuring approach with or without relaxation. If you decide to use relaxation, use either muscular or imagery induced relaxation and put yourself into deep relaxation prior to asking and answering counterdepression questions. When you feel relaxed with the questions, satisfied with your responses, and uninfluenced by the belief you are questioning, move to the next level and repeat the sequences.

Because there are similar self-depressing ideas on each rational desensitization form, you will be able to repeat many counterdepression questions and responses. Consequently, you will have an opportunity to overlearn counterdepression questioning methods to the point of habit.

Obviously, counterdepressive questioning is important, but it is still insufficient without countering depressive actions. Making yourself become involved in productive actions will help create a clearer picture of your capabilities, motivation, and ability to act. This positive triad is the stuff out of which a positive self-concept, tension tolerance, and behavior skills are forged. So, work to turn constructive thinking into constructive actions. Rational desensitization by itself will not do this for you. The system merely provides an *approach*.

Case Examples

By targeting our counterdepressive efforts toward specific situations, the message is delivered that although depression may seem omnibus, there are specific circumstances to which the depressive feelings seem tightly linked. By isolating them, we can realize the problem, and through our division of the depressive elements, we can conquer the problem.

Three case examples are used to illustrate the rational desensitization process. The formats of each are modified to fit the requirements of each of the three persons who applied the technique. These modifications have been chosen because:

1. In real life, most problem-solving formats must be modified to mesh with the problem-solver's situation and abilities.
2. Mastering the approach is more important than rigorously adhering to the format.

Jeff's Example

Jeff was mainly depressed over his interpersonal relationships. When he felt depressed, it was primarily about participating in group meetings (coin club, staff, and such), and family picnics. Jeff also feared each situation. Thus, he logically used the rational desensitization approach to deal with his fears and his depression.

Jeff followed the usual procedure for rational desensitization. He began by isolating his fear-depression reaction toward group meetings. Following are his fearful and depressing thoughts about group meetings.

1. I'm always so tense.
2. I'll never get my ideas across.
3. I won't appear brilliant.
4. People will think badly of me.
5. People will think I'm a nervous person.
6. I'm so inhibited.
7. I can't find anyone to feel comfortable with.
8. People will ignore me.
9. I'm dull and boring.
10. I'm too quiet a person; why can't I be extroverted?
11. I have too many emotional hangups to change.
12. I'm stupid and a fool for being the way I am.
13. I'm too uncomfortable.

Although collapsing various fear-depression thoughts into a few nonoverlapping categories is not required, sometimes it proves helpful because it clarifies the major mental concoctions underlying a fear-depression play-off. Jeff took the approach of collapsing his ideas into categories.

In analyzing his list, Jeff noted that ideas 1, 2, and 11 have the theme of hopelessness. Ideas 4, 5, and 8 refer to people disapproving of him. Ideas 6, 9, 10, and 12 are self-blaming statements, and 6, 9, and 10 are statements that need to be completed because there is a hidden conclusion in each. The conclusion is that Jeff thought he was worthless and that his behavior confirmed that hypothesis. Ideas 7 and 13 are discomfort ideas. Idea 3 suggests that Jeff has perfectionistic leanings, a possible thread that weaved through his fear-depression thinking.

Because of overlapping ideas, it was possible for Jeff to collapse his thinking into the categories of hopelessness, disapproval, self-blame, discomfort, and perfectionism. Although not directly stated, the ideas of helplessness and self-pity are implied in many of his statements.

Next, Jeff decided which thoughts bothered him the most, second most, and so forth. Following is the rational desensitization program that Jeff devised.

In the structuring of this systematic rational desensitization example, a section listing Jeff's responses to the provocative con-

Rational Desensitization Program

Activating Event	Depressing Ideas	Confrontations	Results
Group meetings such as the coin club, department staff meetings.	*Hopelessness* I'm always so tense. I don't get my ideas across well. I have too many emotional hangups to ever change.	*Hopelessness* 1. Where is the evidence that I'm *always* so tense? Are there no exceptions? 2. What ideas do I want to get across? What would constitute an adequate performance? 3. What problems do I need to address and why do I not think I can make progress?	I can change if I want to and I do want to change.
	Disapproval People think badly of me and ignore me because they think I'm a nervous person.	*Disapproval* 1. Evidence that people think I'm nervous. 2. So what if I appear nervous? 3. Evidence that people ignore me because I appear nervous. 4. What behavior do I emit that might put people off and what can I do to change it?	Avoid jumping to conclusions about other people's views. No longer consider myself a mind reader. Took action to change.

Rational Desensitization Program

Activating Event	Depressing Ideas	Confrontations	Results
	Worthless-Self-Blame I'm a stupid fool for being inhibited, dull, boring, and too quiet.	*Worthlessness* 1. What purpose does making the overstatement "I'm a stupid fool" really serve? 2. How can a complicated person be factored down to merely a "stupid fool"? 3. Even if I act foolishly, how do foolish acts make me or any other person a stupid fool? 4. If I act in an inhibited fashion, I will probably appear dull and quiet and feel bored. If I don't like my inhibited reactions, what can I do to change?	Greater self awareness and self-confidence. Take action to change.
	Discomfort I'm uncomfortable and can't find anyone to be comfortable with.	*Discomfort* 1. So what if I'm not comfortable? Who says I have to be?	Acceptance of discomfort.
	Perfectionism I won't appear brilliant.	*Perfectionism* 1. So what if I don't sound brilliant? Why do I have to?	Sense of relief.

frontive questions has been omitted. I believe it is better for a person suffering from a depressive set of beliefs to use an approach that forces him or her to think objectively about and work through the burdensome conceptual problem. Indeed, answers to confrontive questions need to be thoroughly thought through! Consequently, the approach to responding to the confrontive statements and questions included under the objective re-evaluation section of this procedure requires that you reapply the *five criteria for rational thinking* to your answers. If your response meets criteria, you are on your way to more productive thinking.

Stan's Example

Stan's case further illustrates the flexibility of the rational desensitization technique. It is employed with interpersonal difficulties, and shows how to deal with self-depressing ideas that are exaggerated generalities.

In implementing this structured approach, Stan began with interpersonal relations and developed the following systematic rational desensitization chart.

Activating Event	Ideas about Event (listed in order of importance)	Objective Re-evaluations
1. Poor interpersonal interactions.	1. Can't relate to people.	Evaluate what relating to people means. Determine skills that need to be developed. Identify exceptions that counter that statement.
	2. I'll never get better.	If I work to develop interpersonal skills, where is the hard evidence I won't improve?

Activating Event	Ideas about Event (listed in order of importance)	Objective Re-evaluations
	3. I'll never be liked.	Never is a long time. What purpose is served by attributing this quality of changeless-ness to myself?
	4. I'm a bore to be around.	Evaluate in what way I'm boring, what is the feedback I've received to confirm and/or counter this view. Even if I some-times act boring, what can be done con-cretely to increase my congeniality index?
	5. People just tolerate me.	*People* is a very gen-eral term. Specifically, what *people* "just tolerate me"? How is this tolerance shown? Where is the proof that person "Y" only tolerates *me*? What are other reasonable ways to view the same situation?
	6. People who like me have bad taste.	What person(s) who like me have bad taste? Specifically, how is his/her taste bad? Why can't those who like me be valid in their reasons for liking me?

Stan's response to questions he developed on item 6—people who like me have bad taste—resulted in a irrational conclusion: I just know they have bad taste because anyone dumb enough to like me would have to have bad taste. His response is irrational because it is overgeneralized, too abstract, too inferential, not based on hard data or *objective logic*, and unreasonably pejorative. Thus, a question such as "where is the evidence or proof for my *assumption* that people who like me are dumb?" becomes increasingly important. For example, unless Stan can come up with hard evidence that people who like him are dumb, he had better learn to drop the charges against "others" that "their" taste is bad if "they" like him.

Objective logic dictates that specific, concrete, and largely indisputable data are required to confirm the "bad taste" hypothesis. The scientific spirit of this approach requires that in the absence of such data, charges are to be dropped.

Linda's Case

The rational system can be used in evaluating and countering abstract thoughts. The system provides a format for organizing an assault against even the more ethereal abstract and overgeneralized concepts such as worthlessness, helplessness, and hopelessness. Linda's chart illustrates her use of systematic rational desensitization in coping with feelings of worthlessness and hopelessness.

Conceptual Stresses	Ideas that Support the Concept	Evaluation of Concept-Related Ideas
1. Worthlessness.	1. I'm stupid.	1. What is my criteria for stupidity? How come I won't include evidence of my capabilities in my outlook? What is the purpose of blending my performances with my worth?
	2. All my life I've failed to achieve my potential.	2. Even if true, as it is for most people, how does not achieving the height of my potential render me worthless?

Conceptual Stresses	Ideas that Support the Concept	Evaluation of Concept-Related Ideas
	3. I can't do anything right.	3. Spell out "anything" and "right." Making vague references to myself only smudges the issue; better to spell out what I mean and to objectively evaluate the meaning of what I say.

Conceptual Stresses	Ideas that Support the Concept	Objective Re-evaluation
2. Hopelessness.	1. I don't have what it takes to change.	1. *What* does it take to change *what*? What do I need to do to get started?
	2. I've always been a loser.	2. What is a loser? How is my definition of loser a perfect definition for me? What are the exceptions to my loser definition
	3. I'm going to suffer forever. I'll never get better.	3. Where is the incontroversial proof that if I work to identify my irrational thinking and vigorously subject it to a fair, critical analysis, that I won't improve on my ability to disrupt this malignant hopelesssness pattern I've adopted? If I want to get better, I'm going to have to work to do better, so let's see where I can begin.

By frequent practice at countering depressing ideas, you can either permanently rid yourself of them; or should depressing beliefs arise spontaneously, you can apply rational questions previously learned and practiced to increase the likelihood that you will blunt the impact of negative self-depressing ideas and disinhibit yourself from their effects.

Systematic rational desensitization can be applied wherever one is plagued by irrational concepts or ideas. For example, the concepts underlying guilt (failure to meet obligations and self-persecution) are ideally suited to this sort of analysis, as are hostile thinking, exaggerated jealousy, ego fears, and numerous other malfunctional cognitive states growing out of the *self-doubt-downing-low-tension-tolerance-emotional-stress model.*

chapter twelve
BEHAVIORAL STRATEGIES FOR DISRUPTING DEPRESSIVE RUTS

Behavioral technology has existed since the turn of the twentieth century. The movement picked up steam with the publication of John Watson's (1913) *Psychology as the Behaviorist Views It.* Watson's work was followed by Mary Cover Jones's (1924) classic study in which she desensitized a young child to a rabbit he had feared, through the use of behavior technology. Jones's work was followed by the effective habit-breaking method of Knight Dunlap (1928) and Edwin Guthrie (1952). After Dunlap and Guthrie came the behavior modification movement, stimulated by the operant conditioning research of B.F. Skinner (1953). The most recent advocate of behavioral technology is Joseph Wolpe (1969), who through his own research advanced the work of Watson and Jones and created a powerful therapy system particularly well suited for treating psychological fears.

Behavioral approaches are surprisingly thin in their application to psychological depression considering both the high incidence of depression and the many years behavioral technology has been in vogue. Quite probably, as Wolpe and Arnold Lazarus (1971) have noted, psychological depression is a by-product of severe fear arousal. The implication is that by treating the fear, you disrupt the depression. Thus, there has been little direct emphasis on the direct behavioral therapy treatment of depression by behavior therapists.

Of course, it is not surprising to find abundant superficial behavioral advice such as that offered by the "quick fix advocates." This advice is vacuous, rarely helps, and should not be dignified as a behavioral technique. Quick fix advice, like suggesting that the depressed person engage in activities such as swimming or going to a restaurant does not cut it when it comes to overcoming mild depression. Quick fix activities might well help a person rebound from a depressive mood, but such solutions for alleviating a mild depression commonly fail. Undaunted, national magazines and newspapers optimistically imply that the miracle cure for depression is near at hand by taking "expert" advice such as "just pick yourself up," "smell a flower a day," "take a walk along the beach," "get involved in a hobby," and so forth.

When a person's self-perception is riddled with a pervasive sense of despair and anguish, he or she can hardly *focus* attention on a flower, let alone enjoy it long enough to disrupt depression.

Learning Behavioral Desist Skills

People who are psychologically depressed sometimes indulge depressive thoughts and overwhelm themselves in such thoughts, then add to their problems by avoiding responsibilities, acting like walking wounded, and whining and complaining to others about their depressive plights. Such depressive behavior will influence others to respond with: sympathetic concern (poor dear); encouragement (perk up, life is not so bad as it seems), preaching (look for a better way to act, like stop acting glum and act happy), aggravation (get on the stick; stop complaining), and impatience (when are you going to stop moping? I'm getting sick and tired of your griping). If the depression persists, the depressed individual will begin to notice people behaviorally avoiding him or her. When this happens, the depressed person tends to feel worse because of the "rejections." Then he or she may feel depressed because of the rejections, forget that the depression may have contributed to the rejections in the first place, and consequently attribute the latest depressive feelings to the most recent rejection.

It certainly makes sense under conditions of the depression-rejection-depression cycle to practice developing nondepressive behavioral skills, one of which is a *desist skill*. In developing the desist skill, one works to desist from using low frustration tolerance terminology and depressive terminology from the language. Depressive terminology largely takes the form of complaints, such as expressing how bad off one is. Through the development of a desist technique, you should be able to reduce rejections if they are related to complaining. (See Chapter 4 for a review of coping with low frustration tolerance language.)

Development of a desist skill can be boosted by working to develop a skill for verbalizing your positive observations. Positive expression can be aided by considering benign but realistic alternative views, and expressing them. As you make a positive declaration you will appear uplifted, and increase your chances to receive positive feedback, reduce the risk of rejections, and generate a benign cycle.

Mild depression lacks continuity. There are normally occurring breaks in the pattern. Also, in mild depression, pessimistic thinking is often far from overwhelming and can be disrupted through action. Thus, acting in an uplifted manner may help keep the momentum moving. Incidently, this is precisely the advice of William James, who noted that when there was a break in the continuity of his depression, he would act out happiness, and he found he was able to experience the mood he artificially sought to create.

Disrupting Depression through Self-Reward

Peter Lewinsohn (1974) and associates have suggested that people who feel depressed are likely to be people who receive precious little praise, acknowledgement, or other forms of positive rewards from themselves or from others. However, behavioral studies show that where depressed persons are showered with gifts and praise and use positive self-reward (like patting oneself on the back for a positive act), the depression tends to persist and may momentarily worsen despite the rewards. It is likely that this person's basic pessimistic outlook remains and he feels worse about himself because he has not done very much in his view to deserve the reward. The reward is like a handout. The concept of self-reward for positive actions is, nevertheless, a reasonable behavioral approach if used consistently and *reasonably*.

Self-rewards that seem to be trivial and unearned can be iatrogenic. Reward conditions such as praise, eating a bowl of ice cream, or reading a newspaper, often have about as much longterm positive effects for a depressed person as a drop of vinegar on the tongue of a thirsty person has for relieving thirst. Instead of using trivial, unearned reward, what is required is: (1) identify self-help activities to boost confidence and build tension tolerance, (2) engage repeatedly in the activity, and (3) *appropriately* reward yourself for these constructive actions.

A consistent and reasonable reward system adds to your chances for success in disrupting depression, but it *does not guarantee* success, no more than seasoning guarantees that prepared food will be delicious. The seasoning just helps.

Lewinsohn describes a second behavioral approach for alleviating depression. This approach involves increasing a depressed person's opportunities to participate in pleasant activities. Increasing the number of pleasant activities a person experiences seems to have a paradoxical effect, however, according to Constance Hammer and R. Glass (1975). Their experiments suggest that depressed individuals tend to become more depressed after increased participation in "pleasant activities."

Major problems exist in Hammer and Glass's study. First, it is crimped in time. Second, the presumably "pleasant" activities might be construed by their depressed subjects as trivial or patronizing. More importantly, however, the depressed person may view the activities as pleasant, but irrationally conclude:

1. Even though I'm doing all these pleasant things, I still don't feel happy. There must be something wrong with me.

2. These activities are nice, but the feelings won't last. Woe is poor me, I can never stay happy.

To assure that "pleasant activities" will not be iatrogenic requires *countering unrealistic expectations* about the meaning of those activities. Thus, if you want to get up from down under, you would wisely identify and counter *negetive, self-defeating thinking* as well as take *concrete, purposeful,* and *positive* goal-directed actions.

Acting to do better involves getting into problems as well as joy-creating activities. It also requires changing your self-depressive mental processes so that you can be free to profit from what you undertake.

Learning to Assert Yourself

Most people who are psychologically depressed tend to handle their daily affairs reasonably well. However, in this mildly depressed state, they are reluctant to avail themselves of opportunities if such opportunities appear to present possible conflict or require self-assertion.

As Robert Alberti and Michael Emmons (1974) point out, self-assertive actions such as expressing feelings, commending others, and standing up for one's rights can help change negative self-attitudes. They rightly believe that one need not change one's attitude before acting. (I could not agree more.) For as we see in Chapter 15, waiting to get over feeling depressed or fearful before acting can be an excuse that keeps your wheels spinning. On the other hand, when a person feels depressed, he or she generally does not *feel* like acting differently even if he or she wanted to. Therefore, it seems advisable to combine both cognitive and behavioral methods to increase the likelihood that one will be able to dig one's wheels in and move.

A *hierarchial assertion* plan can help you to organize your efforts so as to coordinate straight thinking with constructive acting.

Sometimes a case example provides a more cogent description of the use of a technique compared to verbal directions. Let us take Dick's case example to explain the system and how to use it.

Dick felt depressed because he saw himself as the brunt of other's jokes, too easily pushed around, and too inhibited to express how he felt. At least part of his problem was fear. He was afraid to express himself and to stick up for his rights. The fact that he was fearful caused him to avoid expressing his thoughts and feelings, led him to feel frustrated with himself, and resulted in a sense of depressive resignation: he thought he was too helpless to act effectively; he thought his situation was hopeless because he was "helpless"; he disliked himself for his "consistent weakness."

Following is the general framework for Dick's hierarchial assertion plan, which combines both cognitive and behavioral change strategies.

1. Identify trigger-assertion deficiencies, such as holding back expressing your feelings, low sales resistance, difficulty accepting legitimate compliments.
2. Order assertion deficiencies from high to low in level of difficulty.
3. Provide target tasks for each trigger-assertion problem and order them from high to low in difficulty.
4. Identify both fear-and depression-promoting ideas for each target task, and order the related ideas from high to low in intensity.*
5. Construct challenging ideas, questions, or statements to deal with each stress-promoting activity, starting with the low intensity items and working up toward the high intensity items.
6. Use these challenges in conjunction with relaxation or without relaxation exercises by your preference.
7. Get into the problem situation and behaviorally test your plan.
8. Record your results and make adjustments as needed.

Of the three major assertion areas, Dick found expressing dissatisfactions most difficult, expressing preferences second, and expressing positive feelings least difficult. Even though expressing positive feelings was classified as least difficult, Dick rarely expressed positive feelings. He was afraid to.

A skeletal outline of Dick's Hierarchial Cognitive-Behavioral Assertion Action Plan follows on p. 202. Dick began with his least troublesome assertion problem, expressing positive feelings (Stage 1), by isolating four positive feeling expression situations (Stage 2), and by specifying the fear and depression evoking ideas he had for

---

*Both fear-and depression-countering measures are combined in this plan because you, the reader, are now familiar with how to deal with both processes; ruts usually involve a combination of fear and depression.

Four Preparation Stages

Stage One	Stage Two	Stage Three
Identify Hierarchy Concepts	*Specify each Hierarchy Concept*	*Identify Fear- and Depression-Promoting Ideas for each Specific Situation*
Dissatisfactions. Preferences. Positive feelings.	Positive feelings expressed toward: Candy: I feel happy when I'm with you. Don: I appreciate the help you've given me. Alfred: I don't know you very well, but what I know of you I like. Ginger: You've been a good friend. I appreciate you very much.	Ginger: *Fear* She'll reject me. I'll come across as being uptight. I'll sound clumsy and stupid. *Depression* I'll never get over this problem. I can't help feeling reserved. I'm such a jerk. I have no control.

Stage Four: Three Action Steps

Step One	Step Two	Step Three
Disputing Irrational beliefs	*Getting into Trigger Problem Situations*	*Recording Results*
(without relaxation) *Fear* I won't know what to say.	Relaxation. Psycho-regulation exercise. Direct expression.	Log results. Make adjustments as needed.
Challenge What idea do I want to get across and what stops me from saying it? What is the worst that is *likely* to happen and what would be so bad if it did? What does not knowing what to say mean?		

the least fear-depression evoking specific situation (Stage 3). He took three action steps for this lowest hierarchy situation (Stage 4), then repeated the process for the next step on the hierarchy.

Following is Dick's initial report on the results of his program.

Goal

Effectively express my positive feelings.

Procedure

Hierarchial Cognitive-Behavioral Assertion Action Plan Approach.

Results

Day One: Developed and tested out program. Had some difficulty in identifying fear and depression-promoting ideas. Used five criteria for rational thinking for an assist. Worked until satisfied that my program was designed to do what I wanted it to do.

Day Two: Confronted my fearful and depressive thoughts about expressing my positive feelings to Ginger. Kept at it until I could think objectively about expressing my feelings to Ginger.

Day Three: Prior to talking with Ginger in person, reviewed objective thinking. Relaxed, then went through psycho-regulation procedure. Met Ginger, and at an appropriate point in the conversation I told her that I appreciated her friendship and very much liked her as a person. The words seemed to flow out naturally and I was really happy I could say them. Ginger was really warm, said she knew I like her, I really didn't have to verbalize, but she was glad I did. She went on to say she felt the same toward me and that I was one of the few people she knew she could depend on.

.
.
.
.
.
.

Day Sixty-two: Told man at lunch counter I was allergic to cigarette smoke and I'd appreciate it if he would blow it away from me. He obliged me by putting it out. The whole event happened so fast, and I acted so spontaneously and matter of fact that I surprised myself.

Dick completed his program and judged he was successful because he had produced positive results: (1) he no longer felt fearful and depressed, (2) he felt he had broken from his rut pattern, (3) he saw himself as in control of his future, (4) he saw himself as able to face uncomfortable conditions, and (5) he saw he could rely on himself and, therefore, had little cause to doubt himself.

In a follow-up session, Dick attributed his progress to: (1) psychological *tools* for objectifying his thinking, (2) having clear *goals* for what he wanted to accomplish, (3) establishing workable *objectives* to meet the goals, (4) a high *structured* procedure that required action, (5) *consistency* in applying the procedure, and (6) using an *approach* that was flexible. Dick also reported that what he learned generalized to other trigger-assertion problem areas he had previously avoided confronting: seeking job advancement, and facing up to and dealing with the demands of his parents. He found that he actually enjoyed working with the program because of the variety of activities involved and the fact that he was able to learn positive things about himself through its application.

V

GUILT, ANGER, AND RUTS

Part V is concerned with the two remaining emotions presented as part of the wheel of misery described in Chapter 3—guilt and hostility.

People differ in their need for variety and change. Some like to change location; some like a more predictable existence where they stay put. Some are base-builders; they like to try new things, but they also like a home base to come back to. Some are advancers, who want to build on what they have done and move forward without looking back. Each style has its own value and may reflect the temperament of the person who adopts it.

Guilt is an impediment to developing a temperamentally suitable style because the guilt-ridden person moves in a state of agitation or inhibition. Free of guilt, a person can exercise an enlightened morality and be the person he or she really is. Chapter 13 discusses how a person can be in a rut due to guilt and how to break free.

A person can be in a rut due to his or her own hostility. Wrapped in angry thoughts, the person suffering from hostility tends to be condemning and myopic. Chapter 14 considers how to become less condemningly myopic and how to burst out of the hostility rut.

chapter thirteen
EMANCIPATION FROM THE GUILT RUT

A person who is guilt-prone almost certainly will be in a rut and will experience more than his or her share of fear and depression. Therefore, it is important to understand this self-defeating emotion.

What is guilt? How do you acquire it? What are the forms guilt takes? What are the effects of guilt in interpersonal interactions? How is guilt used as a control? How do depression and guilt blend together? These answers can help you to understand and contend with this crippling emotion, which is the aim of this chapter.

What Is Guilt?

Guilt is a belief that one has failed to live up to an obligation and has, therefore, acted immorally. By failing to act morally and properly, one views him- or herself as bad, or no good. This feeling of guilt can arise for almost any reason: thinking one did not show *enough* concern for a deceased friend or parent while they were alive; aggressive thinking; forgetting an appointment; believing one has acted offensively; taking unfair advantage; believing one has hurt a friend's feelings, and so forth.

Some people are more prone to guilty thinking than are others. And the more guilt-prone a person is, the more often he sees himself as a transgressor and the more likely he is to think badly of himself for those transgressions. And although some of the "transgressions" require making retribution, on examination, most guilts of the guilt-prone person are invented infractions. They are objectively trivial, even though these infractions may feel like subjective disasters. For example, any one who believes that if she occasionally has angry thoughts she is wicked is a prime guilt candidate. It is almost impossible to go through life without an occasional angry thought! And, indeed, angry thoughts are sometimes appropriate!

The Acquisition of Guilt

Guilt is a learned reaction. It is acquired most often early in life through indoctrination, imitation, and self-invention. Generally, it is the expression of all three types of learnings.

Parents, along with other relatives, teachers, companions, mates, employers, even strangers, can help to indoctrinate a person into membership in the guilt cult.

A parent can help guilt-proneness by telling the child that misbehavior will cause the parent to have a heart attack, become ill, feel like a failure, or be destroyed. Statements such as "after all I've done for you, that I should live to see the day when you would shame your family as you have done" can really get the emotional juices swirling in a guilt-indoctrinated person.

Direct provocative statements such as "you are killing me" can have guilt impact. The "why" question, however, is more subtle and has more impact. For instance, a parent who asks "why do you hurt me?" is often more effective in the guilt-producing area than if he or she used a direct statement, because the implication of the question is that only an ungrateful and rotten person would treat a loving parent in so callous a manner. Direct statements and the guilty "whys" are part of the indoctrination process that continues because it gets results.

Imitation of a "guilt model" can help the guilt-learning process. By watching people control other people through guilt, a person can learn the technique and apply the principle against others and self. But too much credit is attributed to other people as the harbingers of guilt. The guilt-prone person is quite capable of extracting standards from the culture and inventing his or her own guilt system using the materials he or she extracted.

Superego Guilt

Guilt develops from parental-societal teachings of right and wrong and from self-instruction. The association that guilt-prone people make to "right" and "wrong" teachings is that negative acts are synonomous with personal worth.

The harsher and more rigid the standards of right and wrong become, the harsher the self-condemnation becomes when the standards are violated. In psychoanalytic terms, when a person is harshly self-punitive, he or she suffers from a too-strict "superego."

Sigmund Freud, the originator of psychoanalysis, maintained that personality consists of three competing systems: the id, ego, and superego. The id represents the unrepressed impulsive side of the human personality; the ego represents the practical, realistic, and managerial part; and the superego represents the conscience. The superego has what is called the "ego ideal," which sets moral standards and evaluates personal performance against these standards. Superego restraints can be functional. Controlling an urge to needlessly cause harm or damage to avoid guilt is generally preferable to acting destructively. Admittedly, however, it would be better to act out of personal dignity, autonomy, and self-concern compared to acting to avoid guilt.

Naturally, there are not three distinct systems meandering through our minds. Freud did not intend for us to believe that there were. The three divisions were a way of organizing his observations. What he did intend to show was that the propensity to be overly self-critical was inherent in the human condition.

Once acquired, guilt arises when we *believe* we acted against moral standards and are bad or evil for our actions. Guilt progresses in the following way:

1. We become aware that we *have* acted or *intended* to act immorally.
2. We feel we are obligated inflexibly to maintain "moral" standards even if they go against our own natural desires.
3. We *condemn* ourselves for our intended or actual infractions.
4. We swear we will repent.
5. We become distracted by our inner guilty torment.
6. We are inclined to repeat our guilt behavior because
   a. we get so tangled in self-blame that we forget to think things out logically.
   b. learned moral standards may go against our normal preferences and desires, and we are inclined to go with our desires.
   c. we may feel resentment against ourselves or others for our plight.
   d. we may ultimately rebel even though the rebellion may lead to more guilt.

Under this circular condition of moral standard violation—condemnation-rebellion-moral standard violation—it can seem as though we are getting nowhere fast, are tied up in our own emotional underwear, and we can become *depressed* over the seemingly never-ending conflict we experience.

The Three Faces of Guilt

A person can make him- or herself feel guilty over present thoughts and actions, past behaviors, or anticipated actions. Thus, there are three major forms of guilt: guilt over actions in the present moment, guilt over past actions, guilt over anticipated actions.

Guilt over present actions is almost always a mirror of a guilt habit. For example, Bob was taught from an early age by his minister father that sex was filthy and immoral and that he should have only pure, "clean," sexless thoughts. When Bob was in the eleventh grade, he had a major guilt reaction when he found himself lusting for his warm and attractive English teacher. He felt very confused—guilty and "dirty" and yet immensely enjoying his sexual fantasies. Subsequently, Bob felt guilty just looking at a sexually attractive woman.

Bob's guilt was over a *thought*, not a tangible behavioral action. Yet, he declared himself a bad person for having sexual fantasies in

his adult life, even though he did not want to give them up. Fortunately, only short-term counseling was required for Bob to realize
that sex was not dirty or immoral, that his thoughts and fantasies
were not crimes deserving mental punishment, and that he had
every right to enjoy sexual thoughts, feelings, and activities.

Some people live in the past and feel guilty over real or imaginary transgressions. Sally, for example, spent most of her waking
hours in guilty recollection. She guiltily recalled ten years earlier
when she blackballed her best friend Joyce from joining her sorority. She was worried that her steady date, Max, might try to date
her more attractive-looking friend, Joyce, if she were in the sorority. (Max, it seemed, only dated sorority women.) Sally had many
other guilty concerns. She also felt guilty about a time when she
was eight years old and lied to her mother about her brother, who
subsequently was unfairly punished. A major guilt trip episode
centered on the time Sally got drunk and smashed the family car.
She felt strong pangs of guilt when she reminded herself that the
automobile was not insured for collision, so the family members
had to pull in their belts that winter to pay for the repairs. She
hated herself for that episode even though she had long since paid
for the damage.

Sally's infractions were minor, past history, and not worthy of
routine mental re-enactments. Her standards, however, were so
restrictive that she could hardly forget a single incident when she
had acted badly. Thus, a large part of her guilt was a reaction to her
perfectionistic belief that she must be pure and do no wrong.

When Sally finally realized that the nature of the human being
is to be fallible and that she unquestionably would make new mistakes and she could not readily improve on current behavior while
dancing about in the past, she started to regard herself more self-
acceptingly.

Sometimes a person feels guilty over possible future happen-
ings. Milton, for example, felt guilty when he thought he might
have to reprimand one of his crew members. Milton was a supervisor in a steel company and was routinely required to take disciplinary action if a crew member violated company policy: was ex-
cessively late, failed to follow safety regulations, contributed to
housekeeping problems, and so forth. Somewhere in his life, Mil-

ton had acquired a view that it was wrong not to be nice to people because that would mean he (Milton) was not a nice person. He defined disciplining as not acting nicely and so he thought he would be acting wrongly by following company policies. Unfortunately, Milton also thought he would be acting wrongly if he *didn't* follow company policies, so he felt continually in conflict.

Milton's morality interfered with effective functioning on his job in yet another way. Not only did he feel tinges of guilt when he anticipated reprimanding one of his crew, but he was also fearful of being rejected by the crew members if he made justified reprimands and by the company if he did not enforce policy. To complicate matters, Milton feared repercussions from the union stewards, who often turned routine disciplinary matters into a cause for filing a grievance. Milton feared feeling discomfort in facing a possible grievance issue and feared appearing foolishly inarticulate, tainting his reputation and thereby losing control over his crew.

Milton resolved his conflicts by facing up to his "be nice" standard. He quickly came to see that if he wanted to be nice, he would have to get another job. Since he liked his job, was good at teaching the crew, and conscientious about checking their work, he decided to get practical and accept the reality that his function was to be effective, not "nice."

Guilt in Interpersonal Interactions

The following case of a married couple, Jane and Bill, illustrates how guilt can be prompted in interpersonal interactions.

Jane and Bill entered therapy because their marriage was in a rut. Each reported feeling snarled in a conflict that appeared to be a no-win situation. Both persons reported their relationship as brimming with tension, particularly coming from strong feelings of guilt. They found they could not respond sexually to each other. Indeed, the relationship was like a bomb that was ready to explode. As might be imagined under those conditions, the couple's interactions were manipulative and mutually destructive. The following vignette shows this destructive guilt-evoking pattern.

In a tone of purest innocence, Jane turned to her husband and asked, "Why don't you ever touch my hair? Is there something wrong with it?" Bill felt his stomach drop and a pang of guilt as he thought, "How insensitive I am—I'm hurting Jane's feelings. I should have been more sensitive." In the midst of his self-blaming, he turned to Jane and contritely touched her hair.

Later that night the couple got into a squabble over who was responsible for buying the groceries that week. After many minutes of verbal smoke and fire, Jane cuddled up to Bill and said in a tone of sweet hostility, "Let's make up and stop all this fighting. Tell me you love me." Caught off-guard but still fuming, Bill spontaneously retorted, "I don't feel like cuddling." To which Jane coldly replied, "You don't care about me anymore. You're incapable of showing love."

Bill once again felt his stomach drop, experienced fluttered speech, felt helpless, sheepish, blocked, and angry. Jane had touched a second sensitive nerve. For her part, Jane's initial victory evaporated as she soon blamed herself for acting so manipulatively.

Predictably, Jane's guilt surfaced in still other ways. For example, when she busily blamed herself for acting manipulatively in the present moment, her current guilt trip triggered past "guilt" recollections. She thus recalled past transgressions, berated herself for her prior faults, and soon felt hopelessly depressed. Some of the ideas that flashed through her mind and contributed to this depression were:

What a rat I am for having conned Bill into marrying me.

I'm not sophisticated, and it's my fault for not having gotten a better education.

I'm just faking my way through life and fooling people; I'm so stupid.

I should have been kinder to my father before he died.

Bill is so kind to me; he really cares. I don't deserve him; he deserves better.

I don't read quickly enough. I should have taken speed reading. I'll never have anything relevant to say to people. They're bored with me and it's my fault.

What a terrible person I was for having gang sex after my sixteenth birthday party. I'm a real degenerate.

Because I didn't watch my brother as I should, he broke his collarbone when he tripped over the fence. He'll never forgive me. I'm so irresponsible.

I'll never change. I'll go on forever making myself and others miserable.

With such a self-downing mental broadside, it is little wonder that Jane felt depressed when she got into guilt thinking. When Jane felt guilty and depressed, she often found herself in a Catch 22 situation with double locks: guilt led to depressed thinking, which stimulated guilt recollections. Since Jane's guilty infractions were always in the past, she felt helpless to redeem herself and, therefore, felt condemned to live her life tortured by her own thoughts.

Jane's behavior strongly suggests that her guilt provocations reflect insecurity. Her guilt thinking and provocative actions reflect her many self-doubts, her fear of tension, and her belief of herself as unlovable. To sidestep her problem, she created crises in her marriage by fabricating unnecessary conflicts and drawing Bill into them. The result of this sidestepping was that she blamed herself for "acting like a hostile bitch" and felt guilty because she thought she had failed to act properly. Because of her own guilty mental webs, she could not see that the "bitchiness" was a reflection of self-doubt, tension intolerance, and belief that she was unlovable.

Jane's inner guilt and insecurity were a result of her attempts to cover up her self-doubts. They reflected misconceptions that she was basically unlovable and *no good* because of her poor actions. Although her actions *were* unlovable, they were definitely not reflective of her personal worth. As she learned to clear up her misconceptions and to accept herself, her sidestepping ceased and her relationship with Bill dramatically improved.

In contrast to Jane's backward looks, Bill's efforts were mainly to avoid acting badly. Although he would occasionally guiltily dwell on an episode from his past, more often he acted in an overly socialized manner and restrained himself from taking assertive actions for *fear* he would offend someone and *feel guilty*.

Bill normally behaved in a self-effacing manner. Whenever he felt slightly aggressive or thought his actions would cause someone hardship, he experienced negative physical sensations and avoided acting even though he might be ninety percent sure he was right. For example, his employer at a sporting goods store was inclined to make snap judgments, which were often wrong. When this person decided to stock up on snowshoes for the spring snows and to understock tennis rackets, Bill kept quiet. He was afraid that if he were to assert a wrong opinion (buy more tennis rackets), he might injure the business and would not be able to live with himself.

To avoid the possibility of experiencing guilt, Bill acted like a "yes man." He was a yes man who feared making an error and feeling guilty over making the error. Thus, he avoided any form of risk to avoid the possibility of error.

To rid himself of the self-restricting mental virus of guilt required "psychological antibodies" targeted toward disrupting guilt and *avoidance*. These antibodies specifically included strategies to attack Bill's sense of worthlessness and his fears. Bill's guilt was reflective of his self-doubts and need to avoid the tensions of guilt. It was also predicated on a misconception that he was absolutely responsible for the feelings of others and if he acted short of exhibiting perfect awareness and highly supportive actions, his behavior would make other people feel bad. This belief was so entrenched that it was like a heavy bank of smog, clouding his judgment. Because of this mental smog, for example, Bill failed to see Jane's guilt-provoking tendencies as a clear signal that she had emotional problems. Instead, Bill took her actions seriously, accepted the blame, felt guilty, and gave himself emotional problems.

Bill overcame his guilt-proneness when he learned to objectively evaluate his perfectionistic, self-imposed attitude that he was not allowed to even unknowingly transgress against the standard of complete goodness and humanity toward others. By closely examining his "goodness" standard, Bill came to modify it. He convinced himself that he would *try* to avoid acting in a manner that would upset other people, but: (1) sometimes people have their own problems and their upset is a reflection of those problems, not of Bill's actions, (2) it is wise to discriminate between one's own problems and the problems of others, (3) acting in his own self-interest doubtless will occasionally (but unavoidably) result in conflict with others, (4) he is not a worm if he fails to be 100 percent perfect, (5) if he needlessly causes others to feel upset, he can certainly do his best to render some form of retribution, (6) the only way he is obligated to be is to be himself, and (7) he is not obligated to follow arbitrary rules and standards if they are strictly in opposition to the normal pathways for finding happiness (or if they reflect normal and unavoidable human tendencies).

Contending with Coercion

Guilt-proneness artificially restricts a person's freedom of thought and *action*. The person views him- or herself in poor self-control, as a wrong doer, and a bad person. He or she tends to display unappealing defenses meant to protect him- or herself against discomfort. Consequently, the person diverts from actualizing true desires by acting in an unauthentic manner.

Because many people are susceptible to thinking they are bad because of poor behavior, guilt becomes a very powerful form of controlling people. Generally, democratic societies allow for considerable flexibility in human behavior. Indeed, human behavior such as playfulness, curiosity, inquisitiveness, and self-expression are often valued by society. Members of the guilt cult, however, tend to shun such activities for *fear* of reprisal and guilt. These people are overcontrolled.

Self-control is most societies is highly desired. Otherwise we would run the risk of having frightening civil disorder and chaos. And the more functional, long-term forms of self-control are those based on realistic moral and ethical principles, not coercive principles. Guilt is a coercive, destructive form of self-control, which can and often does lead a person to feel depressed, resentful, fearful, and rutbound.

Some people are skilled in evoking guilt in others to *expediently* control the actions of others. Karen Horney (1950) illustrated how coercive control is enacted when a person makes *irrational claims*. An irrational claim is a claim that sounds logical, but the premise is faulty. Such claims are levied by those seeking expedient solutions to achieve their "needs." For example, an irrational claim is represented in the following statement by a mother to her daughter: *"Because I am your mother* and have sacrificed myself for your welfare, *you have an obligation to call me* every day, and if you don't you're ungrateful, don't care about me, and are no good." The irrational claim is groundless and can be countered: (1) there is no law that says a daughter *must* daily telephone her mother, (2) whether the mother sacrifices herself for her daughter is irrelevant; it was her choice, (3) whether the daughter telephones legitimately has nothing to do with whether she is grateful or good as a person, and (4) the mother's criteria for "caring" is really a psychological lever for coercion, and it practically guarantees resistance, antagonism, and other forms of negativism on the part of her daughter, even if the daughter initially dutifully complies.

Irrational claims often dominate the consciousness of the coercive person. These people are often quite unaware that in their scramble to get what they want, they act in an unappealingly defensive manner; they show their lousy side, are unaware of doing so, and expect to be lovingly obeyed. Almost always baffled by the resistance to their "claims," these individuals often are in a narrow rut repeating a form of human relations with antihuman undertones. These undertones give them the rightly deserved image of guilt-mongers—ruling through guilt, fear, and various other manipulations.

Although it is possible to stay away from or confront other people who are guilt-mongers, what if you are your own guilt-monger and suffer from a too-rigid set of standards? What do you do?

One of your choices is to complicate your situation by depressing yourself, thinking that you are hopelessly shackled by your guilts, and dare not move from the narrow confines of your rut lest an army of negative self-blaming thoughts descends over your mind like hungry locusts.

Naturally, there is a better way. You can work on building self-regard. Part of building confidence involves recognizing and questioning the foundations of your guilt.

1. What is my *obligating* standard?
2. Why must I *unfailingly* adhere to it?
3. How is my past, present, and future doomed, and me long with them, if I have transgressed against an "obligatory standard"?
4. How can I accept myself even if I can legitimately condemn my behavior?

There are, of course, many more questions you can raise to gain proper perspective and to stop guilt-proneness.

Questioning Guilt over Depression

Sometimes a person feels guilty because he or she is depressed. The scenario goes something like this: (1) I am so depressed and it's my fault, (2) I'm just no good for drawing this depression down on myself, (3) I can't do anything about these awful feelings, (4) I'm so weak and helpless, (5) I keep doing the same thing over and over again, (6) I'll never change, and (7) I'm such a hopeless creature.

When guilt is worked into the scenario of depression, the irrational claims require objective evaluation. Start by asking yourself these questions:

1. *What* am I telling myself to depress myself?
2. In *what* way am I responsible for my problems and *what* can I do to solve them?
3. *How* does making myself depressed render me a bad person?
4. *Where* is the evidence that I can't effectively confront my self-depressing assumptions?
5. If I'm so weak and helpless, *how* come I've been so successful in keeping myself down?
6. If I work hard to develop rational problem-solving skills, *where* is the proof I won't make progress?

7. *What* purpose is served by declaring I'll never change?
8. In *what* way am I hopeless and in *what* ways am I capable of change?
9. *What's* so terrible about having less than perfect control?

Objective questions need to be raised and answered to buck the guilt-depression trend and reverse it.

Rational self-questioning is helpful, but it is only part of the battle. To dislodge guilt requires behavioral action. Ethical, healthy, and self-advancing actions crowd out guilty restraints. Examine where you have been holding yourself back from doing because of a pseudo-guilt. Let us say, for example, that you think:

1. It's wrong to enjoy (you fill in the blank) ——————————
2. It's wrong to express my opinion.
3. It's wrong for me to compete with others.
4. It's wrong for me to assert my preferences.

Then you should determine if such actions will:

1. Cause you or others *needless* physical harm.
2. Cause you to legitimately lose stature in the community.
3. Illegitimately interfere with another person's ability to function and/or to earn a livelihood.
4. Represent a clear departure from generally accepted ethical behavior (purposefully misrepresenting yourself to gain unfair advantage, falsely debasing the character of others, and so forth).
5. Result in legitimate legal reprisals.

In short, will your action(s) advance your interests and preferences and not needlessly cause physical harm to yourself and others and not needlessly interfere with your rights or the rights of others?

chapter fourteen
FREEDOM FROM THE ANGER RUT

In Dr. Seuss's book, *How the Grinch Stole Christmas* (Random House, 1957), the Grinch was a homely, bitter, angry creature who sought revenge against a group of valley people whom he thought made too much noise. His revenge consisted of stealing the children's Christmas presents. In *Snow White and the Seven Dwarfs*, the wicked witch, jealous of Snow White's beauty, expressed her anger and bitterness by giving Snow White a poison apple, which put her to sleep until the Prince woke her with a kiss. In these children's stories and many other tales, anger and revenge are portrayed as prime motivators of human behavior. Anger is introduced in these stories because it exists in everyday life and can lead to the kind of ruts enveloping the Grinch and the wicked witch.

Anger is a state of emotional excitement characterized by strong displeasure. Anger is honest when it reflects a person's displeasure and is uncluttered by self-doubts, intolerances, and contempt for self or others. The following examples describe honest angers. A person who expresses anger toward a friend for walking too close to a dangerous machine is hardly condemning the friend for his or her actions. Quite the contrary, the person is expressing strong displeasure that generates from concern. The person who is overcharged for a service, feels taken advantage of, then angrily takes the matter to court also lets words and actions reflect his or her feelings. And although the person may not condemn the protagonist, he or she determinedly presses the cause. His or her anger is also honest anger.

But some forms of anger are neurotic angers, which are states of emotional excitement generating from self-doubts and tension intolerances blended with contempt, condemnation, and coercion. In neurotic angers, the affected person looks at life's situations as through darkened and cracked prism glasses. The following examples describe neurotic angers. The person impatiently leaning on a horn in a traffic jam while damning and condemning other drivers exhibits neurotic anger. The spouse who shouts and screams at his or her mate for squeezing the toothpaste from the middle of the tube also exhibits neurotic anger.

Neurotic anger patterns are irrational patterns. The neurotically angry person tends to perceive him- or herself as contemptuous or others as contemptuous—slobs, creeps, useless, wicked, and so on. His or her view is that contemptuous people need to be punished.

The angry person is usually a most unpleasant individual. However, in contrast to the destructively hostile person, this person's behavior is tolerable. The destructively hostile individual is the Hitlerian character who tries to organize his or her environment to conform to his or her destructive madness. This person analyzes, plans, organizes his or her efforts, and effects a plan to produce a destructive result. Such characters include Charles Manson, New York's Son of Sam killer, Jim Jones, Jean Harris, and Lady MacBeth. Sometimes these destructively hostile individuals can appear quite charming and disarming. The following story of the scorpion and the frog describes this "charming" destructive striving.

There is a folk tale of a frog who swam in a large friendly pond and a scorpion who walked the land. One day they happened to meet near the shore of the pond where the frog was stretching out on a large green lily pad. "Mr. Frog," said the scorpion, "I would so appreciate it if you would let me climb upon your back and swim me to the other shore." The frog was naturally wary of the scorpion and said, "If I swim you to other shore, you'll try to sting me and I'll surely die." "But no," said the scorpion, "I can't swim and if I sting you, I'll drown, too." The frog was a friendly fellow and what the scorpion said was logical, and so he agreed to swim the scorpion across the pond. About halfway across, the scorpion stung the frog. As the frog was sinking and the scorpion drowing, the frog gasped, "Why?" To which the scorpion responded, "It's my nature."

Sometimes in real life, the ending is as the story says. More often, we find the scorpion has water wings and can be seen to swim toward the next frog, while the stung frog barely manages to survive by grasping a branch for dear life until the poisonous effects wear off.

The person who is destructively hostile generally is not in a rut, according to my definition. This person's lifestyle pattern is dedicated to destruction, so he or she has a strong sense of mission or purpose. His or her approach to life is filled with risk, challenges, and opportunities. In my view, this destructive lifestyle hostility pattern is virtually incurable, and fortunately very rare in pure form.

So, let us dispense with the destructively hostile and concentrate on the sorts of anger problems that can be altered—neurotic angers. These are emotions that are mechanisms for ruts: people get into ruts when they consistently avoid channeling their honest anger or overindulge their neurotic angers.

Anger Variations

Anger differs between people as will as within each individual. We perceive events differently; we reason about what we see differently. Furthermore, each person's world is like a kaleidoscope of experiences, physical energies, and emerging thoughts that change second by second and hour by hour. But with all this change, there is a certain consistency in a person's reaction patterns that render him or her predictable and that differentiate the person from other individuals. The person who is self-righteous, for example, is likely to display self-righteous forms of anger compared to the timid individual, who most likely will suppress his or her anger or ruminate over grievances and keep them to him- or herself.

Anger and the Nature of Power

Regardless of the style of anger, whether healthy, neurotic, or hostile, much of what appears as angry thinking and behaving revolves around the issue of *power*.

True power is the by-product of competency and confidence. Those who have competency and confidence express their displeasures (and pleasures) in a healthy, adaptive way. People who do not have true power typically experience and express neurotic anger or hostility. Neurotic anger, born of tension intolerances and self-doubts, is a defensive anger, a compensation for a sense of powerlessness.

Neurotic Angers

Vindictive perfectionism.   One form of anger is the self-righteous anger of the vindictive perfectionist, the person who seeks to punish others who do not live according to his or her expectations.

Self-righteous anger is an emotional attitude that grows from the belief that to be right means to be safe: people who don't play by one's right rules deserve to be condemned, avoided, or changed to make one's life safe. Power is sought by the self-righteous by attempting to control through coercion and through phony moralism. Unfortunately, the personal motives underlying self-righteous anger are often obscured. Instead, the person focuses on the "external causes" and not upon his or her own tendencies to think self-defeatingly.

People who act to achieve control through coercion, condemnation, or other forms of intimidation suffer from emotionally disturbed thinking. Robert Ringer, (1974), who wrote *Winning Through Intimidation*, palatably espouses this coercive philosophy. However, this practice, although sometimes pragmatic, is generally unprincipled and is a major mechanism for a rut. Admittedly, it is a better rut to be in than the rut of the person who hides at home behind closed doors.

Helpless anger.   Helpless anger appears in the form of whining and whimpering. This is yet another type of manipulative anger. Like vindictive perfectionism, whining, whimpering anger is motivated by the desire to gain control through coercion. Unlike the vindictive perfectionist who tries to win through strength, the whiney whimperer tries to win through weakness. She tries to gain strength from controlling others whom she thinks are stronger than she by frustrating them with her helplessness. In this guise of helplessness, she often acts stupidly if asked to perform. She does this to show that she is too helpless to be depended on. For example, Ruth is a whiney whimperer. She apperars to be overwhelmed with the day-to-day responsibilities of living. She whines and complains her employer doesn't give her a promotion; she appears to nearly fall apart emotionally if her mate does not accommodate her wishes; she acts hurt and angry if people do not comply with her hidden agendas. Ruth's anger reflects her expectation that the world should be as she wants it to be, and that she should not be frustrated. In her view, people who don't act as she thinks they should are condemnable and contemptible. She thinks that: "One way or another, I will get them to do it my way." While Ruth's ego is certainly involved in this anger-creating process her helpless-anger problem is most closely tied to her low frustration tolerance.

Anger and Depression

Jackie lives alone with her pet canaries and feels agitated about living in a lonely state. She feels alienated and estranged from others. In her interpersonal communications, she places silent demands on her friends. These demands predominantly reflect her expectations that these friends should contact her frequently and explicitly verbalize her demands. She nonverbally shows signs of hurt when "they let me down." Her friends are oblivious to her silent expectations, but not to her visibly angered and hurt appearance.

Jackie exhibits a similar pattern at her job. She expects the people who work with her to be like an extended family. When this expectation does not materialize, Jackie mopes and complains, but never comes right out and explains her expectation.

The expectations she holds for her friends and those with whom she works are no less in evidence than in her interactions with members of her immediate family. Indeed, she appears perpetually angry with her father, mother, sister, and daughters because "no one seems to care about me. If they cared, they'd call, invite me over, be more like a family."

Jackie's life is wrought with crippling depressive ideas that her life is a hopeless mess and she cannot do anything to change her circumstances.

The key to understanding Jackie's anger and agitated state of depression is found in the word *expect*. Jackie *expects* people to respond to her in a warm and caring manner. *Expect* is a demand term that is readily translated into people "should," "ought," "must" behave toward me as I want them to. While there is no law against making such demands, there are consequences.

People will tend to feel pushed if an expectation is leveled against them, and they will resist the pressure.

Expectations lead to exasperations and renewed expectations to try to reduce exasperation.

Expectations reflect and promote rigidity.

Frustrated expectations deflect from problem-solving because of the "expector's" insistence on others changing or upon circumstances changing, rather than self-change.

Failure is routinely assured as efforts expended in expectations prove to be efforts in futility.

Repeatedly frustrated expectations can leed to a sense of angry helplessness and agitated depression.

Coping with Anger

In Albert Ellis's (1962) view, anger is the outcome of a four-part thinking process. His analysis of anger is roughly as follows:

1. It's awful to be treated unfairly.
2. I shouldn't have to put up with this nonsense.
3. People who act unfairly are condemnable rotters.
4. I can't stand what is happening.

Ellis' analysis merits consideration. For if your thinking pattern mirrors Ellis's four-stage neurotic anger process, you can question each of the four parts, prevent yourself from overgeneralizing, and, therefore, heighten your chances of adaptively expressing yourself.

Identifying and dealing with neurotic angry thoughts while in the midst of an angry reaction is desirable but hard to do. The very nature of neurotic anger is that it disrupts clear thinking and reasoning.

George Bach and Herb Goldberg (1974) take a contrary approach to Ellis. They claim that the traditional approach to resolving conflicts through rational discussion first requires that each party have an opportunity to uninterruptedly air frustrations and to be clear about complaints.

Both approaches have merit. Being aware of and challenging neurotic thinking and taking the initiative to air complaints with others is an adaptive way of dealing with anger. This adaptive style is different from a view that prevails in some psychological circles; if you feel angry scream it out; do anything, but don't keep it in. This view seems naive. Neurotic forms of anger or hostility are often invented angers against phantom problems. And although getting manufactured neurotic angers out in the open may subject them to objective feedback, unrestrained neurotic anger reactions invite and incite counterattack, and often more unwanted trouble. If you find you are neurotically angry or hostile, *don't condemn yourself*. Instead of being hard on yourself, get tough with the problem instead.

The reason you are in an anger rut is that you have incorporated misconceptions. Neurotic anger comes from ideas that have unfortunately stuck and have influenced your feelings and behavior.

If you put poor information into a computer, it will function ineffectively, although accurately, based on the information it was fed. But poor programming does not make the computer a bad computer. The same is largely true for a person operating with poor information about him- or herself. The person is not a bad person, but is a person with correctable self defeating angry thoughts.

Once you can agree to be compassionate with yourself, start to work at being hard on the problem. Start by:

1. Examining your expectations; how relevant and realistic are they?
2. Determining why you think people *should be* punished for their infractions against your rules.
3. Having a talk with yourself about whether your anger is compensation for a sense of powerlessness (helplessness).

4. Considering how you can build upon your competency and reduce your self-doubts and intolerances.

Don't *expect* perfection in this antianger process. Some neurotic anger and hostility are normal. It is only when neurotic anger becomes part of a predictable pattern that it becomes a problem. Problems are to be solved, not condemned!

VI
RUTS AND PROCRASTINATION

People impede their own success by putting off the very tasks that would assure success. The following chapter discusses how you can become successful in achieving your goals and desires by acting in timely and helpful ways.

Ruts and procrastination go hand in hand. A person, for example, is in a rut because he or she puts off getting out of it.

In this final chapter procrastination is defined and described, and the defenses that blur a person's awareness of his or her procrastination rut are identified. A self-management strategy is spelled out to help the reader over this deadly obstacle.

chapter fifteen
HOW TO GET OUT OF A PROCRASTINATION RUT

Procrastination is encountered everywhere: the student who puts off studying; the businessperson who marks down an item after the time is past when it can be sold; the overweight person who expects to start a diet after the holidays; the person who says he will mow his overgrown lawn next weekend; the person who shows up late for appointments; the qualified person who *complacently* seeks advancement—all are procrastinating.

This pattern is also observed in the *closet procrastinator*, a person who holds others responsible for his or her procrastinating. The closet procrastinator takes advantage of the human tendency to procrastinate by putting pressures on others to work more proficiently. He believes that the reason he always seems to fall behind on his own projects is because he has to keep after others so they won't fall behind on theirs. For example, this *tyrant of the task* can be a parent who continually pressures the kids to clean up, do their homework, dress properly, and so forth, all the time feeling overwhelmed by the incompletions in his or her own life.

Some people procrastinate because they hate to waste time. For example, Mildred hates to shop for clothing or do routine cleaning chores as she thinks these tasks are a waste of time. So she puts off procuring needed clothing and lives in a disheveled apartment. And while she puts off attending to these details she doesn't stop thinking about these and other small tasks that continue to accumulate. As she continues to dwell on the details she has shelved she feels overwhelmed by the magnitude and number of small daily burdens that do not disappear.

To one extent or another, everyone procrastinates. Thus, it is the atypical individual who regularly gets his or her work completed well in advance of deadlines. Indeed, as Parkinson's (1973) law predicts, people who are given more time than they need to complete a task will take it. Since procrastination is part of the human condition, most people will at least ısionally put off until the last minute. Tax returns and Christmas cards flood the mails just in the nick of time for delivery. Typically, however, this form of delaying is minor.

Procrastination (derived from the Latin words *pro*, meaning "forward," and *crastinate*, "until tomorrow") is a much more expansive problem than simply delaying until the last minute to meet a deadline. Sometimes it is moderately serious, as when a person puts off self-improvement projects because she is afraid, depressed, thinks she is inadequate to the task, or discomfort dodges.

A person who routinely procrastinates lives in the debris from his past and undoubtedly finds himself in a rut that he procrastinates breaking. As he drags his feet facing his rut, he is often beset by oppressive thoughts and feelings about the unsavory incompletions from his past that drain time from his present and from his future.

What Is Procrastination?

Procrastination is a complex problem to understand and a simple (not necessarily easy) problem to deal with. Once understood, the pattern need not loom as the major hurdle to getting out of a rut and into a love affair with life. However, to deal effectively with the procrastination problem requires:

1. A comprehensive understanding of its definition and the general forms procrastination takes.

2. An understanding of potential causes.
3. A recognition of the diversions that obscure the problem from a person's own awareness.
4. A recognition of an effective action *approach* to get right to the heart of the problem and overcome it.

Dealing with procrastination begins with defining it. My definition: procrastination is a needless delay of a relevant activity. Often this delay reflects substituting a low for a high priority activity. For example, procrastination is looking to see if you have any crabgrass on your lawn as a substitute for studying for the examination you want desperately to pass.

There are procrastination acts and procrastination patterns. Procrastination acts generally are isolated everyday occurrences such as delaying paying a bill. Such acts are typically tolerated and are of minor significance compared to a procrastination pattern, which is a habit pattern where a person more or less automatically puts off and puts off. The pattern can concern a specific aspect of living (a pattern of feeling uncomfortable returning phone calls and thus procrastinating on calling back) or it can be generalized, a pattern of showing up late for appointments, delaying follow through on commitments, or a pervasive sense that one is dragging one's feet through life).

In contrast to a habit pattern of needlessly delaying relevant activities, there are, of course, numerous downright unnecessary activities that are correctly left untouched. Not routinely sanding and polishing the rafters of an unfinished basement crawl space hardly justifies identifying one's behavior as procrastinating. Also, there are purposeful reasons for delaying; if the delay is legitimately strategic or due to illness, the person is not procrastinating.

Procrastination is obviously not the central issue in all forms of delays for yet another reason. For example, the least of our concerns about a five-year-old boy who is hyperactive would be whether the child is procrastinating on reducing his hyperactivity level. So, another feature of procrastination is that it is a behavior *largely* under the control of conscious processes, and the person theoretically has a *choice* to delay or to act.

Procrastination Categories

Acts and patterns of procrastination fall into two broad, often overlapping categories: maintenance functions and self-development functions. *Maintenance function* procrastination occurs when people put off routines they view as onerous, unpleasant, or mundane, such as housecleaning, auto inspections, filing merchandise guarantees, paying bills, or discarding unwanted materials (old clothing, newspapers, furniture). When this pattern is deeply entranched, people will often report feeling depressed, partially because their living environment appears in a mess and they perceive themselves as hopelessly disorganized.

Self-development procrastination is observed when a person routinely: (1) delays dealing with a troublesome personal problem (fear of leaving one's home, excessive cigarette smoking, overeating, remaining in a destructive relationship, suppression of self-expression), (2) delays taking advantage of leisure time activities (planning a vacation, joining a pottery class, going on a picnic, building a stamp collection), or (3) delays improving career opportunities (seeking to improve work skills, seeking challenging opportunities). When self-development procrastination is pervasive, the person will often report feeling fearful, immobilized, or in a "rut."

The wide variety of maintainence and self-development procrastinations suggests that the problem is multifaceted. But what are the causes of this multifaceted problem?

What People Say about the Causes

Procrastination has been characterized as a time problem. Alden Wessman (1973), for example, viewed people who procrastinate as suffering from a form of time urgency. They seem to be hurrying to get nowhere and often feel overburdened. According to Wessman's formulations, procrastinators tend to be undisciplined, careless, and disorderly. He also thought that they are timid, lack confidence, and suffer from anxiety. And the more serious the procrastination problem, the more exaggerated the symptoms. Sidney Blatt and Paul Quinlan (1967) also explored the relationship of time to procrastination. They found that procrastinating students differ from nonprocrastinating students in that the latter were better able to anticipate future events, plan their time, and avoid distraction.

Perhaps interest in the time factor in procrastinating behavior is greatest in academic circles, on college campuses that are built around programs called personalized systems of instruction (PSI). In PSI the student is required to move at his or her own pace in mastering instruction-supplied materials. Sidney Bijou (1967) discovered that students who participate in PSI, where attending lectures is not required, will tend to procrastinate. However, if students are given instruction on how to organize time and in self-control procedures, they are less likely to procrastinate.

How to organize time effectively has been the backbone of Alan Lakin's (1974) method of *How to Get Control of Your Time and Your Life*. Lakin and other time management people have sought to reduce procrastination by teaching time management principles, and have emphasized how to set priorities and avoid distractions.

Gregory Raiport (1976) presents an interesting time-space typology that provides a framework for understanding why we procrastinate. Raiport classifies people into two categories based on whether they are dominated by time or space considerations. "Time people" he sees as dominated by memory, intellect, and abstract thought. They are inclined toward depression and physical passivity. They are, therefore, likely to be imprisoned in a world of thought where action is de-emphasized. People who are "spacebound" tend to be impulsive, spontaneous, and expedient; they live in the present. Space-oriented people generally focus on immediate gratification and thus put off long-term gain. Both time and space individuals procrastinate for different reasons. Thus, both fail to act in the interests of their future. Ideally, according to Raiport, when space and time dimensions are harmonized, creativity, productivity, and spontaneity result and there is no time or space for procrastinating.

George Bach and Herb Goldberg (1974) believe that procrastination is a sign of hidden aggression. This mask for aggression they see exhibited when the procrastinator delays others, refuses to get pinned down to a fixed date or time, and attempts to induce guilt by parlaying the problem to others by blaming them for their impatience.

Time, space, and hostility explanations for procrastination are helpful but limited. They explain procrastination at a descriptive level. One procrastinates, for example, because one is hostile or does not know how to manage time properly. One could just as easily say that one is hostile because one procrastinates and, therefore, does not manage time properly. In short, descriptive explanations may appear to define causes, but they really don't.

To obtain deeper insight into procrastination, we must next move to a broader overview of the multidimensional procrastination process. What follows is a case of a procrastinator, which will help to introduce the multidimensional view.

The Multidimensional View

Harry regularly spoke at conferences on how to start your own small business. As a conference speaker, he was magnificent— erudite, articulate, and knowledgeable. He conveyed to his eager listeners knowledge of how to assess a business opportunity and how to act upon the assessment. From the enthusiastic expression on the faces of his listeners, they obviously walked away having enjoyed what they heard and, probably, much wiser.

Ostensibly, the presentation was the secondary reason for Harry's journey to the conference. His stated purpose was to sell cat food franchises, for which he earned a sales commission. Oddly, his franchise booth at the conference consistently had a poor floor position. As a consequence, few could locate Harry and make inquiries about his product. He made few sales.

No one can reasonably conclude that Harry lacked the ability to sell franchises. What is clear, however, is that he failed to use his knowledge wisely. The question is why would a wise person act so unwisely? It is tempting to diagnose Harry's problem as a fear of failure. We could argue that he repeated his pattern of failing to get visibility for his product because he did not want his audience to see that he was "only" a cat food salesman and not a great businessman. In Harry's case, this diagnosis would have been largely incorrect. The bottom line for Harry was that *he feared succeeding at the wrong thing*. At any rate, his procrastination reflected his lack of enthusiasm for selling franchises, and his great enthusiasm for public speaking suggested that helping him to overcome procrastination in selling franchises might be missing the boat. How might he instead use his public speaking talents more advantageously?

When Harry considered this forward-looking question, he discovered that his procrastinating on selling franchises took a different twist in meaning. When he examined his situation, he came to see that what he really wanted was to stop serving as a reluctant distributor, marketing someone else's cat food franchise, and instead to operate independently, working at what he enjoyed. The business he was best suited to start was a seminar business where he would set up seminars on how to start your own small business. It was also what he most enjoyed doing. So, he decided to set up small business seminars. Today, Harry is a happy and successful man. He is doing what he enjoys most—public speaking. He actively sells his program, is booked well in advance, and has made himself exceptionally successful.

Procrastination is a multidimensional problem, as Harry's case helps illustrate, because it has different levels of meaning. For example, procrastination can be at a very simple level. Mailing Christmas cards late may reflect general indifference toward getting the cards out early and thus may be a simple and trivial problem. In Harry's case, the procrastination was a more complex symptom that had meaning at a deeper level. It proved to be a healthy signal because the procrastination behavior provoked an analysis of his career status and career interests. This analysis lead to a fresh awareness that pointed to a highly preferable career direction. It is probable that Harry would have continued procrastinating on selling franchises until this helpful signal was heeded.

At other levels, procrastination can signal time mismanagement or, most commonly, self-doubts and discomfort fears. It is this level that is emphasized in this chapter, because this level is more universal.

A Procrastination
Reciprocity Explanation

Procrastination can lead to a rut, and ruts and procrastination blend together, so it should not be surprising that factors contributing to one process contribute to the other. Procrastination and ruts have many causes, but, in particular, they reflect two attitudes that work together against progress—self-doubt-downing and discomfort dodging.

Complex problems can sometimes be factored down to a few major and several minor mechanisms. Procrastination is not a simple problem and factoring it down has limitations. Harry's motives for procrastinating, for example, do not fit easily into the following model. However, most procrastination-type problems can be understood and dealt with using the Procrastination Reciprocity Model. (Figure 19). The model is my proposal that procrastination (and most other forms of self-destructive behavior) and the self-doubt-downing-discomfort-dodging sequence are reciprocals. Understanding and effectively employing this model can help you to stop procrastinating, but also improve your self-view and ability

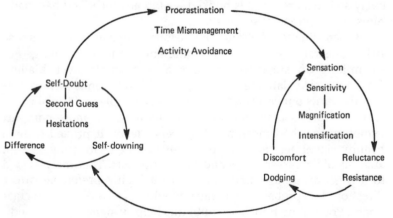

Figure 19   Procrastination Reciprocity Model

to deal with tension.

According to this model, self-doubts may result in discomfort fear,

238

which results in procrastination. The model also supports the opposite: an aversion for tension can lead to self-doubt, self-devaluation, and procrastination. Procrastination (or poor self-organizing) can be the vehicle by which a person comes to negative conclusions about himself feels tense, and *diverts* himself by engaging in self-defensive or low priority activities to avoid the tension.

This reciprocal-transactional pattern can be relative, variable, situational, multifaceted, or multidimensional. What Brendon Maher (1966) and Paul Lang (1969) reported about psychological fear, that it is not the consequence of each threatening circumstance or always expressed in the same degree, is true of procrastination. A person who procrastinates under one form of stress can act quite efficiently under different forms of stress.

According to the Procrastination Reciprocity Model, positive changes in any one of the major dimensions should influence positive changes in the remaining dimensions. Thus, if one comes to prioritize her activities and follows through on priorities, her confidence should grow and her frustration tolerance should increase. Whenever one builds tolerance for the sensations of frustration, one is freer to engage in productive action and likely will come to think better of him- or herself. In other words:

1. If you are not afraid of discomfort, it will reflect positively in your willingness to take action and in an improved self-concept.

2. If you are self-accepting, your positive self-view will reflect favorably in your ability to tolerate frustration, and you will procrastinate less.

3. If you build and use counterprocrastination skills, you will increase your stress tolerance; simultaneously you will have less to be stressed about, and your confidence should grow.

If one has developed a *coordinated* awareness-action program to isolate and face up to *procrastination, self-doubts,* and *discomfort dodging,* he or she will progress more affirmatively compared to the person who emphasizes one dimension and ignores the others. For example, a person could develop a fine time management plan, but fail to implement it because he lacks faith in himself and fears the discomfort of change.

Diversionary Ploys

Self-doubts and discomfort dodging can be translated into irrational self-statements to lay bare the coalescing beliefs and attitudes sparking the procrastination process. However, these irrational self-statements are often obscured by a diversionary defensive style that people who procrastinate readily adopt, to protect themselves against self-doubts and tension.

By making excuses and engaging in substitute activities, the procrastinating person often defocuses from his or her doubts and tensions. So, prior to considering counterprocrastination strategies, the diversionary-defensive processes need to be identified, clarified, and faced.

The procrastination reciprocity model is logically expanded to include the diversionary self-protective tactics taken by people who procrastinate. The expanded model is shown in Figure 20.

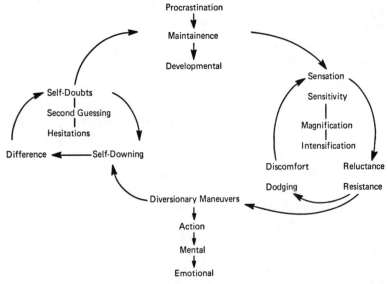

Figure 20   Expanded Procrastination Reciprocity Model

The addition of the diversionary system makes the model complete. So, if one confronts and reduces his diversionary tendencies, he can more clearly see his real problems. If he faces his real problems, he will have less to be defensive about and have more emotional freedom—confidence, tolerance, spontaneousness, and goal-directedness. The following describes the diversionary system.

We clever humans can throw out "red herrings" and sidetrack ourselves by distorting facts. This tendency is certainly legendary, as the fable of the emperor without clothing emphasizes.

In the tale of *The Emperor's New Clothes*, a vain leader commissions a tailor to fashion him a fine suit of clothing. Instead of creating fine clothing to befit an emperor, the tailer creates a fine myth. He tells the emperor that the clothing will be invisible to all who are impure of mind. In truth, there is no clothing at all. But not wanting to admit that he cannot see the clothing (and, therefore, must be "impure"), the emperor marches naked through the streets to show off his new suit.

The excuses that people who procrastinate use to cover up needless delays are like the emperor's clothing; anyone can see through them unless he or she chooses to look away and ignore the obvious. Frequently, even the procrastinating person sees transparencies in his or her excuses.

A procrastination, self-doubt-downing, and discomfort-dodging syndrome is often shaded by diversionary ploys that people muster to divert themselves from these unpleasant states. Such diversions, however, frequently lead to future pain and suffering, even though in the short term they *may* reduce tension. They need to be exposed and dealt with.

Diversionary ploys seem naturally to fall into three categories: mental, action, and emotional.

Mental Diversions

The best-known mental diversion is the *mañana attitude*, where procrastination is cloaked by a decision that a timely activity would be better done later, tomorrow perhaps, when one is in a better mood or better prepared.

George is into the mañana habit and feels like he is in a perpetual rut. His weekly routine is painfully redundant: he goes to work, returns home, sips a cocktail, tosses a frozen dinner in the microwave oven, watches the news on television, and fantasizes about a more active life where he would socialize with new friends. Each night he tells himself that he is going to have to do something to " . . . straighten out my life; tomorrow, I'll turn over a new leaf." And, of course, when tomorrow comes, it proves no different than the day before.

Some people are routinely late for appointments and late in completing projects. As both forms of procrastination promote stress, a person can make a mañana-type New Years' resolution to reduce his tension. The procrastinator will swear he'll reform tomorrow, but odds favor that this good intention will not be translated into practice. The procrastinator adopts this passive mañana posture, because he often separates promptness from the process of stress reduction and personal development. Under such circumstances, promptness is frequently viewed as an onerous obligation. And when the procrastinating person views onerous obligation and promptness as one and the same, he is likely to feel stressed when it comes to getting things done on time, and thereby procrastinates. In contrast, if promptness is seen as tied to a process of stress reduction and self development, the person is likely to be prompt.

The decision to put off until tomorrow conveys a false sense of security that the task will eventually get done. This same diversionary decision is evident in a more elaborate ploy, the *contingency mañana*, where the uncomfortable activity is put off pending the completion of an invented preliminary step, which is also put off. Let us use George's case again to illustrate.

George afflicts himself with contingency mañana reasoning by setting up tough preconditions for action. He believes that although he wants to make new friends and share experiences with them, he cannot proceed until he fully understands himself and knows "what makes me tick." He is afraid that anything less subjects him to certain rejection. But, he believes, if he fully understands himself, he will be able to make constructive changes and ward off rejection. So, George's socializing is dependent upon developing complete self-understanding. Sensing the impossibility of ever obtaining complete self-understanding, George puts off taking the steps to learn about himself.

An important contingency mañana is the happiness contingency. People who are malcontented with themselves often strive to obtain perfection, control, approval, and comfort as a means of obtaining inner peace. These individuals believe that attainment of all of these four happiness contingencies will make their lives wonderful and will make it possible for them to do what they have been putting off. Unfortunately, mental efforts are absorbed in this impossible dream, while action awaits the date when the contingencies are met.

A more extreme form of a mental diversion is the Catch 22 system in which a person traps him- or herself in a no-win situation. For example, Janace expressed: "I really want to date attractive men, but they only want to go out with women who are more intelligent and beautiful than I am; so I can't see trying to meet one." Since Janace was demeaning toward men she viewed as unattractive and since there was no middle ground, she gave herself no basis to establish a workable relationship with a man.

A most debilitating Catch 22 is observed in the "mental prison trap" where a person thinks himself into inaction primarily by engaging in self-critical ruminations. He then comes to identify with his poor self-evaluation, thinks he is inept, believes he cannot change because he is inept, and fears change because he fears losing his identity and losing himself. The obvious outcome of this trap is that the person strongly avoids engaging in personal growth activities, strives to keep "everything" the same, and is miserable about the sameness of his situation.

Action Diversions

Action diversions are low priority, sometimes irrelevant, activities substituted for high priority, relevant activities. They are activity traps that occur in three forms: trivial diversions, life-style substitutions, and self-defeating habit formation. Each variation can contribute to a rut.

Trivial diversions occur when a trivial, low priority activity is substituted for a high priority in order to avoid discomfort or feelings of uncertainty. For example, Albe puts off planning a survival strategy for his Hobby Center Store; sales have slackened, costs have risen, and a recession is beginning. When he thinks about sitting down to think out and to formulate his options, he feels anxious and replaces planning with mowing his lawn, phoning a friend, cleaning, or almost anything but sitting and planning.

Albe does what Alan Lakin (1974) describes as substituting "c" or "d" priorities for the "a" or top priorities.

The *lifestyle substitution* almost assures that its architect will engulf him- or herself in a woeful rut. The action diversion in this lifestyle rut is evidenced in situations where a person fails to seek satisfaction and settles for mediocrity or worse. For example, Sue runs away from men with whom she could feel intimate and emotionally attached. Instead, she marries Rick, a "safe" person to whom she feels only mildly attracted. Not surprisingly, within a year Sue feels in a rut with Rick.

Ron is another lifestyle rut victim who puts off seeking career satisfaction. He fantasizes about getting a college degree with a major in oceanography, a long-standing ambition. Instead, he substitutes selling men's suits (he has convinced himself that attaining a college degree would take too long and entail too much expense). Currently, Ron is a high risk candidate for "burnout" on his job; he doesn't like his work and feels stressed because he is frustrated.

Both Sue and Ron procrastinate on taking steps to get what they want in life. And when a capable person substitutes "safe" for desired goals or weak for strong interests, he or she becomes a prime candidate for feeling unfulfilled, stressed, and "burned out."

Self-defeating habit formation occurs when a substitute activity becomes like an addiction. Carl, for example, procrastinates on facing and resolving his "shyness" problem. When he thinks of his interpersonal activities, he snacks on chocolate ice cream, feels tense about gaining weight, then goes on a binge to forget his anxieties. His food-a-holism is now a worse problem than his shyness, and only adds to it. Carol is an alcoholic. Like Carl who eats to avoid tension, she started drinking to avoid thinking. But by putting off facing her personal problems, she created a worse problem—alcoholism.

Emotional Diversions

The third version of the trip-yourself-up-trilogy is the emotional diversion. Like mental and action diversions, emotional diversions are a substitute reaction; what is substituted is a diversionary activity for a productive action. The diversionary activity is an oversensitivity to emotional tension.

Alice is in a rut because she repeats a pattern of becoming overly absorbed in her feelings. For example, when Alice decided to ask her employer for a raise, she worked herself up to an emotional frenzy by ruminating that her employer would argue down her request and by deliberating on how unfair that would be. In the midst of her wearisome deliberations, Alice noticed how upset she was feeling. Next she thought that her upset feelings would make her sound foolishly out of control if she spoke up to her employer. Then she began to feel upset because she was not "composed." At this point, Alice struggled to gain composure by controlling her feelings; first by trying to squelch them. When she failed to squelch her "upset," she became more upset. Then she tried to ignore her upset. But trying to ignore her upset had the effect of concentrating on those unwanted feelings, and the harder she tried to ignore them, the more intense they became. Now thoroughly engulfed in a mixed bag of anger, fears, helplessness, and depressed feelings ("upset"), Alice's work performance rapidly deteriorated.

After weeks of emotional smoldering and steadily declining work performance, Alice received a warning from her employer that she was beginning to skate on thin ice; her performance was down and other employees were complaining about her moodiness and irritability.

Once again Alice tried to stifle her feelings. Simultaneously, she felt angry at the thought that "it could take a year" to redeem herself before she could ask for a pay raise. However, the more she thought about her situation, the angrier she got, and the angrier she got, the more she tried to control her feelings. Naturally, in the meanwhile, her productivity slid and she felt forced to work longer hours to keep pace with the other workers.

Preoccupied with her continuing upsets and new frustrations over having less time for pleasure and recreation (due to longer work hours), Alice refocused her attention on asking for a raise to financially compensate her for the extra hours on the job. At this point, she again involved herself in an inner power struggle to gain freedom from her tensions and to gain composure. Finally, she abruptly quit her job, rationalizing that she wasn't appreciated. Soon she obtained another job and repeated the same pattern.

In the midst of her internal conflicts, Alice allowed her apartment to fall into disrepair; she felt too uptight to meet with her friends. She felt upset about her failures in these more personal areas, but *believed* she must be in charge of her feelings before she could organize her apartment and rejoin her friends.

Most persons like Alice, who are engulfed in emotional diversions, are overly sensitized to their feelings, particularly negative feelings. Faced with a situation that smacks of stress, these sensitized persons become quickly aware of even minor bodily tensions and escalate the tension by mentally inflating the importance of the situation. By trying to squelch their feelings to appear *"cool"* or *"composed"* or in "control," they add to the escalation.

Absorption in this emotional diversionary process requires time and effort that takes time and effort from productive projects. Paradoxically, this struggle leads to a rut pattern rather than a creative, constructive pattern. This happens despite the usually great interest of the emotionally diverting person to be in control and command of his or her destiny and to be productive.

Emotional diversions like other diversions are not an all-or-none process. Typically, there are breaks in the pattern. Also, the levels of severity differ. Thus, the pattern can exist at three different levels of intensity.

- *The level of minor inconvenience*: one indulges his or her feelings of tension and puts off until it is convenient to act differently.
- *The handicap level*: one overindulges his or her feelings of tension to the point where acting is less onerous than delaying; then he or she mobilizes into action.
- *The level of immobilization*: one greatly overindulges his or her feeling of tension, becomes awe struck with the magnitude of self-inhibiting emotive forces, feels immobilized, and fails to act.

The three diversionary systems operate in profusion. While one may clearly dominate, the other two are almost part of the procrastination pattern. As fear and depression, self-doubt-downing and low tension tolerance play off each other, the three diversionary systems also tend to interact.

Because of this *dynamic profusion*, a person may spend much time analyzing his or her procrastination symptoms in an attempt to unravel the mystery of why he or she acts so self-defeatingly. In this process, he or she comes to know everything about the symptom and makes the symptom into everything. In so doing, the person is trapped into a labyrinth of interlocking emotional, mental, and action complications, where he or she knows much about the symptom and precious little about how to break the procrastination habit.

Ego and Comfort Priorities

When a person procrastinates it is because he or she substitutes a low priority or diversionary activity for a priority activity. This substitution process may be viewed from a second point of view. This second angle is one of ego and comfort priorities, a view that can add clarity to the procrastination issue. Ego priorities reflect security needs like being approved, being perfect, or being in control. Comfort priorities reflect a need for, familiarity, freedom from unpleasant emotional sensations, and feeling good. When ego priorities reign, the person will avoid activities that could tarnish the self-image. When comfort priorities reign, the person reacts like an ergophobe.

Although there are many reasons why a person may come to view himself as inferior, comfort prioritizing is ofen the catalyst for the adoption of self-defeating ego priorities. Explained differently, a person sometimes comes to view himself as inferior when he routinely sees himself backing away from things that are uncomfortable, and failing to savor the good sense of accomplishment which is instrumental to a healthy self-concept and freedom from entrapment in a rut. In the following section a self-management system is described that can be used in the service of eliminating ego and comfort prioritizing and other acts of procrastination.

Overcoming Procrastination

Once the procrastination habit is understood, there are many ways to counter it and to break from the procrastination rut. I have described hundreds of counterprocrastination approaches in two previous books: *Overcoming Procrastination* (1979) and *Do It Now* (1979). Thus, the reader has two solid resources that go beyond this chapter if he or she needs additional self-help assistance.

In *How to Get Out of a Rut*, I emphasize using systematic self-help problem solving approaches. To rid yourself of procrastination requires that you also employ a systematic approach, this one called the Management System Approach.

The Management System Approach traditionally involves five integrated activities:

1. *Analyzing*: identifying problem causes and potential solutions.
2. *Planning*: developing strategies, engineering use of resources.
3. *Organizing*: establishing schedules, delegating responsibility,
4. *Implementing*: translating the plan into action following established procedures. Directing and controlling one's activities to obtain the desired result.
5. *Evaluating*: assessing the impact of the plan in terms of the results it produces. Using this data to improve the plan or as a basis for establishing a new analysis-planning-organizing-implementing-evaluating cycle.

Before you use the five-stage management process, naturally you will have to identify the procrastination habit pattern you most *want* to change. The major requirement in identifying the procrastination pattern is that the pattern and the desired change be clearly specified: for example, maintenence procrastination: paying bills late and getting late-charge penalties, change behavior so that bills are paid on schedule; self-development procrastination: delaying on beginning a master's thesis, the completion of which would bring a desired salary increase and promotion, change to immediately initiate efforts to complete the master's thesis.

When you think about the procrastination problem you want to beat, level with yourself about how important it would be to break out of that particular rut. Will breaking out, for example, help improve the quality of your life, reduce unnecessary strain, help you in achieving important long-term objectives, and aid you in building self-confidence? If so, the goal of breaking your procrastination pattern is well worh pursuing if:

1. You have the motivation to break the pattern.
2. You have or can acquire the necessary psychological and technical skills to begin.

Once done, you are ready to move to the first stage of the five-stage management process.

Analyzing.   Using the Procrastination Reciprocity Model (Figure 19 earlier in this chapter), spell out each of the four conditions. Start by writing down any self-doubts you may have that contribute to your procrastination problem. Self-doubts could include such self-statements as:

1. I can't act until I'm sure.
2. What's wrong with me that I can't persevere with greater consistency?
3. I must be a real loser.
4. The situation is too tough for me to handle.

Second, identify low frustration tolerance language that is associated with your procrastination activities. These discomfort-dodging statements could include such self-statements as:

1. I don't feel like it.
2. I can't help myself.
3. It (the task) is making me feel uncomfortable.
4. I can't stand it (my feelings, my thoughts, and so on).

In this initial part of your analysis, the following two observations may help.

1. Maintenance procrastination usually reflects boredom, depression, discomfort dodging, and disorganization.
2. Self-development procrastination usually reflects fears, self-doubts, discomfort dodging, and sometimes depression.

Third, try to identify diversionary actions. They may include:

1. Mental diversions such as telling yourself you will start later or you have to get other matters out of the way first.
2. Activity diversions where you engage in low priority or downright trivial activities to avoid your priority activities.
3. Emotional diversions where you become so involved in avoiding feeling uncomfortable that you bog yourself down.

Fourth, look at the activity you are procrastinating about doing. Do you:

1. Think you lack the skill to begin?
2. Believe you have to complete it perfectly and rapidly?
3. Tell yourself you can't make the time because, for example, your favorite television show is due to begin?
4. Claim you don't have the energy?

When this diagnostic sequence is completed, you are positioned to analyze your procrastination problem further by specifying:

1. Positive traits and qualities you possess that can be mustered in the service of countering self-doubt, discomfort dodging, diversions, and malfunctional procrastination actions. This includes qualities you have noticed in yourself when you are performing well: perseverance, problem focus, mental flexibility, and so forth.

2. Analysis of the procrastination pattern that identifies the weakest links in the procrastination chain. For example, the weakest link may be the feeling of tenseness associated with procrastination. The weakest link may also be an obviously absurd idea that you don't have energy to begin. Clearly, unless you are very ill or have gone for days without sleep or food, some energy is there!

At the completion of this part of your analysis, you are in a position to decide on the course of action you will follow both to start and to sustain your counterprocrastination program. For illustrative purposes, let us say you have decided to begin by clearly defining your counterprocrastination goals and by using the Idea-Sensation-Action (ISA) approach described in Chapter 8 to accomplish them. You decide, for example, on the ISA approach because it has face validity and provides a structured method for countering procrastination.

Planning.   Planning is a very pivotal step in a counterprocrastination program because without good planning you simply cannot *expect* good results. And where a good plan can be subverted by bad luck, a poor plan typically requires very good luck to work. Clearly, it is better to have a good plan that only poor luck can defeat and for which good luck is not a necessity.

To begin the counterprocrastination planning phase, start by clearly stating your goals in achievable terms. "I want to become a nonprocrastinator" simply won't do as a viable goal because it is just too vague. Instead, a goal such as the following is more attainable: to complete my master's thesis within the next six months. Attaching a time frame that is realistic gives credibility to the goal and rids one of the opportunity to procrastinate because there is no deadline.

Second, determine *how* you are going to proceed in countering self-doubts and/or low tension tolerance talk and/or diversions. For example, in using a ISA approach, normally you would use rational confrontational methods to counter procrastination-promoting self-restricting mental myths. You would also practice relaxation in preparation to action. Then you would use countering and relaxation strategies in conjunction with engaging in problem-solving activities (see Figure 21).

The problem-solving activities, however, need to be spelled out and *sequenced*. For example, if your goal is to complete a master's thesis, the activity needs to be broken down into achievable steps. These steps logically include defining the topic, basic library research, identifying a researchable question, identifying potentially helpful committee members, getting these people on your committee, drafting your proposal, submitting your proposal to the com-

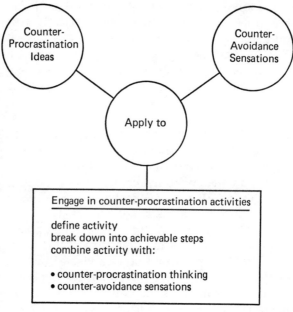

Figure 21

mittee, making revisions based on committee feedback, conducting the study, periodically meeting with key committee members, writing up results, getting the results reviewed, writing up final draft, taking oral examinations, making required revisions, and turning in final thesis.

The steps in the plan are a logical sequence leading to goal attainment. This same logical sequencing can be applied to many procrastination programs. A person procrastinating on dieting, for example, can: (1) research diet plans and select the one that is likely to work best, (2) eliminate, as much as possible, foods from the home that do not fit with the diet, (3) plan meals so that they coordinate with the diet system selected, (4) maintain a posture of forceful resistance to snacking between meals, and (5) recognize that one does not have to be a mindless victim of hunger urges, and so forth.

A person with a general maintenance procrastination problem can block off certain times during the week to attend to maintenance functions. He or she can: (1) order maintenance projects weekly in terms of their priority, (2) penalize him- or herself for unnecessarily deviating from the schedule by, let us say, burning a $100 bill.

Organizing. At this point in this process, we have identified self-stopping ideas and sensations and have planned to counter them. We have described a sequence of action strategies to accomplish the goal.

The sequence of actions serves as subgoals. These subgoals require a time schedule that is realistic and that serves to emphasize a reasonable *time* progression. Unless you are highly antagonistic toward schedules (you have an authority hangup or fear being pinned down), timing and pacing commitments can be quite motivating when you have established achievable objectives. They can provide the basis for a momentum or "positive inertia" that can become a potent force in getting it done.

In your organizational system, you establish the controls that you can use to help foster your goals. The deadline system is a major helpful control system. However, there are many other controls you can build into your system.

1. Use reminders. Write deadlines on your calendar; print cards that you place in strategic locations, such as your wallet; carry a notebook that outlines your plan and schedule. Some of the cards can list mental myths and their rational counters or some particularly relaxing ideas.
2. When possible, handle materials only once. Paper work, in particular, can be a miserable time drain if shuffled about and not efficiently dealt with. For example, put bills and correspondence in a safe place when received; then once a week at a prescribed time, sit down and pay bills, and send out letters as needed.
3. Use the five-minute plan. When you consider beginning to work on your subgoals, commit yourself to begin the task on schedule and work for five minutes. At the end of that time period, decide if you will continue for the next five minutes. The principles underlying this strategy are:
   a. It is easier to begin a task if you initially commit yourself only to short, successive work intervals.
   b. Once you have initiated an action, you tend to gain momentum.
   c. There will be a positive striving to continue with the task, once initiated, because each five-minute step brings you closer to completion.

4. Use a cross-out sheet where you list the steps to your plan in sequence and cross them off after you complete them.
5. Appropriately reward yourself for each major subgoal you achieve, by doing something that gives you pleasure. For example, you can use a contingency reward system, such as agreeing with yourself that you will read your favorite magazine *only* after you have completed step "x" in your action plan sequence. Or, after step "y" you will buy yourself that new jacket you've been wanting.
6. Delegate (whenever possible) to others who may be better able to handle those parts of your project that you would not be able readily to handle yourself. For example, if you were working on your thesis, you might be better able to use your time on research if you hired someone to type up your drafts rather than do the typing yourself.

A good organizing system serves as a viable and efficient system that *you can work* to coordinate your efforts effectively. Your system, if effective, should result in considerable time savings as you are less likely to repeat actions unnecessarily or ruminate about what to do next or ruminate in self-doubts and fall victim to discomfort-dodging urges.

Optimally, your system should be elastic enough to accommodate the unforeseen, errors, and miscalculations.

Implementing. No plan or organizaing system is fool proof. Thus, implementation of the plan will not always run smoothly since there will also be surprises and other unforeseen circumstances intervening on the pathway to your goal. You can use such circumstances to improve your plan and to develop resourcefulness and versatility in the process.

Problem circumstances are inevitable. For example, if your counterprocrastination diet plan causes you to become dizzy or to suffer depleted energy, you will need to change it regardless of how well fashioned it originally may have been.

Implementing your plan means putting your body and mind in coordinated goal-directed motion. It means putting mental obstructions in perspective. Indeed, it means acting despite them or countering them. It means placing your body in a more relaxed state to reduce their impact. It means acting to meet your scheduling deadlines and using your organizational control system to do so.

The self-doubt-downing sequence is a mental obstruction that can be evoked when a person sees what to do, but fails to time and pace his or her actions realistically. Timing and pacing miscalculations constitute *clarity problems* that can precipitate self-doubts. In Carlos Castenada's (1969) book, *The Teachings of Don Juan*, he describes the clarity problem. It occurs when a person's timing and pacing is out of line with his or her abilities or circumstance.

People who see life's possibilities, but don't act, often fear that their actions will not be as swift in practice as in fantasy. Instead of substituting reality for fantasy, they back off. Others attack reality with vigor, expecting perfect progress but they find they cannot proceed without corrections and new learning. Discouraged, they lapse into a self-doubt-downing sequence.

In your implementation phase, the clarity issue will repeat itself many times; thus, adjustment will be required in your scheduling to make it realistic. In your revisions, you will have the opportunity to assess where you over- or underestimate your capabilities. In the process you will increasingly gain in self-awareness and in knowledge of your capabilities.

Evaluating. Evaluation is listed as a separate process. In reality, it is every bit an integral part of every phase of the management system. You evaluate the correctness of your analysis, the goodness of your plan, the relevance of your organizing, and the results of your actions. Almost constantly you are involved in a feedback loop of thought-action-results.

In your evaluations, you attempt to measure your achievement, *not yourself!* Your achievement is relative so you will be able to rate it according to the degree of success your plan and action produces. Normally, you will evaluate your *performance* as you proceed and make adjustments and modifications in your actions. You will also decide whether you will reject the quality of your performance or accept it and move on. In this way you are also evaluating if your system is a workable one for you.

Since you have scheduled your time, you have a straightforward criteria for judging your performance (but not yourself) in meeting your schedule. You will also have realistic data to explain disparities between scheduling and performance so realistic adjustments can be made.

What Next?

As you move toward achieving your counterprocrastination goal, you are simultaneously moving to achieve a positive outcome in yet another way. You are reaching for something positive that you desire. However, as you progress with your plan, new ideas will occur to you and new priorities will take form. Thus, your counterprocrastination program does not end with the attainment of a specific goal or finite series of goals. Instead, the program blends with a life program where one challenge leads to another, which leads to another. There is much to do. Now is the time to start!

BIBLIOGRAPHY

The following references discuss concepts relevant to understanding ruts. There are a number of topics a reader might find helpful in his or her quest to break a rut pattern. These areas are labeled according to the following code in the bibliography:

(B) articles or books that discuss burnout, its causes, and cures.

(D) articles or books that pertain to depression.

(F) articles or books that pertain to fear.

(G) articles or books that are good general references.

(P) articles or books that pertain to procrastination.

Materials that may be of particular reference value are marked with an (*). Books or articles that were used in this work, but that may not be of any particular value to the reader, are not marked as such. However, any books or articles referred to in the text, indicated in the text by the year of publication in parentheses, are listed in the Bibliography.

(D) **Abrahmson, A.,** and **Sackein, H.** A paradox in depression: uncontrollability and self blame. *Psychological Bulletin,* 1977, 84, 838–851.

Abramson, L.Y., Seligman, E.P. and **Teasdale, J.D.** Learned helplessness in humans: critique and reformulation. *Journal of Abnormal Psychology,* 1978, 87, 49–74.

Adler, A. *Understanding human nature.* New York: Fawcett World, 1974.

*(P) **Ainslie, G.** Specious reward: A behavioral theory of impulsiveness and impulse control. *Psychological Bulletin,* 1975, 82, 463–496.

Albert, R.E., and **Emmons, M.L.** *Your perfect right.* San Luis Obispo, Calif.: Impact, 1974.

Allport, G.W. *Pattern and growth in personality.* New York: Holt, 1937.

Arnold, M. *Emotion and personality.* New York: Columbia University Press, 1960.

Bach, G.R., and **Goldberg, H.** *Creative aggression.* New York: Doubleday, 1974.

Bandura, A. *Principle of behavior modification.* New York. Holt, 1969.

————. Self-efficacy: Toward a unifying theory of behavior change. *Psychological Review,* 1977, 84, 191–215.

(D) **Beck, A.T.** *Cognitive therapy and the emotional disorders.* New York: International University Press, 1976.

(D) ————. *Depression: Clinical, experimental, and theoretical aspects.* New York: Hoeber, 1967.

Benjamin, R.L. *Semantics and language analysis.* New York: Bobbs Merrill, 1970.

Berlyne, D.E. *Conflict, arousal, and curiosity.* Toronto: McGraw-Hill, 1960.

(P) **Bijou, S., Morris, E.K.** and **Persons, J.A.** A PSI course in child development with a procedure for reducing student procrastination. *Journal of personalized instruction,* 1967, 1, 36–40.

(P) **Blatt, S.,** and **Quinlan, P.** Punctual and procrastinating students: A study of temporal parameters. *Journal of Consulting Psychology,* 1967, 31, 169–174.

Block, A.M. Combat neurosis in inner city schools. *American Journal of Psychiatry,* 1978, 135, 1189–1192.

Broadman, K. Zar methodik der hypnotischen Behandlung. Zertchrif fur hypnotismus, Psychotherapie, Psychophysiologie und Psychopathologie, Forschungen, 1902, 10, 314–375.

Carson, T.P., and **Adams, H.** Activity valence as a function of mood change. *Journal of Abnormal Psychology*, 1980, 89, 368–377.

* **Cassaire, E.** *Language and myth*. New York: Harper, 1946.

Castenada, C. *The teachings of Don Juan: A yaqui way of knowledge*, New York: Ballantine, 1969.

(F) **Cattell, R.B., Scheier, I.H.**, and **Lorr, M.** Recent advances in the measurement of anxiety, neuroticism, and the psychotic syndromes. *Annals of the New York Academy of Sciences*, 1962, 93, 813–856.

(F) **Cowles, E.** *Don't be afraid: How to get rid of fear and fatigue*. New York: McGraw-Hill, 1941.

Davids, A. Past experience and present personality dispositions as determinants of selective auditory memory. *Journal of personality*, 1956, 25, 19–32.

(P) **Dell, D.M.** Counselor power base, influence attempt, and behavior change in counseling. *Journal of Counseling Psychology*, 1973, 20, 399–405.

Diven, K. Certain determinants of the conditioning of anxiety reactions. *Journal of Psychology*, 1937, 3, 291–308.

(F) **Dollard, J.** *Victory over fear*. New York: Reynol and Hitchcock, 1942.

(P) **Doob, L.** *Patterning of time*. New Haven, Conn.: Yale University Press, 1967.

*(G) **Dunlap, K.** *Habits: Their making and unmaking*. New York: Liveright, 1972.

———. A revision of the fundamental law of habit formation. *Science*, 1928, 67, 360–362.

Duval, S., and **Wickland R.** *A theory of objective self awareness*. New York: Academic Press, 1972.

Elliot, T.S. The love song of J. Alfred Prufrock, in *The American Tradition in Literature*, eds. S. Bradley, R.C. Beatty, and E.H. Long. New York: Norton, 1967.

Ellis, A. *Reason and emotion in psychotherapy*. New York: Lyle Stuart, 1962.

————., and **Harper, R.A.** *A new guide to rational living.* Englewood Cliffs, N.J.: Prentice-Hall, Inc., 1975.

*(P) ————., and **Knaus, W.** *Overcoming Procrastination.* New York: New Anerican Library, 1979.

(B) **Fineman, S.** A psychosocial model of stress and its application to managerial unemployment. *Human Relations,* 1979, 32, 323–345.

Frankl, V.E. Paradoxical intension and dereflexion. *Psychotherapy, Theory, Research, and Practice,* 1975, 12, 226–236.

Freud, A. *The ego and the mechanisms of defense.* New York: International Universities Press, 1946.

Freud, S. *Beyond the pleasure principles,* standard ed. London: Hogarth, 1955.

Friedman, M., and **Rosenman, R.** *Type A behavior and your heart.* New York: Fawcett, 1975.

(D) **Frost, R.O., Graf, M., Becker, J.** Self-devaluation and depressed mood. *Journal of Consulting and Clinical Psychology,* 1979, 47, 958–962.

*(G) **Garcia, E.,** and **Blythe, B.T.** *Developing emotional muscle.* Athens: Georgia State University, 1977.

Goldfried, M.R., and **Trier, C.S.** Effectiveness of relaxation as a coping skill. *Journal of Abnormal Psychology,* 1974, 83, 348–355.

Gong-Guy, E., and **Hammer, C.** Causal perceptions of stressful events in depressed and non-depressed outpatients. *Journal of Abnormal Psychology,* 1980, 89, 662–669.

Guthrie, E.R. *The psychology of learning,* rev. ed. New York: Harper, 1952.

(D) **Hammer, C.L.,** and **Glass, R.** Depression activity and evaluation of reinforcement. *Journal of Abnormal Psychology,* 1975, 84, 718–721.

Harris, J.C. Uncle Remus: His songs and his sayings in *The American Tradition in Literature,* eds. S. Bradley, R.C. Beatty, and E.H. Long. New York: Norton, 1967.

Hartman, H. *Ego psychology and the problem of adaptation,* trans. D. Rapaport. New York: International Universities press, 1968.

* **Horney, K.** *Neurosis and human growth.* New York: Norton, 1950.

————. *The neurotic personality of our times*. New York: Norton, 1937.

Hybl, A.R., and **Stagner, R.** Frustration tolerance in relation to diagnosis and therapy. *Journal of Consulting Psychology*, 1952, 16, 163–170.

Jacobson, E. *You must relax*. New York: Whittlesey, 1934.

James, W. *Psychology*. New York: Holt, 1892.

*(G) ————. *Talks to teachers on psychology: And to students on some of life's ideals*. New York: Holt, 1906.

Jenkins, N. *Affective processes in perception. Psychological Bulletin*, 1957, 54, 100–127.

*(G) **Johnson, W.** *People in Quandaries*. New York: Harper and Row, 1946.

Jones, M.C. The elimination of children's fears, *Pedagogical Seminar*, 1924, 31, 308–315.

Kafka, F. *The metamorphasis*. New York: Schocker, 1968.

Kazdin, A.E. *History of behavior modification*. Baltimore, Md.: University Park Press, 1978.

————. *Self monitoring and behavior change*, in M.J. Mahoney, and C.E. Thoresen. *Self control: Power to the person*. Monterey, Calif.: Brooks-Cole, 1974, 218–246.

Kelly, G. The psychology of personal constructs, Vol. 1, *A Theory of Personality*. New York: Norton, 1955.

————. The psychology of personal constructs, Vol. 2, *Clinical Diagnosis and Psychotherapy*. New York: Norton, 1955.

*(P) **Knaus, W.J.** *Do it now: How to stop procrastinating*. Englewood Cliffs, N.J.: Prentice-Hall, Inc., 1979.

(P) ————. Overcoming procrastination. *Rational Living*, 1973, 8, 2–7.

(P) ————. The parameters of procrastination in R. Grieger, and J. Boyd, eds. *Cognitive factors in psychopathology*. New York: Human Science, 1982.

————. *Rational Emotive Education*. New York: Institute for Rational Living, 1974.

Korzybski, A. *Science and sanity*, 4th ed. Lakeville, Conn.: International Non-Aristotelian Library, 1958.

(D) **Krantz, S.**, and **Hammen, C.** Assessment of cognitive bias in depression. *Journal of Abnormal Psychology*, 1979, 88, 611–619.

* **Kuhn, T.S.** *The structure of scientific revaluation*, 2nd ed., enlarged. Chicago: Chicago University Press, 1970.

(B) **Kyriacou, C.**, and **Sutcliffe, J.** Teacher stress: prevalence, sources, and symptoms. *British Journal of Educational Psychology*, 1978, 48, 159–167.

(P) **Lakin, A.** *How to get control of your time and your life.* Bergenfield, N.J.: Signet, 1974.

Lang, P.J. The mechanisms of desensitization and the laboratory study of fear. In C.M. Franks (ed.) *Behavior therapy: appraisal and status.* New York: McGraw-Hill, 1969.

Lazarus, A.A. *Behavior therapy and beyond.* New York: McGraw-Hill, 1971.

———. *Multimodal therapy.* New York: Springer, 1976.

Lazarus, R.J. *Psychological stress and the coping process.* New York: McGraw-Hill, 1966.

(D) **Lewinsohn, P.M.** A behavioral approach to depression, in *The psychology of depression: Contemporary theory and research,* eds. R.J. Friedman and M.M. Katz. Washington, D.C.: Vitto Winston, 1974.

(D) ———. Clinical and theoretical aspects of depression, in *Innovative treatment methods in psychopathology,* eds. K.S. Calhoun, H.E. Adams, and K.M. Mitchel. New York: Wiley, 1974.

(F) **Lick, J.**, and **Bootzin, R.** Expectancy factors in the treatment of fear: Methodological and theoretical issues. *Psychological Bulletin,* 1975, 82, 917–931.

(D) **Lobitz, W.C.** and **DeePost, R.** Parameters of self-reinforcement and depression. *Journal of Abnormal Psychology,* 1979, 88, 33–41.

*(G) **Low, A.A.** *Mental health through will training.* Boston: Christopher Publishing, 1950.

MacKinnon, N.J. Role strain: An assessment of a measure and its invariance of factor structure across studies. *Journal of Applied Psychology,* 1978, 63, 321–328.

(D) **MacPhillamy, D.J.**, and **Lewinsahn, P.M.** Depression as a function of levels of desired and obtained pleasure. *Journal of Abnormal Psychology,* 1974, 83, 651–657.

Mahoney, M.S. *Cognition and behavior modification.* Cambridge: Ballinger, 1974.

Mahr, BH. *Principles of psychopathology: an experimental approach.* New York: McGraw-Hill, 1969.

Maultsby, M.C. *Help yourself to happiness.* New York: Institute for Rational Living, 1975.

Marcus, L., and **Dowds, B.N.** Subjective evaluation of life's events. *Journal of Consulting and Clinical Psychology,* 1979, 47, 906–911.

(B) **Masloch, C.** Burned out. *Human Behavior,* 1976, September, 16–21.

Maslow, A,H, *Toward a psychology of being* (2nd ed.). New York: Van Nostrand, 1974.

May, R. *The meaning of anxiety.* New York: Norton, 1977.

Mayo, E. *Human problems of industrial civilization.* New York: MacMillan, 1933.

Meichenbaum, D. *Cognitive behavior modification.* Morristown, N.J.: General Learning Press, 1974.

Mischel, W. On the interface of cognition and personality: Beyond the person-situation debate. *American Psychologist,* 1979, 34, 740–754.

———. *Personality and assessment.* New York: Wiley, 1968.

———. Process in delay of gratification, in L. Berkowitz, *Advances in experimental social psychology,* Vol. 7. New York: Academic Press, 1974.

———. Toward a cognitive social learning re-conceptualization of personality. *Psychological Review,* 1973, 80, 252–283.

Murphy, G. *Human potentialities.* New York: Basic Books, 1958.

(B) **Newman, J.E.,** and **Beehr, T.A.** Personal and organizational strategies for handling job stress: A review of research and opinion. *Personal Psychology,* 1979, 32, 1–43.

(B) **Nordlicht, S.** Effects of stress on the police officer and family. *New York Journal of Medicine,* 1979, 79, 400–401.

(D) **Overall, J.E.,** and **Zisook, S.** Diagnosis and the phenomenology of depressive disorders. *Journal of Consulting and Clinical Psychology,* 1980, 48, 626–634.

Overstreet, O.H. *Influencing human behavior.* New York: Norton, 1925.

(P)   **Parkinson, N.C.** *Parkinson's law.* New York: Ballantine, 1973.
(B)   **Pines, A.,** and **Maslach, C.** Characteristics of staff burn-out in mental health settings. *Hospital and Community Psychiatry,* 1978, 29, 233–237.
Premack, D. Reinforcement theory, in *Nebraska Symposium on Motivation,* ed. D. Levine. Lincoln: University of Nebraska Press, 1965.
Raiport, G. Mind conditioning. *Forum,* 1980, July, 82–87.
(P)   ———. *The personality through time space involvement.* Tbilisi, U.S.S.R., 1976.
(P)   ———. Personality typology based upon time space involvement, unpublished paper, 1979.
Reilly, S., and **Muzekari, L.H.** Responses of normal and disturbed adults and children to mixed messages. *Journal of Abnormal Psychology,* 1979, 88, 203–208.
Rilke, R.M. *Letters to a young poet.* New York: Norton, 1934.
Ringenback, P.T. *Procrastination through the ages: A definitive history.* Palmer Lake, Col.: Filter Press, 1971.
Ringer, R.J. *Winning through intimidation.* Los Angeles: Los Angeles Book Publishers, 1974.
Rogers, C.L. *On becoming a person.* Boston: Houghton-Mifflin, 1961.
*   **Ryle, G.** *Dilemmas.* Cambridge, Eng.: Cambridge University Press, 1954.
(B)   **Sarason, I.G.,** and **Johnson, J.H.** Life stress, organizational stress, and job satisfaction. *Psychological Reports,* 1979, 44, 75–79.
Schacter, S. and **Singer, J.E.** Cognitive, social, and psysiological determinants of emotional state. *Psychological Review,* 1962, 69, 379–399.
Schultz, J.H., and **Luthe, W.** *Autogenic training.* New York: Grune and Stratton, 1969.
Seif, M.M., and **Atkins, A.L.** Some defensive and cognitive aspects of phobias. *Journal of Abnormal Psychology,* 1979, 88, 42–51.
Selye, H. *The stress of life.* New York: McGraw-Hill, 1956.
Skinner, B.F. *Science and human behavior.* New York: MacMillan, 1953.
Stoker, B. *Dracula.* New York: Putnam, 1979.

Veiten, E. A laboratory task for induction of mood states. *Behavior Research and Therapy,* 1968, 6, 473–482.

Vogt, O. Die Zielovorstellung der Suggestion. Zertchrif fur. Hypotismus, psychotherpie, psychophysiologie und psychopathologie, Forschungen, 1897, 5, 332–342.

Warshaw, L.J. *Managing stress.* Reading, Mass.: Addison-Wesley, 1979.

Watson, J.B. Psychology as the behaviorist views it. *Psychological Review,* 1913, 20, 158–177.

———. *Psychology from the standpoint of a behaviorist.* Philadelphia: Lippincott, 1919.

(F)   **Weeks, C.** *Simple, effective treatment of agoraphobia.* New York: 1978.

Weinberg, H.L. *Levels of knowing and existence: Studies in general semantics.* New York: Harper, 1959.

Werner, H. *Comparative psychology of mental development* (rev. ed.). New York: International Press, 1957.

(P)   **Wessman, A.** Personality and the subjective experience of time. *Journal of Personality Assessment,* 1973, 21, 103–114.

White, R. *The abnormal personality* (3rd ed.). New York: Ronald Press, 1964.

(F)   **Williams, T.** *Dreads and besetting fears.* New York: Little, Brown, 1923.

Wine, J. Test anxiety and direction of attention. *Psychological Bulletin,* 1971, 76, 92–104.

Wittgenstein, L. *Tractatus logico-philosphicus.* New York: Harcourt Brace, 1922.

Wolpe, J., and **Lazarus, A.A.** *Behavior therapy techniques.* New York: Pergamon, 1966.

Wolpe, J. *The practice of behavior therapy.* New York: Pergamon, 1969.

(P)   **Ziesat, H.A., Rosenthal, T.G.,** and **White, G.M.** Behavioral self-control in treating procrastination in studying. *Psychological Reports,* 1978, 42, 59–69.

INDEX